THE PHILOSOPHY OF SOCIAL RESEARCH

D0165354

LONGMAN SOCIAL RESEARCH SERIES

Series Editor: Professor Maurice Craft, Goldsmiths' College,
University of London.

LONGMAN SOCIAL RESEARCH SERIES

The Philosophy of Social Research

John A. Hughes
Wesley W. Sharrock

Third Edition

LONGMAN
London and New York

Addison Wesley Longman Limited
Edinburgh Gate
Harlow
Essex CM20 2JE
United Kingdom
and Associated Companies throughout the world

Published in the United States of America
by Addison Wesley Longman, New York

© Longman Group UK Ltd 1990
This edition © Addison Wesley Longman Limited 1997

The right of John A. Hughes and Wesley W. Sharrock
to be identified as authors of this work has been asserted by
them in accordance with the Copyright,
Designs and Patents Act 1988.

All rights reserved; no part of this publication may be
reproduced, stored in a retrieval system, or transmitted
in any form or by any means, electronic, mechanical,
photocopying, recording, or otherwise without either
the prior written permission of the Publishers or a
licence permitting restricted copying in the United
Kingdom issued by the Copyright Licensing Agency
Ltd., 90 Tottenham Court Road, London W1P 9HE.

First published 1980
Second edition 1990
Fifth impression 1996
Third edition 1997

ISBN 0 582 31105 5

British Library Cataloguing-in-Publication Data

A catalogue record for this book is available from the British Library

Library of Congress Cataloging-in-Publication Data

Hughes, J. A., 1941–
    The philosophy of social research / John A. Hughes, Wesley W.
Sharrock. — 3rd ed.
        p.   cm. — (Longman social research series)
    Includes bibliographical references and index.
    ISBN 0–582–31105–5 (pbk.)
    1. Social sciences—Research—Methodology.   I. Sharrock, W. W.
(Wes W.)   II. Title.   III. Series.
H61.H88   1997
306'.72—dc21   97–28440
                                                                          CIP

Set by 35 in 10/11pt Times
Produced through Longman Malaysia , PP

CONTENTS

PREFACE

This third edition has been considerably revised in the following ways. First, by inviting Wes Sharrock as co-author. Wes and I have been working together on a variety of projects for a number of years and this third edition would not have been even feasible without his wise and considerable participation. Second, it includes expositions of serious gaps in the second edition, mainly Foucault, Derrida and the post-empiricist efforts to sustain the spirit of positivism. The third, and one of the more important changes, has been in the book's structure. In effect, the review of the arguments now falls more clearly into two parts: the first dealing with positivism and the second examining a range of ideas which constitute reactions to positivism. The thread which runs through both is that of foundationalism and anti-foundationalism which helps to provide some thematic continuity to what can appear to be very different and unrelated issues. The text has been extensively revised throughout and includes two new chapters, both responding to the issues surrounding the foregrounding of language in social science. The conclusion, too, has been completely rewritten to give it an even more Wittgensteinian air.

As usual there are very many people to thank. Ulrik Petersen, an extremely intelligent and companionable politics graduate student from Denmark, has given much needed advice, support and stimulus as well as some serious liquid indulgence. Jon O'Brien and Mark Rouncefield have more than just held the fort while the book was being finished. Their lack of complaint is remarkable testimony to their generosity. Tom Rodden, as usual, has been an immensely generous colleague. Lou Armour, who wrote the best doctoral thesis that either of the authors have seen for many a year, was always insightful and freely giving of his time. Andrew Crabtree, Jenny Ball, Cal Giles, Jason Khan, John Allen, Preben Mogensen, Catherine Fletcher, Karen Gammon, Barry Sanderson and Chris Quinn are others who deserve a special mention for various facilities they have provided during the writing of this book.

CHAPTER 1

The philosophy of social research

Introduction

The relationship between philosophy and what we now refer to as the social sciences has a long history. Indeed, the social sciences have often envisaged themselves as following the natural sciences which originated by separating themselves from philosophy, with the social sciences appropriating as their scientific issues the last unsolved problems of philosophy. Unlike the natural sciences, the social sciences have not, for the most part, been able to dissociate themselves from philosophy. Although the social sciences vary in this respect, philosophical issues continually provide the fundamental questions these disciplines ask about the nature of their appropriate subject matters, their intellectual provenance, their investigative rationales, and above all about the nature of their valid and proper methods. Sociology, for example, seems to consist almost entirely of a succession of approaches and perspectives most of which bear a heavy philosophical tone and which have as their main focus a continuing struggle with philosophical problems, many of which are of nineteenth century origin. As we say, the social sciences vary in this regard, with sociology, perhaps, being the most salient case, existing in near perpetual crisis about its fundamental status and self-conception as a discipline. But, others are by no means exempt. It is common, for example, for training in political science to include courses in political theory, for economics to include the history of economic thought, both heavily philosophical, and for methodological training across the spectrum of the social sciences to include courses in philosophical ideas about appropriate methods predominantly organised under the aegis of the philosophy of science.

We note the involvement of the social sciences with philosophy not by way of complaint but simply to bring to attention the fact that philosophical issues remain of continuing concern in the social and the human sciences. What else this might indicate about their intellectual character is a matter of debate, but it is a central fact about their intellectual life. Nor is this surprising if we look at the formative influences. In sociology, for example, the founding trinity of Marx, Weber and Durkheim spent a considerable amount of their efforts establishing and refining the philosophical bases for their own ideas, the results of which still massively shape sociological debates, not least because of the

differences between the three of them.[1] For them, and this is still probably more typical of the European traditions of social science than it
is of the American, philosophical questions had to be settled in advance
of empirical enquiries. Given this heritage, and the immense difficulty
of bringing philosophical controversies to any kind of conclusive resolution, purportedly fundamental questions at the heart of the human sciences remain unresolved and continually stimulate the necessity to remain
engaged with philosophy.

Of course, the nature of the entanglement between philosophy and
the human sciences has not remained constant over time. As mentioned, the human sciences largely originated in philosophical inquiry
but they were then different kinds of enterprises from those we know
today. The distinctions between metaphysical inquiries, what we now
commonly regard as philosophy, and empirical inquiries, were not so
sharply made as they are today. Prior to the establishment of the natural
sciences, philosophy was regarded as *the* mode of intellectual inquiry
and embraced much of what we now treat not only as separate disciplines but as very different modes of study to those of philosophy. The
emergence of the natural sciences not only shifted philosophy from its
throne as the supreme form of knowledge but thereby provoked changes
in the conception of philosophy itself. Philosophy became more focused
as a metaphysical endeavour rather than an amalgam of the metaphysical and the empirical. Empirical inquiries into the nature of the universe
became very much the province of the natural sciences with philosophy
left with questions which were not empirical in character.[2]

The nature of philosophy

There have been many definitions of philosophy and as many different
philosophical styles as definitions. From the point of view of securing
a definition of philosophy, matters are made worse by the fact that there
are special difficulties about defining philosophy that we shall not be in
a position to understand until we examine philosophical problems about
definition in general. This is not untypical of the way in which philosophy seems to proceed. Its questions quickly seem to assume an aggra-
vating dependence on other questions before we can even begin to see
what an answer might be. What look to be fairly straightforward and
inoffensive questions such as 'What is reality?', 'Are there other minds?'
rarely get answers of the form, 'Reality is such-and-such' or 'Yes, there
are other minds'. More often than not such questions will invite other
questions: 'What is meant by . . . ?', 'How could we determine whether
or not there are other minds?', 'What criteria could we use to distinguish the real from the unreal?', and so on.

Philosophical questions can look simple enough but it quickly
becomes hard to know what kind of answer can ever be given to them,
not least because the business of philosophers largely seems to consist in
disagreeing with each other about what kind of answers could possibly

be acceptable. Philosophical questions about the nature of matter are not the kind of questions physicists, say, can answer. Philosophical questions about other minds are not the kind of questions which psychologists might devise experiments to explore. Philosophical questions about the nature of truth are not answerable by lawyers. Physics, psychology, and law – to stay with the examples – have to assume precisely the kind of things that philosophy wants to ask about. It is physics' task to tell us about the structure of the material world, what it is composed of, why it behaves in the ways that it does, and so on; it is not its task to question the real existence of an external world. Philosophy can accept all that physics tells us about the nature of the material universe and still want to ask its questions whether or not, for example, physics give us its final answer as to the nature of reality. Much contemporary philosophical thought, especially that which affects the social sciences, revolves around the question of whether 'science' occupies a special, privileged place in human thought about reality; whether, that is, science represents a superior form of knowing and, if so, by what means? Let us illustrate with a mundane example.

Occasionally, when driving around the British countryside, one comes across lorries with the word 'Milk' painted on their rear and sides. A fairly obvious conclusion to draw on seeing such a lorry is that this is a vehicle designed to carry milk going about its business picking up milk from the farms for delivery to the dairy. But what is the basis of this inference? The fact that 'Milk' appears on the lorry? More than likely, but what does this presumption depend on? It depends, for one thing, on knowing that 'Milk' refers to what the lorry carries. Yet, as we well know, lorries can have names or words on them which do not refer to what they carry. Sometimes the name of the firm or owner is blazoned on the side, or the name of some product. So, how do we know that the lorry referred to carries milk? 'Milk' may have been the owner of the lorry, or a firm, or even the make of a lorry. How can we be sure about the claim? What kind of claim is it? Is it a claim about what we believe or about what we know? There are, of course, lots of reasons we could provide to substantiate the claim: it was a tanker lorry; 'Milk' is not a usual surname; it is not, as far as we know, the name of a firm, and it would be strange to use it as a pet name, and so on. And, perhaps, an accumulation of such reasons might 'add up' to a conviction that we are right: this lorry does carry milk. But why?

The reasons just adduced include reference to our personal experience, our personal knowledge, the practices of vehicle manufacturers, transportation firms, lorry drivers, and more. How far do we need to go before the link between the sign 'Milk' and the function of the lorry is established beyond doubt? It could be argued that no amount of personal beliefs and reasons are sufficient; what we need to do is look inside the lorry. Again, what makes the results of looking any more certain or corroborative than the reasons we have already offered? We may still be deceived. What should we conclude if the lorry was full of whisky instead of milk? Accuse the driver of smuggling? Conclude that we had misunderstood the label all along and that milk refers to a bright brownish liquid that comes from Scotland and not to a white thick liquid that comes from cows?

But whatever the conclusion arrived at, the point is that we would be embroiled in questions about the nature of evidence and, through these, about the nature of the world: how we know certain things, believe others, how we know things to be true or false, what inferences can legitimately be made from various kinds of experiences, what inferences consist in, what sorts of things make up the world, and so on? Of course, in doing so we begin to lose something of our sense of direction; familiar experiences become doubtful and even the most seemingly self-evident, certain, common-sensical facts appear open to doubt.

Note that these questions arose out of an everyday ability of persons to understand, in this case, what the label on the side of a lorry meant. As such, it does not involve the use of any kind of esoteric knowledge, though we might want to say that it does involve culturally acquired knowledge.[3] We can make such connections routinely and normally without overmuch hesitation. The ability to read road signs, labels on packets or bottles, headlines, street names, and so on, are part and parcel of our everyday competences. In which case why ask the kind of questions just raised?

Of course, at one level there is no reason whatsoever why we should do so. Certainly it is unlikely that philosophical discussion of this ability will make very much difference to the way in which it enters and affects our daily lives. Nonetheless, these philosophical questions continue to exercise a worrying influence, engendering and perpetuating puzzle and anxiety about possible sources of intellectual authority.

Ontology, epistemology and intellectual authority

One of the principal reasons why philosophy and social research remain deeply interconnected is because of the way in which social scientists have adhered to the philosophical view known as 'foundationalism'. This view treats epistemology – the inquiry into the conditions of the possibility of knowledge – as prior to empirical research. The possibility of empirical knowledge needs to be secured against persistent sceptical doubt, the kind of doubt which raises arguments to the effect that we can never truly know anything about the real, external world, can never legitimately, and with full confidence, claim to know anything. To protect against this kind of scepticism it is argued that the possibility and the actuality of knowledge need to be conclusively demonstrated by identifying sound, unchallengeable means, or methods, of acquiring knowledge. If we are to be assured of our entitlement to the confidence that, for example, we often feel about our scientific knowledge, then we need to be able to demonstrate that our system of knowledge is built upon sound foundations. Foundationalism, then, is the view that true knowledge must rest upon a set of firm, unquestionable set of indisputable truths from which our beliefs may be logically deduced, so retaining the truth value of the foundational premises from which they follow, and in terms of which our methods of forming further ideas about the world and investigating it can be licensed.

The influence of foundationalism is sufficiently strong in the social sciences for the priority of the foundations to be deemed not merely logical but also temporal. Thus, it is common for philosophical, especially epistemological, issues to be regarded as the first, preliminary ones that need to be addressed in order that sound methods for enquiry can be laid down in advance of the empirical research itself. As we shall shortly see, conceptions of the nature and organisation of social research are often themselves derived from one or other philosophical conceptions about the nature of scientific enquiry. As a result, research approaches and techniques are often developed as implementations and demonstrations of the philosophical preconceptions. Accordingly, the aim of much of social research is, in effect, to show what difference the adoption of a particular philosophical point of view, especially on epistemological matters, makes. The result is that criticism of research results, and the methods which generate them, is often directed through them against the philosophical conceptions underlying them and often made from a different, conflicting philosophical position. Thus, it is difficult to regard the social sciences as representing disciplines which produce cumulative empirical findings: findings which build upon each other within frameworks which are more or less settled. Instead, what we have, to varying degrees, are philosophical arguments based around and provoked by putative empirical findings.

'How is it possible, if it is, for us to gain knowledge of the world?' is the question which provides the main business of epistemology. Related to it is the equally momentous question, 'What kinds of things really exist in the world?': a question which belongs to that branch of philosophy known as ontology. Epistemology is, to put it briefly, concerned with evaluating claims about the way in which the world can be known to us and, as such, involves issues as to what it is to know *anything*.

As philosophical questions these are not so much questions about particular methods of investigation or techniques of data collection or even about specific matters of fact. They are purportedly general questions which ask about these particular methods of techniques, or the facts which are purportedly established by their use, whether they satisfy the general requirements for being able to say that we do, indeed, know something. Such questions, of course, presuppose that we can identify those general requirements, and epistemological controversies are all about the nature of these supposed requirements.

Quite clearly ontological and epistemological issues are not unconnected. Presumably the capacity of whatever methods or procedures give us knowledge of what there is must depend, in part, upon what there is to be known about. It is important to emphasise, however, that ontological and epistemological questions are not to be answered by empirical enquiry since they are engaged in examining, among other things, the general nature and significance of empirical inquiry. We cannot empirically inquire into the question of whether or not there are such things as 'empirical facts'. We can, it seems, establish some particular facts – such as what the suicide rate in the United Kingdom was in 1973 – but asking what justifies that claim is very different from asking whether there really are any facts at all and, if there are, whether our ordinary ways of finding things out could possibly provide the basis for establishing their existence? This is not an empirical question, for to suppose that one could answer it by assembling facts would be to beg the very question itself. Instead, it invites a response in terms of reflecting on the very presuppositions of knowledge and the identity of facts. This reflection obviously cannot be carried out in terms of facts, for the point is to ask whether there are, indeed, any facts, what characterises something as a fact (if there are any), and how those facts may be correctly identified.

In our daily lives, and in our professional investigative practice, we have plenty of bases on which we are prepared to assert and defend our claims to know something. These ways may variously include reference to experimental methods, correct procedures of analysis, authoritative sources, spiritual inspiration, age, experience, and so on: that is, by reference to those procedures collectively accredited as 'good reasons' for knowing. It is this public collective licensing from which the intellectual authority of our knowledge practically derives, though drawing on this licence is not always a sufficient guarantee that one does know. What is being stressed here is the grounded nature of our knowledge claims and the way in which particular grounds have, under appropriate conditions, an authoritative status; but, in the nature of grounds, they can be challenged and may be refuted. To put it another way, there may be, in the case of any particular knowledge claim, reasons why normally 'good grounds' are not 'good enough'. Seeing if the grounds upon which we ordinarily rely will withstand more intensive questioning is one objective which motivates philosophy.

But how, if we recall the example of the milk tanker, could there be any doubt about the facts of the matter, that it carried milk, or doubts about how we could find out what the facts are? In the practical sense already mentioned, there is no reason at all, except in the cases where, for example, there is suspicion of smuggling, deceit or whatever, cases which are, again, also very practical ones. In cases like these we are merely taking for granted, and not sceptically reflecting on a framework of standards within which we make our judgements, as to whether this is relevant and sufficient evidence to establish facts like these. But such claims, and the evidence on which they depend, are only articulable once there is in place some framework for underpinning them as claims and evidence and about which it is reasonable to ask, 'While this framework may be good enough for all practical purposes, is it really sufficient for establishing an unquestionably true identification of the way things in the world really are?'

In a practical sense, of course, we learn such frameworks as part of what we learn about the world. Philosophically, however, this really gets us nowhere because it is possible that what we learn may be wrong, and systematically so. We might be dreaming, deluded, blinded by personal prejudice or have learned cultural practices and beliefs that are false. In other words, it is deemed possible to be 'deeply sceptical' about the whole framework within which our specific judgements are sited.[4] We can doubt, that is, our whole way of finding out about the world and, in the most extreme, sceptical case, can doubt whether it is ever possible to know anything at all. After all, one can simply point to the variety of views and conceptions about the world which are or have been held by various historical societies – beliefs in witchcraft, gods sitting on mountain tops, procreation as the result of jumping over fires, the power of magic and many more – to suggest that we cannot afford to be complacent about the validity of our own conceptions, for we also might be wrong. In which case, then, questions arise about how we can possibly tell whether the world, in itself, is really the way in which it appears to us; whether, that is, our own beliefs are sound. It cannot be done by offering what, in other contexts, we would count as conclusive empirical evidence, since it is just our reliance upon such supposed evidence that is being questioned. After all, the gods of ancient Greece, for example, were just as real, just as much unquestionable facts, to the members of that society, who might in turn have regarded the facts of our world, such as the internal combustion engine, television, or aircraft, as some species of magic. But, just what this difference might imply about the nature of knowledge in general is by no means clear. Were the ancient Greeks deluded, and how can we show that they were and, even more importantly for us, that we are not as deluded in our way as they in theirs? What entitles us to pronounce against the ancient Greeks given that, to all intents and purposes, the facticity of their gods was something it was impossible for them to doubt? What makes our own certainties any more secure than those equally fervently held ones of the Ancient Greeks? Some of the issues here will be considered more fully in Chapter 6 and succeeding chapters.

Epistemology is particularly troubled by the need to find answers to persistent scepticism. It is directed towards attempting to ascertain whether there are truths which can be secured against all possible doubt, or whether it is unavoidable to concede to the sceptic that, in the end, we can never be truly certain of anything and that even our own most cherished certainties are only a matter of misplaced confidence. Indeed, one of the major activities of theories of knowledge has been to give what Quinton calls an 'account of the logical order of justification' (Quinton 1973: 115). This has often taken the form of a search for the indisputable certainties which can provide secure foundations for human knowledge: that is, thinking of knowledge as a structure like a building which needs to rest on a stable base along with the attendant belief that there are some beliefs more basic than others, and by which these latter beliefs may be supported and justified. If such beliefs, which it would be impossible to doubt, could be formulated, then all beliefs could be arranged in a hierarchical order at the bottom of which are those which, while justifying those above, do not themselves require justificatory support. This particular conception, known as 'foundationalism' and mentioned earlier, has lately been identified as one of the key components in the formation of 'modern philosophy', that is, the period since the seventeenth century and bequeathed to subsequent eras through the work of René Descartes (1596–1650), often counted as the father of modern philosophy. The attack upon and rejection of 'foundationalism' has been a major feature of recent thinking and a key to the radical reconstruction of philosophy itself.

The social and historical rootedness of philosophy

What has so far been said about ontology and epistemology might make it appear as if they were endeavours which were somehow detached from the social and historical circumstances in which they appeared. And, indeed, this has certainly been one of the motivations behind philosophy; that is, to uncover principles which have general, in the sense of universal, application, and can desirably be known in an equally universal way by everyone independently of personal, social and historical circumstance. However, and as briefly illustrated earlier, conceptions of the world have actually changed historically and why should philosophical conceptions be any different from these others? Philosophy has characteristically looked upon its history as a succession of progressive attempts to identify these universal principles. But it is possible, as is now being vigorously and for many different reasons argued, that the notion of progress in knowledge may be an illusion and, therefore, the notion of progress toward valid general principles in philosophy also an illusion. Perhaps Toulmin's advice (1972: 1–14) should be heeded not to treat forms of epistemology, and presumably ontology also, as expressing more about the social and historical nature of the period in which they originated than as saying anything about ultimate truths.

As we have already mentioned, many of the methodological debates in the social sciences need to be understood in relation to the rise, and the success of, the natural sciences and to the way in which philosophers have interpreted the nature and consequences of this success. Descartes and Locke, two of the major figures whose work founded the 'modern period' in Western philosophy, were very much men of their age and discussed the principles of human knowledge against the background of the then current ideas about the order of nature and man's place within it and, in so doing, did much to clarify and elaborate those current ideas. According to Toulmin, they took three 'commonplaces' for granted, 'commonplaces' that were not felt to be in need of philosophical justification: first, that nature was fixed and stable, to be known by principles of understanding equally fixed, stable and universal; second, that there was a dualism between mind and matter, the latter being inert, while the mind was the source of reason, motivation and other mental functions; and, finally, that the exemplar of true knowledge, of incorrigible certainty, was provided by geometry against which all other claims to knowledge were to be judged. We can see how such a conception provided both a basic ontological description of the world and epistemological prescriptions about how that world could be investigated. It directed scientists' and philosophers' attention toward the structure of the material universe, to its quantification and measurement and to its description in terms of rational theoretical principles. Through time it became established as the authoritative version of the world, rather like a set of instructions about how the world should be sensibly assembled. It stressed systematic method, the importance of testing out ideas against nature itself rather than deriving explanations from theological assumptions, communicating knowledge to a fellowship of science, and accumulating facts about the world consistent with the explanatory theories. It became a conception, widely held by scientists and philosophers. More detailed theoretical work within various disciplines was given intellectual validity by the extent to which it was seen as consistent with this conception, and in so doing continually reaffirmed the conception itself. There were many different theoretical schools, even within a single discipline – rationalists, empiricists, corpuscularians, vorticists – taken as consistent with the ontological and epistemological principles put forward. The point is that these principles set the context of debate within which the different schools fought their disagreements. In short, for a time it was these principles which held intellectual authority.

An awareness of the social and historical contexts of claims to knowledge does raise a problem, again one that will be addressed more fully later, which has to do with the relativity of knowledge. It arises from the idea of the social determination of knowledge, which means giving up on the ambition to secure the truth of our own ways of thought against those of other times and places. Although the 'commonplaces' of the seventeenth century view of the world – a view, incidentally, that was specific to learned groups in Europe – retained a strong influence throughout the succeeding two centuries, none of them has the same meaning, or is held with the same conviction, today. The ideas of evolution and of a universe originating in a 'Big Bang' no longer support the conception of a fixed and unalterable universe. Similarly, the distinction between mind and matter, so 'common-sensically' true, no longer has the clear bright force it once had. The invention of non-Euclidian geometries, too, had a devastating effect on the belief that the Euclidian geometrical scheme was the frame of the universe, but allowed geometry, paradoxically, more room as a human creation, useful and powerful for particular purposes but depriving it of a special status as the leading representative of certainty and the embodiment of a universal standard of knowledge. But, if such 'evidently true' principles of past times can be displaced, can the certainties of our own time and place avoid a similarly ruinous fate? Fundamental beliefs have varied from place to place and time to time, and to many there seems no reason to suppose that our own certainties will, in the long term, prove more durable than their predecessors. If they do change then will their displacement involve any progression, an evolution of knowledge towards better forms, or can systems of knowledge only be judged in their own terms as the product of particular social and historical settings? Are we entitled to make negative and dismissive judgements on forms of knowledge alien to our own, such as beliefs in witchcraft, for example, or on medicines which rest on very different conceptions of disease and, yet, have a remarkable efficacy at least in the cultures they serve?

These examples, and there could be many more, sharply pose the issue of the relativity of the criteria of knowledge or, to put it another way, the sources of our intellectual authority. How do we judge between different systems of knowledge? Are there clear and unambiguous criteria, as Plato and Descartes felt geometry represented, by which we can determine whether or not what we know is true? Is there, in short, any universal source of intellectual authority, or is all knowledge simply relative to the society and the period in which one happens to live? Questions such as these, abstract though they may seem, are important in helping us to understand what we are doing when, among other things, we engage in social research to produce knowledge.

To round off this introductory chapter we want to try to relate some of the above general remarks about the nature of philosophy to the process of social research.

Philosophy and the research process

Broadly speaking, research is carried out in order to discover something that is not already known about. However, this *is* broadly speaking. If we look at what counts as research in the social and the human sciences, for example, what we find is a variety of activities ranging from surveys to discover the relationship between various social factors, to persons spending time observing how other people work, to carrying out experiments in laboratories, to scholarly review and criticism of X's ideas, to elaborating a new approach within the field, to a critique of existing work on X, and more. It is hard, in other words, to see quite what these activities have in common that makes them *research*, apart, that is, from trying to formulate or discover something new. What we can say about them is that they are reasoned activities in the sense that they ought to be done with scrupulousness, with rigour, with a careful weighing of the evidence and the arguments, with some methodicalness. That is, that they are scholarly activities.[5] Of course, these activities can be done well or badly – hence the 'ought' – but ideally they ought to have at least the above qualities and will be judged upon the extent to which they do possess them.

However, in connection with scientific activities, and for the present we can include the social sciences under this label, it has been argued that more than scholarship, to use this term, is involved. Descartes and Locke bequeathed to their successors the idea that the distinctive success of scientific knowledge is because it possessed a method, the scientific method, a corpus of sure procedures which, if applied with appropriate scruple and commitment, are sure to produce knowledge of the world. The identification of the scientific method seemed to be a vital part of the solution to epistemology's 'big problem', namely, finding an assured means to knowledge within foundationalist conceptions. All the techniques we typically associate with science, such as experiments, hypothesis testing, theories, the public scrutiny of method and results, measurement, and so on, are seen as embodying the scientific method. But, and this is the point at which philosophical issues surface, it is always open to us to ask, 'why these techniques or procedures and not others?', 'what sort of guarantees do these methods and techniques offer that others do not?' Descartes and Locke therefore bequeathed the quest to figure out just what it is about the practices of science that embody this method, what makes them superior, what lends them greater intellectual authority than others? Relatively recently, however, the idea that this is a quest for a chimera has taken hold. As we shall see, the philosopher of science, Paul Feyerabend, has argued in the most extreme and dramatic way, though his predecessor Karl Popper and his contemporary, Thomas Kuhn, have both promoted the same idea, that there is no 'scientific method' which is in general use among scientists and which is the touchstone of knowledge.

In the social sciences these kind of questions take on an extra dimension, namely, the fact that the topics of the social sciences are topics which, in various forms, are also topics for members of society. Indeed, it is more than plausible to argue that the social sciences emerged out of the political, economic and social concerns of ordinary life. In which case, the problem of intellectual authority for the social sciences is, what makes social scientific knowledge superior to that of the man or woman in the street, the journalist, the politician, the revolutionary, the Trobriand Islander, or the racial bigot? What, to put the question another way, is the basis for their intellectual authority?

It will be no surprise to find that answers to these questions are not straightforward. The difficulties grow if we take even a cursory look at what social researchers do when they say they are engaged in research. The training of social researchers will normally consist in their being required to master questionnaire techniques, the principles of survey design and analysis, the intricacies of statistics, maybe even computer programming and modelling, and so on. Of course, the emphasis given to different techniques would depend on the discipline involved: the sociological researcher might also have to know about ethnography as well as statistical techniques, the economist about even more sophisticated mathematical and statistical modelling, while the historian would probably be more concerned with developing skills in the interpretation of various kinds of documentary evidence. These skills can be learned and used as the skills of a craft. Researching a problem is a matter of using the skills and techniques appropriate to do the job required within practical limits: a matter of finely judging the ability of a particular research tool to provide the data required and itself a skill. In short, it is to treat research methods as a technology and, make no mistake, without this attitude 'normal science', to borrow Kuhn's (1996) phrase, would not be possible.

However, and the source of the relevance of the philosophical issues of the kind reviewed earlier, although research methods may well be treated as simply instruments, in fact they operate within sets of assumptions. Many of these are theoretical claims about the nature of society, of social actors, of interaction. Interviews, for example, depend for their use on 'theoretical' claims about how the interview encounter can be managed in order to maximise the validity of the respondent's answers. The order of questions on an interview schedule or a question-naire is justified in terms of presumptions about the best ways to gain the trust of respondents so that they will answer more intimate questions without too much concern. Of course, many of these theoretical commitments are little more than 'rules of thumb', though no worse for that, but others are much more explicitly theoretical claims. The point is that no technique or method of investigation (and this is as true of the natural sciences as it is of the social) is self-validating. Its effectiveness, its very status as a research instrument making the world tractable to empirical investigation is dependent upon the kind of 'instrumental presuppositions', as Cicourel (1964) refers to them, sketched above. Further, methods and techniques are also dependent upon epistemological justifications. As Sheldon Wolin notes:

The employment of method . . . requires that the world be of one kind rather than another. Method is not a thing for all worlds. It presupposes a certain answer to a Kantian type of question. What must the world be like for the methodist's knowledge to be possible?

(Wolin 1973: 28–9)

What is not so clear, despite the account given earlier of philosophy being concerned to provide intellectual authority, is whether it is capable of providing such authority.[6] What is true is that for most researchers, be they in the natural or the human sciences, philosophical inquiry often looks like an irrelevance to their activities, and it can be suggested that the extent to which they are concerned about what philosophy has to say is motivated more by a search for security, as justification for what is going to be done anyway, than it is for practical guidance. In any case, philosophers themselves are no more in agreement about the status they want to claim for their pursuit than they are about anything else. Some philosophers have quite modest conceptions of philosophy's standing, perhaps regarding it as properly subordinate to science, performing some 'underlabourer' role as John Locke envisaged or as W.V.O. Quine does in our own time. In the underlabourer role, philosophy is an aide to science, clearing up confusions and other obstacles which may inhibit scientific progress. The great metaphysicians, on the other hand, such as Descartes, Kant, Hegel and, more recently, the phenomenologists, Husserl and Heidegger, propounded views on the nature of philosophy as a much mightier venture which would assess the pretensions of science. Husserl, for example, thought philosophy should be the 'first science', an indication of its priority over the empirical sciences. Philosophers have even questioned, as did Wittgenstein and, in their different way, the logical positivists, whether philosophy, or at least the metaphysical part of it, could have anything meaningful or significant to say on its own behalf. Wittgenstein cast doubt upon the very notion that has motivated much of Western philosophy, namely, that knowledge needed foundations.[7]

Since the nature of philosophy, and its relationship to other forms of knowledge, is itself a major matter of philosophical dispute, there is, of course, no real basis for us to advocate any one view on these matters as the unequivocally correct conception of the relationship between philosophy and social research. What can be acknowledged, however, is that many different views about the relationship are themselves represented in social science. Arguing about philosophical issues is not restricted to those with professional qualifications in that discipline, and a great deal of disputation within the social sciences is as much about philosophical topics, often conducted on the basis of arguments derived from the work of recognised philosophers, as it is about properly scientific or empirical matters.

Our concern here is with philosophical issues that are raised about appropriate methods of social research, though many of these issues will have a wider import than social research methods alone, encompassing themes which are theoretical in nature. Much of the discussion will, of necessity, relate to the philosophy of science, since much of social science thinking about method is shaped by one or other conception of the general nature of science. The question of whether any given social science is indeed a genuine science, only a pseudo-science or in some other way lacking in terms of the requirements of proper, mature sciences is a strong driver of disputes about both the nature of the social sciences and of the research within them, with research seen as designed to move the would-be sciences much closer to the standing of a full-fledged science. Because the social sciences commonly insist on measuring themselves against one or other philosopher's conception of the attributes of the most successful sciences, the social sciences have, therefore, since their appearance on the intellectual scene, constantly been accompanied by a sense of failure over their inability to make their achievements match those of the natural sciences they take as their model. The practical as well as the intellectual failings are also grist to the mill: in spite of economics we still have economic crises, a fact sometimes blamed on politicians for not listening to their economic advisors who, in any event, speak with very different voices; politicians blame social scientists for not dealing with the 'problems of our time', and so it goes.

The status of the social sciences remain unsettled. Within sociology, for example, debates range over whether it can be scientific in the manner of the natural sciences which has led, in its turn, to an extensive involvement with the philosophy of science in repeated attempts to understand what it takes to qualify as an example of authentic scientific knowledge, and whether sociology can hope to satisfy those requirements. There is a disquiet, too, about whether the optimism of a decade or so back was really justified, as many eminent methodologists begin to doubt the achievements, and question the direction of procedures for, social research which they had themselves previously endorsed. Even more recently we have the more drastic 'postmodern turn' which seeks to abandon the very premises upon which the ambition for a social science has rested since the early years of the nineteenth century and, before that, the Enlightenment. Whether philosophical rumination on these and other problems will resolve them is doubtful, since the problems are so widespread and multifarious. Nevertheless, what can be said is that some effort at clearing some of the philosophical ground would not go amiss.

The rationale of the book

It could be said that our concern is with the methodology of social research; that is, with an examination of the means of obtaining knowledge of the social world. As far as methods of social research are concerned, we shall endeavour to discuss the kind of claims that can be made about the knowledge they produce. This involves looking at the theories of knowledge upon which they are based and raising questions about their philosophical plausibility. In such a relatively short book as this we can do no more than present selected highlights of what we see as some of the main issues in the philosophy of social research. As we shall see, one of the problems of philosophy, and especially in a context such as the social sciences where philosophical issues are deeply ingrained, is that it is difficult to treat topics in a clearly defined step-by-step manner without seriously distorting them. A remark of Wittgenstein's about language can be applied to philosophy: 'You approach from *one* side and know your way about; you approach the same place from another side and no longer know your way about' (Wittgenstein 1958: para. 203). That is, one of the most difficult things in philosophy – although it is not unique in this – is to get a clear picture of just what the problem is. One might be fortunate to see things clearly from one direction but from another one might as well be enveloped in a fog. Another of Wittgenstein's images for philosophical investigations, that of disentangling a ball of thread which involves pulling first on one thread, then on another, going back to the first, then pulling on yet another, and so on, is that of criss-crossing the same intellectual ground. The implication of this is that it can often be difficult to follow through an argument in a linear fashion. It will need to be taken up, then set aside before being taken up yet again in a different context and from a different angle. This will certainly be a necessity of our presentation here where the same themes and thinkers will appear and reappear at different points in the exposition, and where the same argument will be relevant to quite distinct issues. The consequence is that it is impossible to provide an overview that will include everything that is of concern in the philosophy of social research. As we said earlier, our aim is to provide highlights and what we shall find is that, while we may illuminate one path, in the shadows lurk diversions which can undoubtedly be of interest but which we do not have room to discuss. We shall also find that issues keep surfacing in various guises but guises which are not mere disguise. They appear sufficiently differently to warrant looking at them again from a different vantage point.

The book is divided into two parts which attempts to represent, in a very simplified and schematic way, the main course of events affecting the relationship between philosophy and social research in the period since 1945. The key event during this period, as far as the philosophy of social research is concerned, has been the various reactions against positivism and its associated methodologies and methods. Accordingly, the first part of the book – from Chapters 2 to 4 covers the positivist position, its problems and some of the reasons for its rejection. The second part, beginning Chapter 5, deals with the aftermath of the widespread, though never universal, rejection of the positivist project.

The structure of the book is also intended to be instructive about the relationship between philosophy and methods of social research. It is easy to be confused about, and misrepresent, the nature of the reaction against positivism. In particular, it is too easy to misunderstand it as a denial of all utility to those research techniques of social research allegedly sponsored by positivism, such as the social survey, questionnaires, and techniques of statistical analysis. It is common but, in our view, misguided to present the case against positivism as an argument against, for example, the social survey. Or, alternatively, to suppose that indicating some valid uses to which the social survey may be put in sociology, for example in the kinds of sociology which are very close to data collection for administrative purposes, is to offer a defence against the critiques of positivism.[8] The fact that one can concede some modest, though limited, utility to the social survey is largely irrelevant to the argument over positivism (see Marsh 1982).

The positivist programme was not a modest one easily satisfied by the adoption of some useful, if limited, data collection and analysis techniques. Rather, it was an extremely ambitious and intendedly far-reaching project to achieve nothing less than the drastic transformation of the social sciences, implementing what it saw as the most demanding standards of thought, and bringing their results up to the very highest levels of validity comparable to those of the natural sciences. The positivist idea, as we shall see, is that there is a fundamental unity and foundation to all knowledge which is provided by the unity of science. As a consequence, the social sciences should be basically the same as, and capable of equally towering achievements as, the natural sciences. Thus, it is not the social survey as such – or its ancillary tools, such as statistical analysis, the interview or questionnaires – which is the focus of the criticism of positivism. After all, the social survey, being very much a pragmatically developed and practical device, has no *necessary* identification with the ideals, aspirations or requirements of positivism. This is not to say that the social survey, or any method for that matter, is without any problems or that, as a method, it contains nothing of philosophical interest. The social survey became the focus of the criticism of positivism because of the *status* it was assigned within the positivist project in which it was treated as the very paragon of social research practice, and as the means by which rigorous data could be collected and materials amenable to quantitative analysis could be assembled. In an instantiation of the positivist view and highly important for the direction of social research since 1945, the social survey was envisaged to be the main means of transforming the nature of social science, helping bring it into a new epoch in which theories could be formal constructions expressed in logico-mathematical terms, rather than natural language, and in which data could be analysed quantitatively.

In its heyday during the 1950s and early 1960s, positivism in Anglo-American sociology tended to a marked arrogance, inclined to suppose its own paragon status, and abruptly dismissive of any suggestion that there might be alternative approaches. It is this point which is worth bearing in mind in relation to current attempts to speak up, in reasoned and modest terms, on behalf of the social survey and its associated techniques. The original objection to these methods was that they were not paragons of sociological method. While they might have some practical utility they are, as practised by contemporary social scientists, hardly likely to be the instruments of the transformation of social research as envisaged by positivism. Thus, it was the extent to which the research practices and achievements of the social survey were 'talked up' as an exemplary and progressive movement in the advancement of social research toward authentic 'hard science' status which was the problem. Accordingly, scepticism about the extent to which (a) survey research embodied any particularly exceptional degree of scientific rigour relative to other possible research methods; (b) the positivist ideals were practicable and appropriate within social research; and (c) survey research was actually solving – as opposed to fudging – profound problems of method, can coexist, more or less comfortably, with the view that survey research is not devoid of all utility and that, in the foreseeable future, it may be as practically effective a method for tackling certain kinds of research problem – as opposed to the only legitimate method for tackling *all* the problems of social science – as one is likely to get. Divested of any connection with the positivist project, and therefore from the suggestion that those who adopt the survey and make use of the latest techniques of statistical manipulation are taking the first steps on the royal road to a truly successful science, survey research can continue to be used. But it becomes an activity without any particular significance for the social sciences. It is also deprived of its alibi: that its current results may be problematic and deficient, even by its own standards, but these failings may be overlooked against the fact that the effort is being made in service of the highest and most demanding of standards and ambitions. Thus, one achievement of the critique of the social survey was to sever its connection to the policies of the positivist project.

We have spent a little time overviewing the different places occupied by the critiques of certain methods of social research, using the survey as an example, and critiques of the positivist project, as an illustration of the often unclear connection between what a method can practically achieve and the kinds of claims that can be made on its behalf. As we shall see, the overselling of the survey and its associated methods as paragons of scientific social research obscured its real, if modest, utilities drawing upon itself a virulent attack that should have been directed at the pretensions of the positivist project. However, the important point for present purposes is that it is the claims, especially philosophical claims, made on behalf of research and its methods that need to be subjected to the closest scrutiny.

Any feeling that an injustice is being done to positivism in this book by subjecting it to the harshest and most demanding criticism should be mitigated by the knowledge that the project, in its heyday in the social sciences, was often an arrogantly assertive doctrine which was summarily dismissive of all conceivable alternatives, generally dogmatic in its responses to criticism and argument, as well as boastful of its own aims and achievements. Further, although we shall have much to criticise about the positivist project, we do not for a moment suggest that it has been conclusively rebutted. Conclusive outcomes are rare indeed in the social sciences and in philosophy. As we shall see, there are strong elements of the positivist conception which persist in the social sciences, though these days rarely in a full-blown form. However, the reaction against positivism did demote it from its preeminent position and placed it in a much more embattled one as well as, philosophically, encouraging revisionary efforts in an attempt to overcome its problems.

While we have suggested that in social science positivists were less than self-deprecating in their dealings with those who disagreed with them, it would be wrong to suppose that they were unaware of the difficulties confronting their own position; unaware, that is, of the problems in effectively realising, as opposed to programmatically prescribing for, their scientific aspirations. However, the characteristic response was to regard these difficulties as provisional problems to be solved within the parameters of the positivist project itself. Thus, the exposition of the story of positivism will progress through an outline of:

- the formation and elaboration of positivism's fundamental principles;
- the intramural debates over the problem in specifying and implementing positivist doctrines in research methods;
- the extramural criticisms which saw the difficulties with the positivist programme not as manifestations of temporary difficulties in applying a well-formed project, but as fundamental flaws.

It was in the middle and late 1960s that the opposition to the positivist project reached its full force and often led to the development of strong reservations not only about the validity of programmes encouraging the social sciences to emulate the natural sciences but often, and in the end, about even the validity of the natural sciences themselves. One way to challenge the positivist project was to condemn it for presenting 'science' as a unique and privileged venture which delivered ultimate knowledge of reality and to maintain, instead, that science was only one among a plurality of ways in which to represent reality; no worse, perhaps, but certainly no better than, other and even conflicting versions of reality. Relativism became, and has remained, a prominent topic of debate. Certainly, the sense that in the positivistic period there had been an unwarranted sense of certainty attached to the aims and achievements of science became widespread, which meant that epistemological issues were back on the agenda, especially in respect of the extent to which scepticism about 'positive' knowledge was possible. Doubts were not only expressed about the suitability of natural science as a model for social science but some raised the question of whether any knowledge of reality was possible.

In the second part of the book, we consider some of the more profound consequences which arise from the abandonment of positivism and the degree to which this abandonment entails also abandoning the quest for certainty which was so much the hallmark of positivism. It can certainly be argued that positivism had an unduly narrow picture of what was permissible in science and, therefore, sought to exclude from the social sciences activities which could, and quite validly, be done in the name of science. Thus, and for example, the positivists in social research were apt both to overestimate the extent to which the natural sciences were quantitative in nature (physics might be thoroughly quantitative and mathematical, but what about botany?) and grossly underestimated the difficulties confronting serious attempts at measurement in social science, neglecting the extent to which it might be the case that true quantitative understanding might emerge from rich qualitative understandings. At the level of research, as we indicated earlier, the critique of the positivist project was not aimed so much at placing a ban on the use of techniques, such as the social survey, or at primitive mathematical and statistical models, such as causal path analysis, but was intended, rather, to clear a legitimate space within the social sciences for those kinds of predominantly qualitative forms of research work which positivism tended to disparage.[9]

The argument is that the road to quantification in social science, if that is the road we want to go down, may be longer and more round-about than that tried by the positivist project and that it may have to travel through a long period of prior qualitative work. In the present period, those who espouse the validity of qualitative research do not necessarily have to dissociate themselves from positivism's objective of a formal, quantitative social science. Instead, they can treat this as an objective attainable, if at all, only over a much longer term than that envisaged by the positivist project. Moreover, given the remoteness of such a long-term result from the present conditions and practices of the social sciences, there is still no necessity to associate with the positivist project, since its prescriptions are characteristically designed to treat the attainment of formal theory and quantification as short-term matters. As we shall see, in basing this on rather misguided conceptions of the exemplary practices of natural science, positivism's efforts in this respect disregarded the substantive issues in the social sciences since they could not be addressed within the constricting restrictions of method which the positivists sought to impose. Thus one point against the positivist project was that it had the wrong idea even about what it wanted to do.

However, while some may regard themselves as aspiring no less to scientific status than positivism, differing only over the means toward broadly the same objective, there were others for whom the problem was more that of the privileged status accorded to science within the positivist scheme. As we have pointed out, positivism considered science to be very special, to be the embodiment of an authoritative, universal and final understanding of the nature of reality and superior to all other forms of understanding. Dissociation from this privileging conception of science has been a key feature of many of the movements of thought in the social sciences in the post-1960s and it is the consequences of some of these attempted dissociations that we shall look at in the second part of the book.

One view, discussed in Chapter 6, is that the positivists are inappropriately fixated on the provision of explanation, as is exemplified in their enthusiasm for the hypothetico-deductive scheme of theory, and therefore neglected the extent to which historical study and social research are actually about a different matter altogether than the subsumption of social life under lawlike generalities. They emphasised explanation at the expense of *understanding*. This point needs to be put in a couple of different ways to avoid as far as possible the confusion which can arise over the different meanings that 'explanation' and 'understanding' can have.

It can be argued that 'explanation' is a form of understanding and, accordingly, we need to put the criticism of the positivist project in the following way. The positivists identified understanding with only one form of it, namely, that provided through a formal, general theoretical scheme. They did not, in other words, appreciate the diversity of forms of understanding, the different kinds of explanation that could validly be given. Above all, they failed to appreciate that the kinds of explanation and understanding sought of other human beings is not of the theoretical, nor even necessarily of the scientific, kind at all.

It can also be argued that 'explanation' is distinct from, and the opposite of, 'understanding', if we understand the latter as the kind of transaction which goes on between people, in a way that it does not with inanimate phenomena, as they attempt to comprehend each other's meaning, that is, see the sense and significance of what they say and do. It is the kind of 'understanding' that is sought by other parties to a conversation, for example, and which arise in the social sciences insofar as these involve understanding 'other cultures' as a primary, even their main, task.

In either case, it is possible to argue that the problems of the social sciences are much closer to the problem of attaining a reciprocal understanding in a conversation than they are like those of the natural scientists seeking to attain exceptionless generalisations for natural phenomena. That is, the methodological problems and solutions for the social sciences are of a kind involved in comprehending difficult or obscure communications and not of the sort involved in attaining valid statistical generalisations. This view is often seen as expressing the 'hermeneutic' nature of the social sciences. Hermeneutics was precisely a method of 'understanding', a method for dealing with obscure and problematical communications, namely, those which originated in the attempt to understand ancient texts as clearly as possible but which came to be applied to all kinds of communication. It attempted to develop valid methods for understanding biblical and related writings, and so the idea of hermeneutics as a general conception is one of developing valid methods for understanding others, especially those from whom we are historically and culturally remote.[10]

It is entirely possible to regard hermeneutics as an important part of social science without necessarily rejecting the notion that these sciences are nonetheless scientific, as was argued by Max Weber and Alfred Schutz, for example. However, it is also possible to regard the 'communicative' character of social exchanges as indicating that they have an essentially different kind of subject matter than the sciences and that accepting the hermeneutic approach displaces any sort of scientific conception for the social sciences, as Winch and Gadamer do.

One can also regard the attainment of 'understanding' in the hermeneutic sense as one methodological phase in a series of phases of inquiry. Weber, for example, thought that attainment of an understanding of the actor's meaning was a stage in research to be followed by a phase establishing causal connections that validated connections only hypothetically made through understanding meanings. Rather than thinking of scientific concepts as putatively replacing those used by the members of a society, the hermeneutic emphasis on 'understanding' can lead to an argument about the extent to which social science concepts are *dependent upon* and *derivative from* commonsense concepts and not rivals to them. This can also lead on to the further argument that the relevance of commonsense understandings is as matters for social scientific study rather than from an invidious assessment of them against the supposed universal standards provided by science. This issue brings us to the rationality debates.

The notion that science is authoritative and universal has been taken by many social scientists, and not just those formally positivistic in their orientation, to mean that science can provide a standard for the evaluation of conduct, one which we can use to judge whether others' activities are fully, or at all, rational. 'Rational' is thus sometimes used to mean: in accord with the current scientific knowledge. This has to do with the connection, or 'rationality', to the idea of effective action. People seek to adapt means to ends, and they can be effective or not in this. Science tells us what the nature of the world is, how things really work. If this is so, then science ought to be able to tell us whether any given set of means can indeed be effective in attaining the end that is sought. If people have conceptions which differ from, even defy, those of science, and if they base their actions on them, then they ought not to be able to attain the goals. For example, if science tells us that there is no such thing as magic, then people who seek to achieve goals through magical means are doomed to fail. Those who use magic are, in this sense, irrational.

This idea that science provides a universal standard for all people and does so on the basis of a definitive grasp of the nature of reality, has become a particularly obnoxious feature for many. The question has been raised, and will be aired in Chapter 7, as to whether science can legitimately occupy its purportedly privileged position, and whether the notion of rationality outlined above is actually appropriate and helpful in the attempt at *understanding* other human beings. The rationality debate is almost an inevitable one which leads to charges and counter-charges on the issue of relativism. Does the refusal to privilege science mean that it is only as good as, no better than, primitive magic?

Refusing to privilege science can provoke the feeling that profound certainties are being lost. Science seems to offer the prospect of a stable point of reference outside the turbulence of otherwise contending points of view, an all-encompassing God's eye view of things, and one which is objective in being above the partialities and perspective that otherwise pervade human life. Such a view seems to deny the fact that science is, after all, one more human activity, and to presuppose what cannot just be unquestioningly conceded, namely, that science can rise above the human condition. Science is a cultural phenomenon, and if cultures are local, partial and perspectival, then perhaps science is just the same, expressing particular points of view but attempting to pass itself off as something special. It makes its moves in the rivalry of cultures, not on the basis of its grasp on the true nature of reality itself, but by its effective performance in presenting itself through its large claims and persuading, by fair means and foul, other people to accept them. Thus, the aim is not to begin from assumptions about science's presumed objectivity

– its universality, superiority or finality – but to bring these into question at the outset. The question is not only whether science is entitled to the privileging claim for it, but whether the objectivity sought by science is possible at all.

This kind of scepticism has consequences for the views of those who have supposed that they can reestablish the social sciences on the basis of a concern with 'meaning' and through hermeneutic type methodologies, for if all objectivity is being conclusively denied, then there cannot be objectivity about meaning either. Chapter 8 expands on this theme.

One final word. By training we are sociologists and so, on the principle that authors should write according to their strengths, such as they are, most of the examples and ideas are derived from this particular social science. However, it should not be thought that other social sciences do not experience the problems we will discuss; on the contrary. Throughout, unless accurate exposition dictates otherwise, we have used the term 'social science' for convenience, and would remind the reader that the scientific status of these disciplines is an issue in what follows.

Notes

1. See Hughes *et al.* (1995) for an exposition of the thought of these figures and their impact on contemporary thought. Also, despite its self-avowed emphasis on psychology, Smith (1997) is an excellent source for the history of the social sciences.
2. This is very much a summary of what were deep and complex changes over many centuries. What is certain is that we cannot extrapolate our present disciplines back into the past. What also needs to be taken into account are the historically very recent processes through which disciplines, as we know them, were formed and established along with their boundaries. See Smith (1997).
3. We mean by this no more than that one needs to have experience of a culture in which such lorries ply their trade in the way described. Ordinary puzzlement of this kind is not the issue here.
4. The phrase 'deep scepticism' is taken from Phillips (1996) which is an excellent introduction to philosophy and its problems.
5. We do not intend to imply that care for these kinds of things can only be manifested by academics. Such care can, of course, be shown in all sorts of occupations and activities. Our point is to emphasise the quality of the activities rather than tying them to some institutional role.
6. The issue of philosophy's own intellectual authority has recently come under attack from the social constructionists who argue that philosophy itself is culturally shaped and, hence, no more secure than any other form of knowledge. See, for example, Bloor (1976). Earlier, Wittgenstein set out to challenge the nature of philosophy itself in his later work.
7. Wittgenstein (1958). See also Anderson *et al.* (1988, ch. 8) for a summary of Wittgenstein's ideas.
8. On the development of the social survey, see Ackroyd and Hughes (1991).

9. In some cases, qualitative research was expropriated by so-called positivist methods by seeing them, for instance, as useful preliminary, pilot research to aid in the design of research using more quantitative methods, such as the social survey.

10. Note that 'hermeneutics' names a particular tradition, and not all those, such as Peter Winch, who want to make similar arguments, would want to count themselves as recommending this tradition.

CHAPTER 2

The positivist orthodoxy

A word of caution is in order about the title of this chapter. The critics of positivist social science, among whom we wish to be counted, like all critics have a tendency to present a picture of the opposition, in this case positivism, as if it were not only stupid but without any subtlety and variety. Although it is necessary to give a summary, hence simplified, picture of positivism, the reader is warned that it is neither a stupid position, though it might be wrong, nor a monolithic school of thought. What we here refer to as 'positivism' includes or overlaps with positions which identify themselves by other names – 'empiricism', 'behaviourism', 'naturalism' – and some which even identify themselves as *the* 'scientific approach'. Just to make things more complicated, some of these same names are sometimes used to identify antipositivist positions. 'Positivism' is also a term, as indicated, associated with a number of rather disparate philosophical schools. Nevertheless, we shall continue with the label 'positivism' since it is so widely used in the way we deploy it here, and shall draw attention to differences as and when necessary.

We refer to 'the positivist orthodoxy' because, in some of its versions, it was for some time, and until recently, the nearest thing to an orthodoxy in the social sciences, and probably even now is the philosophical epistemology that holds intellectual sway within the domain of social research methods though, these days, this hold is no longer as strong or unquestioned as it once was. Since it has been vehemently attacked since the late 1960s, there are few brave enough now to embrace the positivist label with any great gusto. Nevertheless, despite this marked decline in its preeminence, social research's most used research instruments, such as the survey, the questionnaire, statistical models, the idea of research as hypothesis testing and theory corroboration, to mention but a few, all embody the formative influence of positivism. As one commentator says of the relationship between positivism and sociology, 'even if in its simpler philosophical forms it is dead, the spirit of those earlier formulations continues to haunt sociology, in a full range of guises . . .'.[1] Also, while in some social sciences, such as sociology, its authority is less than absolute, and probably always has been so, in economics it is not easily challenged even now.[2] Political science had its 'behavioural movement' rather later than its compatriot disciplines and this still holds a strong position. In psychology, too, positivism's hold is weakening but is still immensely strong and perhaps continues to prevail. History is beginning to make more use of statistical methods classically associated with social research and, to this extent, is entering into a more positivistic orientation. The growth of such fields as educational research, management studies, marketing – as endeavours within higher education institutions, and associated with the human sciences – have revived positivism's fortunes in some ways.[3] So, it is still worth looking at the philosophical character of positivism not out of some archaeological interest in a decayed civilisation but because it is very much alive.[4]

However, the authority of positivism did not arise overnight, but grew out of a long intellectual debate.

An intellectual background

Although it is customary to trace philosophical ancestors back to the early Greeks, the more proximate origins of positivist epistemology lie in that blooming of European thought in the sixteenth and seventeenth centuries. Even though the Renaissance and Enlightenment picture of the intellectual darkness of the Middle Ages was overdrawn, these later centuries saw tremendous changes in ways of thinking, particularly through the beginnings of modern science but also in social and political thought. European thought was gradually freed from the theological cage erected by an alliance between political Absolutism and the Roman Catholic Church. Although 'natural philosophers', and Newton is a good example, often saw their endeavours as primarily religious rather than purely scientific, giving a means of understanding the mind of God and the nature of his perfect creation, the allegorical world picture of medieval times was replaced by a scepticism over whether nature could be properly explained by reference to the Bible or to religious dogma. Though religious elements were still strong, the groundwork was being laid for a secular vision of the traditional theological images of the natural and the social worlds.[5]

Two figures stand out sharply: Francis Bacon (1561–1626) and René Descartes (1596–1650). The former continued the Aristotelian legacy of empiricism as the account of the foundations of human knowledge, while the latter continued the Platonic rationalist tradition. Both were looking for an intellectual method that would defeat scepticism and, in doing so, provide a new certainty for knowledge of the world. Bacon argued for the authority of experience, experiment, induction and painstaking observation as the way toward a reliable basis for scientific ideas, thus rejecting the *a priori* method of medieval scholasticism. For him, a theory of knowledge had to emphasise the methodical accumulation of experientially tested findings. True knowledge of nature required the scrupulous design and conduct of experiments, patiently working to the 'most general axioms, ridding the mind of false notions', opinions and received tradition. Descartes, on the other hand, placed his faith in the certainty of mathematics, especially geometry, as the fundamental basis for scientific knowledge. For him, mathematical principles were timeless and unchanging and, therefore, the most suitable language for expressing the laws of nature. Though the doctrines of each of these were very different, they both supposed that knowledge must rest on foundations.[6] Descartes, along with other rationalist philosophers, such as Spinoza and Leibnitz, while not denying the value of sensory experience, experiment and observation, stressed the role of logical deduction from self-evident premises, while Bacon, Locke, Hume and other empiricist philosophers took the view that the search for knowledge started with direct sensory experience, and it was this latter branch of the epistemological divide that was carried forward by positivist philosophy.

Comte's positivism

In the social sciences the first self-conscious proclamation of the positivist view came from Auguste Comte (1798–1857). He followed the optimistic impulses of Diderot and other French Enlightenment *philosophes* in extending Bacon's ideas about the study of nature to the social. It was Comte who coined the term 'positivist philosophy' and, as well, 'social physics' and 'sociology'.[7] Comte's work was influenced by the major philosophical attacks on metaphysics made by Hume (1711–76) and others, in the eighteenth century, and by the new ideas of progress and order emerging from the French Revolution. Comte's positivism is also a theory of history in which progress in knowledge is itself the motor of historical change. Comte saw the task of philosophy as attempting to express the eventual synthesis of all scientific knowledge in which the sciences would be unified into one great system. His own theory of knowledge stressed that science consisted of precise and certain method, basing theoretical laws on sound empirical observation. For him the social sciences were kin to the natural sciences, sharing the same epistemological form and equally free from the speculative dross of metaphysics, an aversion shared by most positivistic views. Although Comte was sufficiently a child of the Enlightenment to reject theological criteria for knowledge, he also rejected the rationalist's claim that knowledge could be derived from thought alone, and, instead, pressed the claim that knowledge is derived only from empirical evidence.

Though Comte's explicit doctrines have little more than historical interest these days, his spirit was carried forward later in the century in the work of John Stuart Mill (1806–1873), Herbert Spencer (1820–1903) and Emile Durkheim (1858–1917), and is still, though diffusely, represented in the style and manner of some parts of the social sciences today. Of Comte's claims, perhaps the most influential was his assertion that society, including values and beliefs, could follow the same logic of inquiry as that employed by natural science. Comte's explicit espousal of a unity of method between the natural and the social sciences was timely and fateful. It gave impetus and strength to the view that the explanation of social phenomena, that is, all that is studied by the human sciences, was not, in principle, different from the explanation of natural events: a view endorsed by Mill. Indeed, for Comte, the development of all sciences followed a historical sequence from mathematics, through astronomy, the physical and the biological sciences, to reach their apogee in the rise of the social sciences.[8] Sociology was to be, in Comte's terms, the Queen of the Sciences. Phenomena in both the human and the natural worlds were subject to invariant laws. Though there were differences between the human and the natural sciences arising from their respective subject matters, the development of appropriate research methods in the former would remove these irritants so that the social sciences could take their rightful place at the head of the hierarchy of human knowledge. As indicated earlier, Comte himself stressed the importance of indirect experimentation, observation, and the comparative method. More deeply than this, his view encouraged a deterministic conception of people and society by effectively underplaying those factors normally regarded as uniquely human: free will, choice, chance, morality, and the emotions. Human social life was simply the result of a coalescence of forces interacting so as to produce a particular sequence of behaviour. History, too, was simply a theme with variations in which human and other factors combined to work themselves out through time (see Toulmin and Goodwin 1965, especially ch. 5).

Throughout the nineteenth century this conception gained an authority continually reinforced by the amazing successes of the natural sciences and their applications. The landmarks of this progress are familiar, the most famous being the publication in 1859 of Darwin's *The Origin of Species,* which gave a systematic statement of the idea that could be used as a resource for the claim that humankind was irretrievably part of nature and subject to the same laws of process, adaptation and change. It was not long before the social sciences began to use these insights to develop theories of human society. Marx (1818–1883), for example, although born and bred in the very different philosophical tradition of Hegelianism, wished to dedicate his monumental work on capitalism to Darwin. Herbert Spencer (1820–1903), explicitly borrowed from Darwin's work as a vindication of his own theory and method. By the end of the century positivism's scientific-deterministic view was firmly entrenched as the ambition of the social sciences. However, although, as far as the human sciences were concerned, it was positivist systems which became dominant, there were rivals. There was, in philosophy, towards the end of the nineteenth century, a revolt against positivist thought and a resurgence of idealism and romanticism, a movement particularly strong in Germany.[9]

The questions we now want to address are what positivism implied for the practices of the social sciences beyond the ambition and exhortations to pursue it. What rules of investigation, what techniques and methods of research did it justify and authorise? What kind of knowledge did it claim was the proper goal of social science?

The elements of positivism

According to Giddens, in its widest sense 'positivist philosophy' refers to those perspectives that have made some or all of the following claims.[10] First, that reality consists in what is available to the senses. Second, philosophy, while a distinct discipline, is parasitic on the findings of science. Associated with this is an aversion to metaphysics as having any rightful place in philosophical inquiry proper. As a philosophy, therefore, positivism is as much concerned to establish the limits of knowledge as its character. Hume's petulant outburst against metaphysics captures the general spirit well:

If we take in our hand any volume; of divinity or school metaphysics, for instance; let us ask, Does it contain any abstract reasoning concerning quantity or number? No. Does it contain any experimental reasoning concerning matter of fact and existence? No. Commit it then to the flames: for it can contain nothing but sophistry and illusion.

(Hume 1975: Sec. XII, Part III)

Third, that the natural and the human sciences share common logical and methodological principles. This is not to say that they share identical research techniques since their respective subject matters differ and so require rather different investigative practices, but this is a matter of pragmatic adaptation of a general procedure, not one of logical or principled difference. Fourth, that there is a fundamental distinction between fact and value, science dealing with the former with the latter belonging to an entirely different order of discourse beyond the remit of science. As we shall see later, the positivists did not think that all distinctively human qualities were beyond the reach of scientific understanding. While scientific knowledge has its limits, these do not exclude knowledge of the mental or 'inner' life of human beings. Science can study and describe human values, but cannot assess their ultimate truth.

This résumé of the main elements of positivist thought as it applies to the human sciences cannot, obviously, do justice to the variety represented by its many versions. From the perspective of social research the important questions turn on what positivism implies, first, for the methods of studying society; second, what it claims about the proper knowledge to be gained from such study and, third, the criteria necessary to assess that knowledge and distinguish it from beliefs and understanding which cannot qualify as knowledge. These are wide-ranging questions, and there are many styles of social research equally consistent with the broad precepts just discussed. However, as a system of thought with pretensions to authorising versions of the world, both the natural and the social (and positivism is particularly strident, not to say intolerant, in its views of what knowledge is), some of its main manifestations need closer examination.

The revulsion against metaphysics was bound up with a strong commitment to scientific knowledge which dealt – ideally – with facts, systematically discovered, and rigorously established which could then serve as adequate grounds for theories. In order to make and maintain the distinction between empirically grounded knowledge and mere speculation, demarcation criteria were needed.

Positivism recognised only two bona fide forms of knowledge, the empirical and the logical: the former represented by natural science and the latter by logic itself and also by mathematics. By far the greater importance was attached to the empirical. In this it took its inspiration from that philosophical tradition which claimed that all our ideas come in one way or another from our sensory experience of the world; any idea that cannot be shown to be derived from this was not a genuine idea. Clearly, such a view is dependent on a presumption that the external world acts on our senses and, in this way, is made known to us at least in a 'brute' form. It also served as a criterion by which to determine what was knowledge and what was merely superfluous speculation; ideas only deserved the appellation of knowledge if they could be put to the test of empirical experience. There was no knowledge prior to experience which itself was informative about the world. As we shall see, mathematics presented a problem for this view.

Though this view of the source of knowledge had some plausibility as an account underpinning natural scientific knowledge, there were difficulties in applying it to human life. The notion of fact, especially when posed in opposition to value and the kind of entities conjured up by metaphysicians, had strong connotations of the material world, the world of fixed, tangible, permanent *matter*. To this extent, positivism had to overcome a distinction expressed in a number of ways between 'things material' and 'things human' (or, in the realm of the mind); a distinction massively important in the history of thought involving, as it did, legal, religious and ethical as well as political implications. Given the all-embracing imperial ambitions of positivism, if it was to encompass social phenomena it had to invalidate the view that the human and the material world comprised essentially different orders of phenomena. Some positivists denied the distinction altogether by insisting that what we would regard as distinctively human phenomena were either themselves only illusions or misleadingly appeared to be different from the facts of material nature. This meant reducing human activities which appeared to be other than material in nature to phenomena of an intrinsically physiological, chemical, biological or behavioural nature. Others, however, were not reductionists in this sense, claiming instead that human and material phenomena were equally real, but the former were not amenable to reduction to purely material facts – Durkheim was a major proponent of this view as we shall see – though this did not detract from the fact that the two kinds of phenomena were to be known through the same general methods of scientific inquiry.

The difficulties of applying the general method in the case of human and social phenomena were manifold. For one thing phenomena in the material world, if only as a matter of common sense, seemed to have a nature and character independent of the observer, while so much of human phenomena seemed entirely relative to the observer. How could one reach an understanding of beliefs, systems of magic, emotion, morality, legal codes, legends, public opinion, and the like, in the same way that one could of the moon, the stars, skeletons, gases, chemical compounds, and so on? Do the former possess the same attributes of permanence, durability, and independence of human volition and perception as do phenomena of the external material world? These were some of the questions that had to be answered before positivism could successfully claim that the human world, like the physical, operated according to natural laws which could be discovered by a scientific method taken from the natural sciences.

So, the questions were: 'What in the human world corresponded to the "hard facts" of nature?' 'What procedures were appropriate for discovering and studying these facts?' And, assuming these questions were satisfactorily answered, 'What were the laws corresponding to the laws of nature?' By the early nineteenth century there were some straws in the wind. Some scholars were beginning to take seriously the observation, now seeming rather self-evident, that human action is not random but conforms to predictable patterns. One of the great insights, late in the eighteenth century, was Adam Smith's formulation that individuals acting on their own self-interested preferences could, as if controlled by an 'invisible hand', produce generally beneficent large-scale social regularities (Smith 1970). The very notion of society, it came to be realised, strongly implies a set of phenomena which, though involving individuals with all their uniqueness, independence and unpredictability, nevertheless, exhibit stable large-scale regularities as real and as predictable as individuals are unique and different. In short, there were ideas around which made it plausible to conceive of society as a level of reality *sui generis*. The problem was to implement this idea.

There were, and still are, many puzzles here and it is opportune at this juncture to look in more detail at one exemplary attempt to solve these, that of Durkheim, which was of pivotal importance in promoting positivist aspirations within sociology. Like that of other great thinkers, Durkheim's work displays many contradictions, inconsistencies, dubious arguments and other deficiencies, but he did attempt to think through the positivist approach and inspired much of the spirit that has since enthused positivistic social science.[11]

Durkheim's positivism

Durkheim was the first sociologist since Comte, to whom he owed a considerable intellectual debt, who in a serious though much less imperialistic sense carried forward Comte's vision of sociology, zealously justifying sociology as an autonomous discipline characterised by the application of the scientific method. Durkheim shared Comte's empiricism, his views on the unity of science, his devotion to rational social reform, and his distrust of psychology, but rejected as bordering on the metaphysical many of Comte's pronouncements about the laws of the historical progress of knowledge. Durkheim's own work encompassed philosophical discussions on the nature of sociology as well as his more substantive enquiries into the division of labour, suicide, religion and education. In significant respects his work builds a bridge between the nineteenth century and the twentieth. Many of his ideas – including the centrality of the division of labour for social organisation, the recognition that society represented a level of reality in its own right, that society was fundamentally a moral order – had their roots in Comte and his contemporaries. Other scholars, too, particularly J. S. Mill, Herbert Spencer, Ferdinand Tönnies, had their influence on Durkheim's ideas. However, although Durkheim was very much a child of nineteenth century thought, he was to modify that tradition in consequential ways.

Durkheim insisted that society was an essentially moral phenomenon in that it was the shared, collective ways of thinking, perceiving and acting that comprised the 'hard facts' of social life, and which had a constraining effect on individuals through obligation, a constraint that was as powerful as that set up by physical forces. Society, therefore, predominantly consisted in a collective moral consciousness. This, he held, was expressed in religion, in law, in the division of labour, in institutionalisation itself. Yet, like a true child of positivism, he wanted to show that the fact that society was primarily a moral reality did not detract from the idea that it should be studied by the same methods as those of the natural sciences which were demonstrably superior to other methods of conjecture and speculation. The latter included social philosophy which, in attempting to study the moral association of society, had endeavoured to forge a unity between idealism and materialism. This philosophy argued for a strict duality between nature and human life, thereby rejecting the positivistic idea of a unity of method between the natural and the social, or human, sciences. For his part, Durkheim wished to retain a distinctive conception of humankind as having an essential moral existence, but to study this by using the methods of natural science without their materialistic implications which, unfortunately in his view, led to a reduction of the distinctively human to the material. Herein lies the importance of his efforts to establish sociology as an autonomous discipline defined by its object of study and to avoid the tendency in much of nineteenth century thought to reduce the moral and the social to an epiphenomenon of material forces, a tendency most marked in Marx. Moral phenomena, such as law, religion, and morality itself, were regular, orderly phenomena and could be the object of a natural science if studied in the correct way. 'The aim is to bring the ideal, in various forms, into the sphere of nature, with its distinctive attributes unimpaired' (Durkheim 1953: 96). These aspirations left Durkheim with two related problems to solve and to do so within the framework of positivism: first, to establish the reality of the social and, second, to discover ways in which it may be scientifically investigated.

Science, for Durkheim, was the study of 'things' and could only proceed on the basis that it had first accurately described and classified those 'things' which comprised its subject matter. Having done this, it could then go on to explain the ways in which they were connected. The notion of 'things' is contrasted with ideas:

Things include all objects of knowledge that cannot be conceived by purely mental activity, those that require for their conceptions data from outside the mind, from observations and experiments, those which are built up from the more external and immediately accessible characteristics to the less visible and more profound.

(Durkheim 1966: xliii)

A most important characteristic of 'things' is that they are not subject to our will, but resist our attempts to change them, showing, according to Durkheim, that their existence is independent of our beliefs about them; 'things' in Durkheim's sense are entities of the world external to the individual's awareness.

Sciences deal with 'things' and sociology and the social sciences should be no exception to this. So, turning from the general properties of 'things' in general we must now examine the way in which Durkheim tries to demonstrate the facticity, the 'thingness', of the social. 'Social facts' take on properties of 'things' in general: they are external to us, are resistant to our will, and constrain us. By way of illustration he cites the French language, moral rules, economic organisations, laws, customs: all social phenomena but which are independent of and constrain individuals. We cannot, as individuals, alter or change them as we please but must live within their frame.

Here, then, is a category of facts with very distinctive characteristics: it consists of ways of acting, thinking, and feeling, external to the individual, and endowed with a power of coercion, by reason of which they control him . . . the term 'social' applies to them exclusively, for it has a distinct meaning only if it designates exclusively the phenomena which are not included in any of the categories of facts that have already been established and classified. These ways of thinking and acting therefore constitute the proper domain of sociology.

(Durkheim 1966: 3–4)

These facts are not reducible to other disciplines, for example, to biology or to psychology, which have their own order of facts. 'Social facts', nonetheless, are 'things' in that they possess the requisite characteristics which make them facts in the world and not states just in the minds of individuals: externality, constraint, diffuseness and generality, and – because they are facts of collective life – are distinctive to sociology, belonging to no other discipline or science. Sociology is an independent discipline which studies a distinctive kind of fact which is not, and cannot be, properly investigated by any other science.

Durkheim's conception of society is a 'realist' one because it holds that there exists, within the realm of nature, an entity defined in terms of a system of relations responsible for generating collectively shared norms and beliefs. Society is a reality 'in itself' and 'social facts' exist 'in their own right' quite apart from manifestations of them in and by individuals. It is individuals, for example, who commit suicide but the suicide rate indicates a 'social fact' independent of individual suicides. It is the interaction and association of individuals which gives rise to the emergent phenomena of the social, and which is not reducible to psychology (a fate Durkheim particularly wanted to avoid) or to biology. For Durkheim this means that the explanation of 'social facts' has to be in terms of other social facts.

Society is not a mere sum of individuals . . . the system formed by their association represents a specific reality which has its own characteristics . . . It is, then, in the nature of this collective individuality . . . that one must seek the immediate and determining causes of the facts appearing therein.

(1966: 103–4)

The task of the sociologist, according to Durkheim, is to describe the essential characteristics of social facts, explain how they come into being, enter into relationships with one another, act on each other, and function together to form social wholes. Durkheim's 'realism' did not equate to 'materialism' in the way that, for example and on some readings, Marx's did. It is possible to read Marx and some of his followers as holding that only material phenomena are real and that, therefore, 'ideal' phenomena, such as beliefs and ideas, are not as real as material phenomena and, hence, cannot be effective causes of the behaviour of material things, such as human beings. Durkheim's realism includes ideal phenomena. For him, social reality consists, in the main part, in ideas and beliefs, albeit collective rather than individual products, and the fact that these are 'ideal' rather than 'material' does not detract from their reality or from their capacity to exercise causal influence on the behaviour of individuals. By acting together individuals produce linguistic symbols, religious beliefs, moral codes, laws and the like, shared by most members of a particular society or group. Accordingly, when individuals think and act on these shared ideas or 'representations' they do so not as isolated individuals but as members of a larger cultural whole. Moreover, in doing so they produce and reproduce a structure or pattern which gives that group or society its characteristic morphology; that is, its arrangements, for example, by the way a society is differentiated into social groups each of which has the same characteristics as others, or whether the constituent groups are differentiated from each other, each having distinctive characteristics from the others. Social life consists of collective 'representations' – which include the ways of thinking about and portraying both natural and social reality – and which are states of the 'conscience collective' operating according to their own laws distinct from the psychological laws which govern the individual consciousness of its members.

Having established, to his own satisfaction at least, the reality of the social, Durkheim's next task was to show how it may be made known by a social science. To this end he devoted one of his most famous studies, that of suicide, to elucidating the procedures for a definitive study and explanation of 'social facts'. The broad outlines of such an endeavour were already there in the notion of 'social facts' as 'things' but there were essential details of method and methodology arising out of the particular nature of the social. His conception of 'social facts' as external to the individual led him to reject the view that a satisfactory explanation of a social fact was to describe its present role in society, that is, the point or the use it had for those who were dependent upon it. As a corollary, it was entirely unsatisfactory to try to explain the existence of an institution by supposing that it was intentionally brought into being on the basis of benefits it might bring to individuals. Durkheim eschews this and any forms of teleological explanation which seek to explain things in terms of the ends or purposes they are imagined to serve: 'social facts' require explanation by causes (and ones of which individuals are not conscious) that are deterministic rather than purposive.

Earlier it was remarked that Durkheim, in his efforts to establish an intellectual warrant for sociology, had to overcome the 'materialist' view that tended to deny reality to 'ideal' phenomena. This step was necessary in order to bring the world of 'ideas' under the inquiring eye of science. Science, for Durkheim, dealt with that which is 'subject to observation' (Durkheim 1966: 27). Scientific observation was, however, and as Durkheim realised, no straightforward matter. 'Things', or in the specific case of sociology 'social facts', did not just appear to our senses. On the contrary, what appears directly to our senses is often misapprehended, even illusory. For Durkheim, the members of society – though subject to or bearers of 'social facts' – more often than not are deluded about the nature of social reality. They are more likely to substitute the 'representations' of 'social facts' for the real thing. These *notiones vulgares* or *idola* are illusions which distort the perception of real social processes and are entirely the products of the mind 'like a veil drawn between the thing and ourselves' (1966: 15). To build firm foundations sociology, like any science, must break away from these mental illusions to uncover the real. Scientists must, then, be prepared to approach the social world as if they were looking at it for the first time: 'He must feel himself in the presence of facts whose laws are as unsuspected as were those of life before the era of biology; he must be prepared for discoveries which will surprise and disturb him' (1966: xiv). Thus, Durkheim draws a firm contrast between the way in which the world appears to the untutored understandings of those who live in society, and who encounter social facts as part of their everyday life but have only a partial and superficial awareness of their nature, and the way the world will appear when understood in terms of the deep and general knowledge that will result from the systematic examination of those same facts using the proper methods of science.

The point that Durkheim is making here is an important one. In saying that the members of society do not really know what 'social facts' are because they have only a superficial and distorted familiarity with them, Durkheim holds fast to the idea that truly to know something is to have discovered it through the application of the scientific method. He is not saying that they have no idea whatsoever of them, simply that their ideas are impressionistic, vague and confused as to their real nature. Especially revealing in this connection are his remarks on defining 'suicide' as a scientific construct:

We must inquire whether, among the different varieties of death, some have common qualities objective enough to be recognisable by all honest observers, specific enough not to be found elsewhere and also sufficiently kin to those commonly called suicides for us to retain the same term without breaking with common usage.

(Durkheim 1952: 42)

However, what is also clear from this quotation is that the social scientist cannot ignore common conceptions despite the fact that they are vague, often unclear, ambiguous, rough and in need of clarification. On the contrary, the concepts of ordinary life are a source of social scientific concepts and the task of social scientists is to transform them into scientific ones by dealing with the phenomena they denote as 'things' and try to rid themselves of the prejudices and other preconceptions common-sense knowledge contains and which, for Durkheim, are impediments to scientific knowledge. 'Social facts' must be observed from the 'outside', as it were, as dispassionately and objectively investigated as if one were examining physical facts.

Durkheim is making more than the point that science comes about because the scientist adopts a particular *attitude* to the world, as his dictum 'social facts must be regarded as things' might seem to imply. Important as this posture is, he is also claiming that it is efficacious in making the real nature of the world known. However, attitude and stance are not enough; other methods are required to enable the sociologist to recognise 'social facts'. What these are are already provided in his notion of a 'thing', and its embodiment in the concept of 'social fact', which provides some criteria for distinguishing phenomena that are 'social facts' from those that are not; 'social facts' are general, external, collective and constraining. So, beginning with what might be the appearances of 'social facts', the 'illusions' – which are all that is available to start with, not the direct apprehension of 'social facts' – the social scientist must be rid of preconceptions. The second task is to look for the phenomena that display the characteristics of 'things' and, third, define them scientifically. Definition is an essential procedure in Durkheim's epistemology since it is the means by which the scientist establishes 'contact with things' (1966: 42). It is also the way in which the scientist avoids the risk of taking a misleadingly partial view of the phenomenon in question. A correct definition must be all-encompassingly general, catching the distinctive characteristics of all the phenomena that come under the term. Thus, a definition of religion must encompass all phenomena that are called religious which it would not do if, for example, 'belief in a divine being' were used as a definitional characteristic. This would fit Christianity but would exclude other religions, such as Buddhism, which do not include belief in a divine being.

A scientific definition of a phenomenon is constructed by grouping together common external and objective characteristics and, once having formulated a definition, including in the investigation all those phenomena that conform to it. To define crime, for example, it is first observed that crime can be recognised by particular external signs and that what distinguishes crime from other social phenomena is that it provokes a reaction 'from society', namely, punishment. Punishment is not an individual act though individuals are its operative agents. It is a matter for the society, embodied in legal and moral codes and, as such, a sign that the 'collective conscience' is involved in some manner. Similarly, 'suicide' is defined as 'all cases of death resulting directly or indirectly from a positive or negative act of the victim himself which he knows will produce this result' (Durkheim 1952: 44). This definition, according to Durkheim, denotes a homogeneous group, distinguishable from others, and delimits a phenomenon for investigation as a 'social fact'.

To effect the move from external appearances to the real phenomenon Durkheim invokes the principle of causation, an axiom essential to his epistemology. Durkheim had closely attended to John Stuart Mill's methodological writings and agreed with him on the difficulties faced by the social sciences in devising suitable experiments to test their theories. Yet, since Durkheim insisted that the hallmark of science was that it dealt with causes, then this must also be a normal procedure for sociology. The explanation of social facts should be tested on the assumption that a given effect always proceeds from a single cause despite the fact that, in actuality, causal relationships were entangled in complex ways. Thus, once a category of social fact has been defined, it will be possible to find a single explanatory factor for it. Or, as in his study of suicide, Durkheim could identify subspecies or types of suicide in terms of their different subspecies of causes.

Since direct experiment to establish cause was not possible for the social sciences, resort must be made to the comparative method. For Durkheim this meant, effectively, 'concomitant variation' or, as we know it now, correlation; that is, the parallel movement of the series of values presented by two phenomena as accomplished through statistical manipulations. This alone, provided that the relationship has been shown in a sufficient number and variety of cases, is proof that a causal relationship exists. The constant concomitance of two factors is sufficient to establish a law (Durkheim 1966: 130–1). By itself the discovery of a lawlike relationship was not sufficient for any profound understanding, but only to indicate that a connection of some causal kind existed. A third factor might be responsible for the correlation between the original facts, and further investigation would need to deal with this possibility. But, through successive refinements, a closer and closer approximation could be effected towards uncovering the true relationship between 'social facts'.

One point that needs to be repeated and stressed here is Durkheim's insistence that the causes of 'social facts' must be sought among other 'social facts'. Thus, the social fact of a stable suicide rate must be a manifestation of, and explained by, equally persistent properties of the social structure, such as the distribution of the populations between religious faiths or into household units. This explanation of one social fact by another is one of the conditions on which the very existence of sociology as an autonomous discipline depends; it must not be reducible to the phenomena which belong to the domain of another discipline, such as psychology or biology. Each science deals with its own domain and cannot look beyond itself for explanatory causes.

One of the important aspects of Durkheim's work from the point of view of this book is the way he endeavours not only to provide ontological and epistemological foundations for sociology but, not content to rest with such programmatics, tried to apply these to problems in both sociological theory and social reform. This latter concern builds on the moralistic and reforming tradition represented by Comte, among others, in the rational, that is, science-based, and ameliorative intervention to ensure society's well-being. In which case it was vital to demonstrate the scientific status of sociology as a means, not only of understanding the origins of the various pathologies that society was heir to, but also to justify corrective intervention. Showing that social processes were subject to causal laws and gaining knowledge of these through disciplined inquiry would, in Durkheim's view, provide at last a scientific basis on which to base social reform. His 'rules of sociological method' were intended to go beyond the merely illustrative use of historical and social examples, as he claimed that Comte, Spencer and others had done, and to ground sociology as a systematic science.

Of particular interest is Durkheim's study of suicide, which impressively displays the relationship between his philosophical ideas about science, the nature of sociology and their application in the investigation of a substantive phenomenon. The decision to study suicide was particularly courageous given Durkheim's assertions about the nature of social facts. Of all human acts, suicide seemed so personal, so much a product of individual will – a point of view he fully recognises in his definition of suicide – that it is hard to see how it could be studied as a sociological rather than a psychological matter. Nonetheless, he strongly maintained that explanation in terms of individual psychology was insufficient. Concomitant variation shows that there is no relationship between the suicide rates in different populations and the rates of certain psychopathological states. For example, suicide is often thought to be a result of mental illness, but that cannot be the basis for a general, lawlike relationship because, for example, the proportion of neurotics and insane persons among Jews is relatively high, yet the frequency of suicide in the same religious group is low. By a similar logic of argument Durkheim disposes of explanations of suicide in terms of heredity and imitation. By the elimination of alternative explanations and by the assembly of other evidence he intends to demonstrate that the only remaining and possible explanation for suicide must be in terms of social, not psychological, biological or geographical, facts. Among the positive indicators he points to is the constancy of the rate of suicide in various societies over significant periods, how the rates differed between societies, and how the rates varied in a constant manner with variations in certain social conditions. Thus, though the individual no doubt had private experiences connected with suicide, these could not explain the remarkable statistical concurrences exhibited by suicide rates. These rates must, therefore, be due to their association with conditions prevalent in the groups to which the individuals included in the rates belonged. Variations in these general conditions gave rise to different types of suicide, the altruistic, the egoistic and the anomic. In this way Durkheim was able to move towards a relationship of constant concomitance between a single cause, the degree of the social integration of social groups, and a single effect, the propensity towards suicide; the latter varying inversely with the former.

Although Durkheim contributed little, if anything, directly to the production of statistics – these were developed by others – nevertheless, his ingenious use of descriptive statistics made a large contribution to seeing how such materials could be used in sociological analysis as indicators of the nature and extent of social conditions (Shaw and Miles 1979, Halfpenny 1982). Suicide rates, population figures, and the like, were for Durkheim the observable sediments of the moral state of society, 'social life consolidated', making it possible to study social reality through these quantitative manifestations. He saw suicide rates, for example, as the product of the 'suicidogenic current', or those 'social facts' which establish that there will be, in particular groups, a certain number of voluntary deaths of one sort or another. By using these 'objective manifestations' according to the principle of correlation to establish causal connections, the sociologist was thereby able to exhibit previously undetected patterns of causal order beneath the appearances of everyday social life.

Some lessons of Durkheim's positivism

It is impossible here fully to appreciate the many subtleties of Durkheim's thought, or rail against its crudities. He is important here because he confronted many of the issues that positivist social science had to solve if it was to establish itself as *the* way forward for social science. It should go without saying that Durkheim is not the only figure of importance within this tradition. His debts to Comte and Mill have already been noted. Nor was his influence in subsequent years to remain unmodified and undistorted, as scholars found in his work what they wanted to read to justify their own ideas. Founders always run the risk of misrepresentation as their authority is drawn on to lend credence to less impressive productions, but, as far as the philosophy of social research is concerned, what is Durkheim's importance?[12]

The first feature to note is what his work implies about the relationship between social science and philosophy. Though rejecting, like

Comte, the metaphysical tendencies of much of nineteenth century social thought, Durkheim did see fit to justify his own conception of what empirical social science should be like in philosophical terms. The picture of science he proposed was actually a philosophical one. The problem for sociology is to reconcile idealism and materialism in order to identify its own distinctive domain of inquiry. In this respect, his concern was to establish the social, the collective, as a reality in its own right that was not reducible to phenomena at some other level and belonging to some other discipline, such as psychology or biology. He endeavoured to show how 'social facts', though moral facts, were as much a part of nature as biological, chemical and physical facts. This 'social relational realism' enabled him to argue that the social could be studied with the same scientific methods used in the natural sciences, with suitable modifications, without, as said earlier, reducing social phenomena to material 'things'. Thus, ontologically speaking, natural and social realities were of the same order – 'thing-like' – and being so could be studied in accord with the same general epistemological principles. Once he had established the independent reality of the social and the unity of method he was able to argue that social life could be studied objectively through the method of science.

A second feature of his work caused him rather more difficulty though his solution is both ingenious and consequential. Science dealt with the objects of sensation, with phenomena which were external to individual consciousness but which could experience its existence; it was this which effectively marked science off from metaphysics and established it as a valid and superior form of knowledge. In espousing this view and claiming that 'social facts' were 'things' – though not material things like rocks, tissues, cells, or whatever, but taking on the characteristics of 'thingness' as objects in an 'external world' beyond ideas – Durkheim had to deal with the fact that though the external world was experienced as 'thing-like' by those who dwelt within it, nonetheless, their acquaintance with social facts did not obviate the need for science since this experience could not serve as an adequate basis for knowledge of the social world. Though people in their everyday life directly encounter and experience the effects of social facts, they do not, thereby, come to an understanding of the true nature of those facts. Consequently, he had to undermine this common-sense view of society as illusory, while retaining the conception of science as dealing with 'objects of sensation'. To this end, therefore, he had to develop a theory and method for explaining why society does not appear in its true nature to its members.

This he tried to do, not altogether clearly, in a number of ways. He urged the adoption of a particular attitude by the social scientist towards social phenomena: an attitude of objectivity, strangeness, surprise, shorn of prejudice and preconceptions. Further, the notion of 'thing' when applied to the social provided an ontological criterion by which the real processes in society could be identified. They were to be identified, using the principle of correlation, through their collective manifestations, the sediments and other traces they left behind them, and the effects this had on the world of appearances. In this way the laws of society were revealed by a properly constituted science. So, he retained the idea of science as dealing with observables but these served only as indices of underlying structures of social organisation which were not themselves directly observable though they did exercise causal force over the actions of individuals.

Durkheim stands out in the history of social science because he tried to make legitimate a conception of social science consistent with the prevailing image of natural science, at least as he understood that. This image was not an accurate one, as we shall argue below, but his stress on laws and causal explanation, objectivity, and rigorous method is important and gave authority to his own substantive investigations. It had a powerful influence on succeeding generations even though, and even in his own time, his ideas did not escape criticism. It was claimed that the price of Durkheim's scientific approach was that it overdid the 'thing-like' character of society, that is, that it reified society by attributing properties to it that it simply could not possess. Certainly, much of what Durkheim had to say could give the strong impression that he did think in terms of group minds, or of society as an organism in more than just a figurative sense, though he himself insisted that nothing could be further from his mind. Nevertheless, in spite of these and other criticisms he does represent what is the core of the positivist interpretation of social science. It should become apparent in succeeding chapters that this view is not without its difficulties.

Notes

1. Halfpenny (1982: 120). More recently, Pawson (1989) echoes the same sentiments when he suggests that positivism lost the battles but won the war.
2. American and European traditions of sociology are different in a number of respects. Many of the methods now used in empirical social research were pioneered in the United States, fed by a long tradition of social reform which based itself on fact gathering to inform policy. By contrast, European sociology has always been more theoretically than empirically oriented. British sociology, as might be expected, sits midway between the two though, in recent years, it has become even more influenced by European, especially French, social theory. See, as background, Turner and Turner (1990), Ackroyd and Hughes (1991).
3. The position of marketing is an interesting one since a number of the most commonly used methods of social research, such as sampling, questionnaires, opinion polling, were originally developed in this field and later taken over by social researchers. See, for example, Bulmer (1984).
4. See, for further example, Phillips (1987), where he remarks that 'some of the most boisterous celebrants at positivism's wake are actually more positivistic than they realise . . .' (p. 44).
5. Becker (1932) is still one of the best accounts of the intellectual consequences of these changes in European thought. See also Nisbet (1974).

6. And, in this, sustained a conviction, as will be seen, which has lasted down the centuries, so much so that even some of the most recent tendencies in social thought still regard it as important to be 'antifoundationalist'.

7. Interestingly, in using these terms Comte was trying to distinguish his proposals from the developing science of statistics under the guidance of Quetelet: a major irony given the significant role that statistics plays in contemporary social research.

8. The one human science missing on Comte's pantheon is psychology which he rejected as a species of metaphysics, believing that it would eventually be replaced by 'cerebral physiology'.

9. See Hughes (1967), Manicas (1987), Mommsen and Osterhammel (1987). Schnädelbach (1984) is a valuable and short overview.

10. Giddens (1977). Halfpenny (1982) identifies 12 positivisms in his examination of this tradition.

11. Apart from Durkheim's own writings, useful accounts are Aron (1970), Lukes (1973) and Hughes *et al.* (1995).

12. Also, it is as well to point out that the development of what we now regard, not always informatively, as positivistic methods of social research, such as questionnaires, surveys, the use of methods of statistical inference, owe little directly to Durkheim, at least in Anglo-American sociology, as we shall see in the next chapter. French social science on the whole has taken more notice of his structuralist proclivities than his methodology.

CHAPTER 3

Positivism and the language of social research

As mentioned, much of positivism's motivation came from a strongly held view that the social sciences should endeavour to emulate the most advanced of the natural sciences. Accepting this ambition was one thing, realising it another. It was not clear what it was about the natural sciences which made them apparently so superior as forms of knowledge. It was generally accepted that physics was the most advanced of the natural sciences and so embodied most clearly what must be the scientific method, but quite what it was about physics which marked it out was a matter of debate. However, not much attention was given to the actual practices of the natural sciences by those who would follow their example. Social scientists, in the main, took their ideas about the natural sciences from the philosophy of science, with positivism as their main inspiration. Following the supposed 'scientific method' as described by positivism was the main route through which social scientists, through the 1930s to 1960s hoped to move in the direction pioneered by the most successful of the natural sciences and, eventually, equal their achievements.

It must be noted, however, that among positivistically inspired social scientists there were debates (as there still are, for although direct allegiance to positivism has declined since the 1960s, it continues to have influence and adherents) over such questions as the nature of scientific explanation, whether social science theories could attain the categorical certainty of natural science theories or could only reach probabilistic conclusions, whether falsification or verification was the fundamental criterion distinguishing scientific statements from nonscientific ones, and so on. These debates, at one time, formed some of the core issues in the philosophy of social science (see, e.g. Papineau 1978, Ryan 1970). However, some positivists were interested in converting the programme into practice and doing some of the empirical research which their philosophy deemed so all-important. They tried to design proper scientific instruments for social research. It is with these attempts to figure out how to do this that this chapter is concerned. If the example of the natural sciences was to be followed, then how was this to be done? In what way could the positivist's general idea of scientific method be applied to social life?

The language of observation

One of the important features of positivist philosophies of science was the preeminence accorded to empirical research in the production of knowledge. All the major scientific advances, it was claimed, had resulted from the patient accumulation of facts about the world to produce the generalisations known as scientific laws. Science, above all else, was an empirical pursuit and its basis lay in the observation of what we can term 'brute data': that is, data which are not the result of judgement, interpretation, or other subjective mental operations (see Anscombe 1957–8 and Taylor 1978: 60). In the same manner as natural scientists describe and classify phenomena by noting such 'brute data' as shape, size, motion, and so on, so should social scientists define and chart their phenomena of interest.

Positivists argued, then, that the objectivity of science depends on the fact that there is a theoretically neutral 'observation language' in which investigators can give the barest description of their direct experience of the world, thus presenting data of which the scientist can be most certain since it describes what has been directly observed. However, scientific theories seek to go beyond what is simply observed to explain the observed phenomena and, accordingly, must therefore hypothesise about that which has not been directly observed but which, for example, can only be inferred from what has been observed. Thus, the observation language is both ontologically and epistemologically primary: ontologically because it reports phenomena which have been observed, and epistemologically because it is these observed phenomena which present the objects of explanation for and the data of science.[1] Statements in the observation language can be directly assessed as true or false simply by relating them to the observed 'facts' of the world.

The notion of an 'observation language' established, for the positivists, the connection between language and the world and implied a 'correspondence theory of truth', namely, that statements in the observation language have a direct match with observed phenomena. Therefore, the truth of a statement, including theoretical statements, is to be determined by its correspondence with the observed facts. From the theoretical statements, implications as to what occurrences ought to be observable could be deduced and matched against observation statements. Thus, a choice could be made between rival theories by seeing what observable occurrences should follow from their different principles and then matching these against observation statements to see which predicted consequences best matched the observed facts. The importance of the 'theoretical neutrality' of the observation language is now apparent: the facts can be stated in terms which do not depend or derive from the suppositions of either of the two rival theories, so enabling them to be compared against *independent* observational evidence. The theories must, therefore, be of such clarity as to permit an unequivocal comparison with the facts so that one could definitely tell whether the occurrences logically implied by a theory did or did not prescribe what was observed to occur. If it did correspond then the theory was true; if not, then it was false. Later, in the hands of the logical positivists, whether or not a theory could be 'cashed out' in terms of such unequivocally confirming or falsifying observation statements would become a criterion for the very meaningfulness of the theory and a way, thereby, of distinguishing scientific statements from metaphysical ones.

The logical positivists

The logical positivists propounded what is perhaps the clearest and most influential version of positivism in the twentieth century. The group began in Vienna in the late 1920s under the leadership of Ernst Mach, Mauritz Schlick and Rudolf Carnap.[2] They were to give positivistic philosophy of science a shape and system which served to make it the predominant view of the first half of the twentieth century.

As with other forms of positivism they rejected metaphysics by recognising only two kinds of proposition: the analytic and the synthetic. Analytic propositions include those of mathematics and logic which themselves say nothing about the empirical facts of the world but are true or false by virtue of the rules and definitions of the formal system to which they belong. Thus, the proposition $2 + 2 = 4$ is true because of the definitions contained in the number system used, in the same way that 'This red book is coloured' is tautologically true by virtue of the connection between the words 'red' and 'coloured'. 'Red' is one coloured word among others, and so to use one of the coloured words is just to say that it is coloured. To say 'This red book is not coloured' would be to contradict oneself. By contrast, the truth of synthetic propositions is verified by empirical observation: that is, by determining whether or not what the proposition says corresponds with the facts of the world. The truth of the proposition, 'This book is red' does not depend on the meaning of its constituent words, but on what the actual colour of the book so identified is. If the book is, in fact, coloured green, then the proposition is false. Whether the proposition is true or false can be determined by looking to see what the colour of the book is. However, statements which are neither tautologies nor empirical statements are not propositions and are meaningless.

Religious, moral and aesthetic statements along with metaphysical ones were consigned to the dustbin of meaninglessness or, a slightly better fate, reduced to statements about personal taste or preference, since they were verifiable neither by empirical observation nor by logical deduction. For example, the statement 'This picture shows two dogs and a cat' is an empirical, synthetic statement. It states something which is directly observable about the painting. We can look at the picture and see whether or not there are two dogs and a cat in it. But the statement 'This picture is beautiful' says nothing of the sort. There is no directly observable thing in the painting that we can point to as observable evidence for the truth or falsity of the statement. Therefore, for some logical positivists, the latter kind of statement says nothing at all but is meaningless. As mentioned, others would allow such statements as an expression of personal taste. It says nothing about the painting but about the person who utters the statement and is equivalent to saying, 'I like this painting'. To use Ayer's example as further illustration, 'the Absolute enters into, but is itself incapable of, evolution and progress' is not analytic and nor is it, even in principle, verifiable: it is an utterance which is 'literally insignificant'.[3] The principle of verification, that is, whether a statement could be compared with some directly observed facts, served as a criterion for deciding whether a statement was meaningful or not.

Logical positivism also differed from nineteenth century versions of positivism by stressing the *logical* character of the scientific method as well as the empirical. Logic had always been a problem for positivist and empiricist philosophies given their emphasis on the empirical as the source of knowledge and, following from this, their rejection of rationalist doctrines as little better than metaphysics. Some, J.S. Mill for one, put forward an empiricist interpretation of logic and mathematics. For him logic and pure mathematics consisted of propositions that were generalisations from experience: a view which rendered mathematical statements, such as $2 + 2 = 4$, susceptible to empirical refutation. It was developments in formal logic from the middle of the nineteenth century onwards that offered a resolution of the suspicions with which empiricist philosophies held logic and mathematics. Logic, and mathematics as a branch of logic, came to be regarded as a collection of formal rules for constructing propositions and stipulating the conditions under which, within the formal system, they could be taken as true or false. Formal logic, in other words, elaborates the relational structure of terms within a symbolic system but is itself empty of empirical content. Logic might tell us that if, say, proposition a is true then proposition p, which follows deductively from it, must also be true regardless of whatever it is that propositions a and p respectively state. Logic has, however, nothing whatever to say about whether a is or is not as a matter of fact true. Thus, although beyond experience, logic and mathematics, unlike metaphysics, expressed *analytical* truths; that is, their statements were true or false by virtue of the rules for manipulating the symbols. Mathematical and logical truths are *a priori* not, as many rationalists thought, because they mirror the way in which the human mind works or belong to a Platonic realm of essences, but because they are analytic and get their truth from the way in which the rules of the symbol system have been laid down. One way of putting this is to say that they state truths which are true by virtue of meaning and another is to count them as true by convention. As analytical truths they could be incorporated into the very structure of science without fear of metaphysical contagion. That is, without risk of importing into science truths which were purportedly true of the empirical world but which were not empirical and, therefore, could not engender unequivocal observation statements. By positivist standards such statements would only uselessly intrude on science because they are meaningless and give only an illusory appearance of stating truths about the empirical world.

As far as logical positivism was concerned, these developments in the reconceptualisation of the nature of logic and mathematics spelt the end of traditional philosophy. Its main pursuit, metaphysics, had sought to discover fundamental truths about reality, ones which were deeper or more general than those which could be reached by science. For logical positivism the only truths about the world were those reached by science because metaphysics was meaningless. Logical analysis, as a method, could resolve philosophical problems and paradoxes by reconstructing philosophical statements in the language of formal logic. They also helped to reformulate the notion of empiricism. Since Hume, empirical knowledge had been conceived in terms of ideas, or concepts, which were the remains of sense impressions, that is, things created in the mind by causal contact with things in the external world. These were the source, and the only source, of our knowledge of the external world, all of which must come to us through the senses. As said earlier, as against rationalists such as Descartes, there were no innate ideas for, if ideas were created in the mind only through contact with the external world, there could be no ideas already present in the mind prior to experiential contact with the world of things.

For the logical positivists, as it was for positivism more generally, empirical observation of the world was the foundation of knowledge and, hence, of science. However, it became clear that empirical observation was no simple matter. Even our commen-sensical 'direct' experience of the world around us − a world of tables and chairs, oranges and lemons, TV programmes, coffee cups, pints of beer, Apple Macs, and the rest − were not simple direct apperceptions but complex bundles of more basic sensory impressions, among other things. Such experiences could not satisfy persistent scepticism and, hence, could not serve as the foundation stones of knowledge. Instead, what was required was the identification of the basic elemental data of observation which could not be doubted, out of which these more complex perceptions were built.

The language of observation and mental states

The idea that knowledge is based upon a primary, or 'protocol', observational language was intended to ground science as an empirical discipline, giving it an objective character by providing, in principle at any rate, statements which were purely about how things are in the empirical world, statements about things which were observable, publicly available for others to observe and purged of all emotional, ideological and theoretical preconceptions, providing a clear criterion of truth independent of human whim and prejudice, and privileging its status as knowledge of the highest order. However, the very difficulties of formulating an adequate basic observation or protocol language suggested that observation was a complex matter. Indeed, there were radical empiricists, including Mach, who were suspicious of the powerful theoretical concepts of even physics such as 'atom' or 'absolute vacuum', since they were beyond experience. But for the more moderate empiricists the idea of a sensory experiential language proved, in the end, a difficult idea to establish. Facts did not just appear. They were not just lying around waiting to be picked up by some wandering scientist; they had to be discovered, assembled and made informative. All the 'facts' Darwin used as evidence for this theory of evolution were 'known' before he used them. Fossils had been noticed by other naturalists many years before Darwin, most of the flora and fauna, too, had been discovered or seen by other travellers. What Darwin contributed was a profoundly radical way of rearranging these 'facts' so that they spoke within a different theoretical framework, namely, the theory of evolution.[4] There was, then, more to scientific observation than simply 'directly observing', however basic or 'brute' these so-called facts appeared to be.

As far as the logical positivists were concerned while most members of the school saw this observation language as consisting of the direct noninferential reports of experience, exactly what the 'protocol' terms in the observational language referred to was a matter of much inconclusive debate. Some argued that these reports of direct observation referred to sense data, that is, referred to the observer's experience induced in his or her sensory apparatus, which meant that 'experience' was experience of an object and required an inference from sense data. But, for our purpose, the point is that whatever the characterisation of these protocol terms, it was the observational language that was ontologically and epistemologically privileged as beyond reasonable doubt. So far as scientific practice was concerned, it was not suggested that all descriptive terms and concepts be couched in this basic observational language. All that was necessary was that if they were to be meaningful, then they should, in principle, be translatable into, or reducible to, statements in the observational language. The positivists could no more agree how such a translation or reduction could be carried out than they could on what the observation reports referred to.

So, while the formulation of a primary observation language proved philosophically elusive, if not illusory, other criteria or principles of observation for determining facts were required. To an extent these were already implicit in the positivist theory of knowledge. The world, whether natural or social, operated according to strict laws and therefore possessed a deterministic structure which it was the business of science to discover; a structure which could be described formally and, as we shall see, quantitatively. Methodologically, then, empirical research, and here one might say that for positivism this meant 'scientific research', amounted to discovering those regular and invariant properties of the phenomena of the world and the relationships between them;

the properties being described, as far as possible, in terms of what is rigorously observable. Thus, the physicist does not deal with billiard balls, falling feathers, crashing cars, boiling water, but with bodies of a particular shape, size, mass, motion, wavelength or whatever. Correlates among such abstracted attributes constitute the basic ingredients of scientific theories. Many such attributes may not be observable unaided by instrumentation, but the principle is there nonetheless.

Carried over into the human sciences this kind of conception faced a number of problems. One of these had to do with so-called 'mental states'. Human beings are not simply external shells of shape, size and motion: they have an inner life not accessible to observation in the normal way, unless private introspection is counted as a publicly available form of observation. Some argued that the inaccessibility of mental phenomena to direct observation meant that they could not be dealt with objectively and so excluded them from the domain of scientific enquiry. Physical objects, physical events, physical processes could be described in more rigorous versions of the five senses and were, accordingly, publicly available. Mental states or states of consciousness, on the other hand, could only be experienced, and truly known, by one person, namely, the person undergoing the experience. Some logical positivists (Neurath's (1973) 'physicalism' in its insistence that science could legitimately only talk of phenomena described in the vocabulary of physics was perhaps the most prominent and extreme of these), claimed that science could only speak of 'mind' in so far as it did so in terms of spatiotemporal phenomena, such as speech sounds, facial expressions, and so on. The social sciences were, in other words, the study of behaviour with the conception of behaviour being construed extremely narrowly and confined only to phenomena which could be described as physical movements. Such a rigorous physicalism was, however, too extreme for most positivists.

A more typical strategy was to argue that though mental states were not observable in any direct fashion, nonetheless particular mental states were associated with specific outward bodily displays and could be inferred from them. For example, we see a person clenching his fists, gnashing his teeth, glaring wide-eyed from a red face, and reasonably conclude that the mental state the person is experiencing is that of anger, indeed, that the cause of all this dramatic posturing is the internal experience of anger and rage. Accordingly, the argument was adduced that all statements referring to mental states could be analysed into a further set of statements referring to overt bodily signs or displays. Mental phenomena, then, could be indirectly observed by treating the corresponding outward behavioural display as an index of the 'inner' mental states.

This sort of account of the relationship between mental states and overt behaviour was comfortable to many empiricists since, seemingly at least, it brought the 'mind' into a scientific frame of reference in which its features could be publicly observed, charted, quantified and correlated. The epistemological principle of sensory experience as the foundation of scientific knowledge was preserved and the mind known through systematic observation of publicly accessible events or behaviours rather than through unsystematic and subjective introspection. However, though this account had some plausibility with reference to anger, pleasure or pain, human beings experience more sophisticated 'mental states' than these. They can desire wealth, status or power, can believe in democracy or the divine right of kings, determine the moral worth of actions, admire the beauty of the Giaconda, worship Eric Clapton, fall in love, and many more. Could these emotions, beliefs, morality, judgements be interpreted in the same way? Do these mental states correlate with determinate bodily displays in the same way that it might be said of anger? For the positivists the answer had to be in the affirmative. The beliefs people hold, the values they subscribe to, the judgements they make, their tastes and their preferences, are all publicly verifiable since they are manifested in publicly observable behaviour, artifacts of various kinds, and so on. These more 'sophisticated' mental states only differ from the case of anger in their degree of complexity. A person who worships Eric Clapton, for example, is likely to have a large collection of his albums, hang posters of him on his or her bedroom wall, make every effort to attend his concerts, and so on: all overt, publicly observable behaviours and indicators of this person's passion. Values are objective in the sense that they are held by persons who can verbally report their values and beliefs. The social scientist does not have to agree or disagree with the values and beliefs expressed but can simply report on them or use them as primary data. In short, the values people hold are as factually 'brute' as geological strata, atoms, gas flows, velocities and the like. By using carefully constructed instruments, such as questionnaires, attitude scales or interviews, subjects can provide responses which are indicative of mental states and in this way provide objective access to important aspects of human mental life.

Developing a methodology for investigating the mental aspects of human life was itself part of a larger issue mentioned earlier of formulating principles of social scientific observation. It was felt that to conform to what natural scientists were able to achieve, the language of social science observation had to consist of objectively defined observables, and had to be generalisable and, if possible, quantifiable: much the same criteria that Durkheim argued for. Since the aim was, in effect, to fulfil the Comtean vision of discovering general laws of social life, the basic terms of the scientific language had to express general rather than particular qualities. One of the important moves in social research in this respect was the adoption of quasi-mathematical terms in which to talk about data, namely, the language of variables. This represented a way of talking about social phenomena within an apparently neutral framework in terms of their general attributes and properties which particular instances did or did not possess, or possessed to varying degrees, and which could be compared in regard to putative causes.

The language of variables

It is difficult today to recapture the revolutionary impact of this formulation of the character of social research and its phenomena, since the language of variables is now so much taken for granted in empirical social research.[5] The developments of the 'language of variables' owed much to the work of Paul F. Lazarsfeld (1901–76) and his colleagues. He himself was an occasional participant in the Vienna Circle prior to the Second World War and his emigration to the United States. Lazarsfeld's major efforts were devoted to developing research techniques and designs in the context of research on, for example, the effects of the mass media and on the determinants of voting choice, both areas in which he did pioneering work. His work was inspired by a particular, though not unique, conception of science and how this could be translated into making social research more scientific in its quest for adequate empirically based theories.

The notion of a variable has a long tradition in mathematics, statistics and, importantly, symbolic logic. It is essentially a simple idea. A variable as opposed to a constant can vary in value within a range of values, even if this is simply of the order of 0 or 1, where 0 indicates the absence of a variable and 1 its presence. The innovative move was to use this idea as the pivot around which a whole way of thinking about social research could revolve. 'No science', declared Lazarsfeld, 'deals with its objects of study in their full concreteness'.[6] Certain properties are selected as the special province of study of each science, among which each tries to discover empirical relationships, the ultimate being those of a lawlike character. Thus, and as said earlier, physics is interested in its objects not in their full concreteness but in abstracted properties of them, such as their mass, length, force, velocity, molecular composition, and so on. Science's connection to the world is an abstracted one describing the properties or qualities of things, not with things in themselves. In this, Lazarsfeld is thoroughly Kantian, espousing the position that things can never be known 'in themselves' but grasped only through their 'surface' appearances or indications. This means that the first task of any science is to identify those few general properties by which all the phenomena in its domain are to be known: no simple task as the history of science attests. It is particularly difficult for the social sciences when they have yet to develop their own standard terminology. Nevertheless, for Lazarsfeld this was not an insuperable problem nor, indeed, one that needed to be solved by epistemological or ontological rumination. What he proposed was an empirical strategy for pursuing this goal for social science by treating properties as variables: that is, using variables as 'devices by which we characterise the objects of empirical social investigations' (Lazarsfeld and Rosenberg 1955: 13).

Briefly, Lazarsfeld saw the research process as one of translating concepts into empirical indicators; that is, indicators based upon what is observable, recordable, measurable in some objective way. The first step was the creation of a 'vague image', or construct, that results from the immersion of a researcher in a theoretical problem. The real work begins by 'specifying' its components, aspects or dimensions, and selecting 'indicators' which can 'stand for' them. Thus, the concept of 'ethnic prejudice' can be manifested in a number of ways: by the overt expression of dislike for persons of different racial or ethnic backgrounds, by an unwillingness to hire persons of different racial or ethnic backgrounds, by refusing to work with them, by voting for political parties which have racialist policies, by refusing to purchase a house in an area where different ethnic or racial groups live, by overt hostility, and more. We might also think of the concept of 'ethnic prejudice' as a matter of degree rather than a property which someone might or might not possess. In any event, in choosing indicators we have to think about the context in which the investigation is to be carried out. Hiring someone, for example, can only be done by a person who is in a position to hire or fire workers. There may be no political parties which explicitly avow racialist policies. The question of buying a house anywhere may not be an issue in particular cases. The point is that the concept needs to be thought about in terms of what appropriate manifestations, were they to occur, would be appropriate indicators of 'prejudice'. The next step is to think of the ways in which these manifestations could be observed as data. In the case of variable analysis this is likely to involve surveys and questionnaires, though it need not. The particular techniques of data collection and measuring instruments used will, nevertheless, depend upon the practical exigencies of the investigation. Most concepts will, likely as not, prove to be combinations of indicators rather than a single measure. As most social research will be interested in more than one construct, it is by finding patterns among indicators in terms of their covariation and interrelationships that empirical descriptions are built up, and out of which empirically grounded theories can be devised to explain the patterns found. Quantification, according to Lazarsfeld, is possible through using the idea of variables if only at the relatively crude level of frequency counts of the presence or absence of some property, since even this modest level allows for the identification of covariations between variables.[7]

As hinted earlier, it is perhaps better to regard Lazarsfeld's endeavours as methodological rather than philosophical; that is, as seeking for a way of making social research an empirically based science. Nevertheless, there is a metaphysics of ontological realism there to the extent that it only makes sense to talk of indices if it can be claimed that they 'stand for' something. However, although Lazarsfeld talked of an abstracted connection between scientific concepts and the world, in practice his strategy is effected by means of correlations among indices and the strength and stability they display, if they do, across studies. But there was no real way of anchoring the connection of indices with the 'objects' or the 'properties' they putatively stood for. Although, for example, the concept of 'ethnic prejudice' has a common-sense meaning, its connection to actions or sentiments – the phenomena which it is supposed to stand for, which are, in a sense, empirically observable through the responses to questionnaires and other instruments – is also a matter of common-sense judgement on the part of researchers rather than a strict theoretical derivation as it would be in, say, physics. Theoretical validity is owed to the sovereign position given to the empirical in that the adequacy of a construct is determined by patterns found among measured variables or indices. Special importance is given to operationalising concepts into observable measured indicators. For Lazarsfeld, indicators are what social science research works with, and they indicate something, to varying degrees, if they show detectable patterns of association with each other. In other words, consistent patterns of association found across a range of studies are, for Lazarsfeld and variable analysis more generally, good evidence that the research has discovered real causal relations between the phenomena of interest.

For empirical social science, then, the language of variables offered a way of expressing relationships in data and, as such, a way of describing phenomena objectively and quantitatively. All phenomena that are of interest to social research, including subjective states, could be conceptualised, measured at some level at least, correlated and variously manipulated by the formal techniques of variable analysis. Hypotheses could be formulated and tested. Although few, if any, of the social sciences could emulate psychology in being able to carry out laboratory experiments, fair approximations in nonexperimental settings of social research to the logic of experimental design could be achieved using statistical partitioning methods.

However, despite the fact that the Lazarsfeldian conception has virtually become the orthodox style of social research, in some quarters regarded as *the* method of empirical social research, it has not been without its critics. Some objected to the way in which the reality of social phenomena and processes, in all their fullness, richness, complexity and flux, were concealed behind what was, in effect, a descriptive apparatus whose character owed more to the technical requirements of developing the measuring instruments and of manipulating the statistics than it did to genuinely capturing the underlying connections between phenomena it was supposed to describe (see Benson and Hughes 1991). Some of these matters will be further developed in Chapter 5.

A further difficulty was that variable analysis was intendedly atheoretical; a ubiquitous method for pattern searching in data as a route towards theory formulation. Theories explained the patterns, but the patterns were needed first in order to obtain better theories. That is, although 'vague' theoretical ideas will inform the kinds of variables that will be investigated, or which will be regarded as independent, as dependent, as mediating variables, and so on, their significance is to be determined by empirically confirmed patterns and correlations shown in the data.[8] The method, in short, turns out to be a strategy for the construction of empirical theories which, as we shall see, fall far short of the kind of theoretical generalisations which were the objective of positivist ambitions.[9]

Nor could the approach avoid philosophical commitments and problems of an ontological kind. It involved not only a conception of the scientific method and how this could be instantiated in research techniques and practices, it also had to face up to problems about the nature of social phenomena. Although the approach was intended to be 'neutral' in regard to theoretical commitments in being proposed as a ubiquitous method for the testing of whatever theories come along, there were doubts as to whether, within its framework, it could adequately deal, for example, with the idea that Durkheim strenuously argued for, namely, that society was not reducible to the properties of individuals.

Social wholes versus methodological individualism

As Durkheim had argued, the social sciences were not concerned with individual phenomena as such but with collective phenomena including, of course, those individual states of consciousness which reproduced the collective understanding and outlook. The social sciences dealt with groups and collectivities of various kinds, institutions, cultures, whole systems of interaction and processes which are, so to speak, more than just the sum of individual phenomena and have, as Durkheim put it, a reality in their own right. Economics deals with institutions concerned with the production and distribution of goods; sociology with classes, groups, institutions, even whole societies; political science with governments, political parties, voting patterns, and more. Yet, as was the case with mental states, such collective phenomena are not themselves what a positivist would regard as directly observable. One cannot, for example, observe social classes, the economic system, capitalism, and the like, so what ontological status could such concepts possess? Again, as Durkheim asserted most forcibly about the reality of collective phenomena: 'Society is not a mere sum of individuals. Rather, the system formed by their association represents a specific reality which has its own characteristics' (Durkheim 1966: 103). Social reality, in short, transcends that of individuals. As in nature, there occur in the social world, and definitive of it, wholes which are not simply aggregates of the individual elements composing them but are organic unities, more than the sum of their parts. Such emergent wholes cannot be reduced to the parts composing them.

A successful substantiation of this kind of claim, it could be argued, is necessary to the viability of the social sciences, and Durkheim did so argue, for without it the proper study of human behaviour, whether deemed to be social or otherwise, would be psychology or one of its branches. Philosophically, the issue is an ontological one concerning the reality of social entities (Lukes 1970, O'Neill 1973, Sharrock 1987). As we have seen, Durkheim claimed that social entities were real 'things' even though they were not material 'things'. However, operationally matters were not so easily resolved. The empirical evidence adduced for social facts was, primarily, derived from individuals. Only individual behaviour could be observed in any direct way, whether this be in the form of responses to questionnaires, attitude tests, ethnographic observations, recorded rates of the frequency of criminal activity, rates of suicide, voting preferences, share buying, or whatever. In short, 'nothing about social facts is *observable* except their individual manifestations' (Lesnoff 1974: 77, italics in original).

The paradox here seems patent: on the one hand, the claim that social wholes were real depended on it not being possible to reduce completely statements about them to statements about individuals; on the other hand, the evidence for the reality of social wholes seemed to depend entirely on evidence derived from observable individual behaviours. Even though Durkheim, among others, had claimed to show that individual characteristics and behaviour varied with, or were determined or caused by, social contextual factors, the data on which such conclusions were based were always traceable back to their origins in observation of individuals.

It is undoubtedly the case that properties can be predicated of social wholes which cannot be predicted of an individual. A society or a group can be said to be stratified, hierarchical, democratic, class ridden, and so on, while the same characteristics cannot be predicated of an individual. Groups, for further example, can be said to maintain their identity in spite of the replacement of members. The character of the groups, too, can allegedly be shown to influence the behaviour of its members. In many legal systems some associations are treated as if they were persons having rights and obligations distinct from their members. Economists speak of, and even have theories about, the firm. However, these observations are, to a degree, beside the point. Though in legal and in ordinary language we can and do speak in this way, the issue is whether this is legitimate *scientifically,* and, if so, what ontological and epistemological justifications can be offered for so speaking? Answers to this affect the interpretations that can be plausibly offered for research operations supposedly measuring or indicating collective phenomena.

Of course, the problem as set out does not require that a choice be made between the reality of social wholes or the reality of individuals; it is not, or need not be, a question of one or the other. To maintain the view that there are both individuals and social wholes, while accepting at the same time that the latter are not observable in any direct way, we need also to be able to claim that, if anything is to be truly predicated of a social whole, this must imply the truth of descriptions of the individuals who, in part, comprise the social whole. Without this condition it would be impossible to test statements about social wholes by observation since these are not observable, though individuals are (Mandelbaum 1955, Lessnoff 1974: 80–1). But, equally, the description of social wholes, though implying true descriptions of individuals, must involve more than this; that is, it must mean that the set of relevant individual descriptions does not exhaust what may be predicated of the social whole. Thus, for example, 'British society' may be offered as the name of a social collective and a number of properties predicated of it, such as 'is a monarchy', 'is a member of the European Community', 'has a low crime rate compared with X, Y, Z societies', 'has a rate of inflation of X%', and so on. The question is, however, whether each of these statements, while implying the truth of a host of statements about individuals – their behaviour in elections, in the market place, their obedience to the law, their attitudes and beliefs, and many more – is reducible simply to a listing of such individual statements however large in number? If not, then what is left that is not so reducible (see Coulter 1982)?

According to the doctrine of 'methodological individualism' nothing is left since all so-called collective facts are, in principle, explicable in terms of facts about individuals. References to social wholes or collectivities are, in this view, essentially summary references to the characteristics and properties of individuals, and the latter could replace the former without residue. The 'real', in other words, is restricted to what can be observed and these are the characteristics and properties of individuals. The most that can ontologically be claimed of social wholes, since they are never concretely given in observation, is a status as theoretical entities having explanatory convenience only (see, e.g. Hayek 1964: 5–15). Ontological reality is attributable only to individuals while social wholes are regarded as abstract or theoretical entities not observable but having an explanatory usefulness rather like similar kinds of theoretical concepts in physics and the other natural sciences.

For some this interpretation was tremendously important, since it seemed to bring the social sciences even closer to the practice of natural science in which a principle of reduction, that is, the logical derivation of generalisations of, say, chemistry from the more inclusive generalisation of those of physics, could be seen to operate through a hierarchy of explanation from the most fundamental physical and all-encompassing general laws about the behaviour of small-scale physical processes, down to those generalities which applied to more molar phenomena, such as the behaviour of objects, including those of living creatures. It appeared, too, to avoid the metaphysical lapses to which the social sciences seemed heir to, particularly that of reifying collectivities and attributing to them qualities which, properly speaking, could only belong to individuals and their relationships with each other. In so far as recourse was made in ordinary language to things like the 'spirit of the people', 'the racial memory', 'the mind of an age', 'class consciousness', 'the people', and so on, then either this was a careless way of speaking done for effect, or, at best, a conveniently summary way of referring to large numbers of individuals in some capacity or, at worst, unscientific and ignorant. In social science, and this was essentially Weber's argument, references to collective entities such as 'the state', 'bureaucratic organisation', 'the spirit of capitalism', and so on were summary expressions used for the convenience of not having to express all the statements about the individuals composing them.[10]

For others, however, 'methodological individualism' was too timorous and, furthermore, seemed to lead to a psychological reductionism in which all so-called social facts, including those social properties and attributes of individuals, were ultimately reducible to explanations in terms of psychological dispositions. Durkheim would certainly have made this objection. Social wholes needed to be given a less ephemeral character than that of mere theoretical entities or summary expressions and given, instead, a conception more consistent with a view of them as real causal factors.

Of course, as hinted at earlier, methodological reductionism does not necessarily imply a psychological reductionism: that is, that the only valid explanations of social life are those couched in terms of human psychological dispositions. George Homans (1967), for example, argued that sociology can be 'reduced' to psychology in the sense that its laws can be logically derived from those of psychology, just as the laws of chemistry can be deduced from the more general ones of physics. Sociology along with other social sciences, on the other hand, claims that human action is, at least in important and irreducible respects, the outcome of interaction with others. That is, it acknowledges that there are 'emergent properties' arising out of individuals *interacting* with other individuals, properties that are not present in the individual alone. Interaction itself is one such emergent property, and all that flows from this, such as the possibility of power between two or more people, exchange, social status, cooperation, conflict, and much more. Indeed, in describing the actions of individuals we often have to make reference to their institutional status in order to understand the actions they are performing. The actions of a person towards his children cannot be understood without the relational description 'father', arrest by a person cannot be understood unless we understand the institutional identity 'policeman'. In short, the whole relational context that is social life is not reducible to psychological dispositions.[11] This does not, of course, dispose of psychological explanations as relevant to the explanation of human social behaviour; but nor is it meant to do so; it is merely to reserve places for the respective disposition of social and psychological explanations.

What does all this amount to methodologically? What are the implications of these views for social research? The problem occurs for the social sciences in the following way: 'individuals' and 'social wholes' are not discrete, separate phenomena, the latter being defined and conceptualised in large part in terms of the former, because only individuals, their attributes and behaviour are observable. If this is correct, then it is extremely difficult to establish, theoretically and empirically, the reality of social wholes independently of the reality already accepted for individuals. But, for the positivist, if an observational basis cannot be provided for social wholes then they are little more than metaphysical entities, and data presumably about such entities are masquerading as scientific data.

The practice of variable analysis was a way of by-passing these issues in research. For its purposes, all that is needed are ways of indicating the properties of 'objects', be they individuals, collectivities, aggregates or even whole societies. However, in by-passing the questions it also begs them. While seeming to offer indicators of collective phenomena it leaves open the issue of how these indicators are to be interpreted: whether, for example, they reflect mere aggregate phenomena, such as those indicated by some averaging operation of the variables derived from individuals as one might calculate an average income to reflect the earnings of a particular group of workers, or whether they stand for authentically collective emergent properties. We can calculate such indices but the ontological claim is prior to choices of indicators since, presumably, the indicator has to reflect the properties of the phenomenon it is designed to 'stand for'. It is not that indicators cannot be produced but, having done so, what inferences does this entitle one to make about the character of the underlying phenomenon?[12] If we lean towards methodological individualism, then the interpretation of the patterns produced will lead to a different kind of theoretical interpretation than if we are persuaded of other conceptions. The empirical patterns of variable analysis will not resolve matters such as these. This is a problem to which we shall return in other guises.

The nature of generalisations and the status of theory

While the positivist tradition made troubled efforts to resolve its philosophical problems the business of variable analysis-based research forged ahead. This is perhaps not surprising given the emphasis placed on empirical observation as the prime ingredient of science. Both Bacon and Mill, for example, and years apart, eager to exploit and advocate the method of experiment, regarded nature and its laws as already in place just there waiting to be discovered by the correct empirical methods. Whatever the questions about the meaning of variable analysis, this certainly looked to many like an authentically scientific method which followed natural science's emphasis on measurement through the generation of statistics and substituting for experimental methods through the manipulation of statistical relationships of correlation and association.

It was widely thought that the aim of science was to produce generalisations or laws stating the causal relationships which held between phenomena in the universe. Natural science had progressed by discovering invariant and necessary connections between phenomena in an orderly and lawful universe. Galileo, Newton, Darwin, later Einstein, and others, had each contributed a precise and universal statement as to how certain phenomena operated and, using these statements, scientists had an ability to predict events in the natural world with astounding accuracy. Such statements, it seemed, were universal in the sense that they specified that all events of a particular kind were invariably connected with other events and having the basic logical form of 'Whenever A then B'. The problem was to understand how these statements worked. Do they, for example, express a necessity that is inherent in the nature of things themselves or, as the eighteenth century philosopher, David Hume proposed, a natural psychological propensity to project such connection onto nature? Understanding why laws involve both invariance and necessity proved less than straightforward. Invariance of regularity was the lesser problem since laws could be seen to apply *ceteris paribus* (i.e. 'other things being equal'), and operating subject to simplifying conditions. Variations from what the law stated could be explained by special circumstances which could be elaborated under the *ceteris paribus* provision. For example, the generalisation that water boils at 100° centigrade assumes, even though any particular statement of the law might not mention these, that the air pressure must be equivalent to that at sea level, that the water is sufficiently pure, and so on. The real problem was necessity. As Outhwaite points out, the most obvious way was to see the source of necessity as inherent in the nature of things, yet others saw this as anthropomorphic or trivial.[13] The positivist tradition, with its presupposition that empirical knowledge was the only possible knowledge of reality, was to give laws an empirical interpretation following the ideas of Hume and other philosophers of the British empirical tradition.

Laws as empirical generalisations

Hume argued that the idea of cause is no more than the outcome of repeated observations of one object following another, or one event following another event. For Hume ideas were impressions gained from the senses and his interpretation of cause was consistent with this point of view. Knowledge of causes was the result of sensation and habit. Reason alone, for example, could not arrive at the idea of heat causing water to boil, or of gravity causing bodies to fall, without experience to work on. To say that A causes B is to say that A and B are 'constantly conjoined', that is, always occurring together, in our sensations; the causal connection being attributed to, but not observed in, nature. Through repeated observations of similar conjunctions one comes, by habit, to expect that they are causally related and will always be so.

The idea of cause and effect is deriv'd from experience, which informs us, that such particular objects, in all past instances, have been constantly conjoin'd with each other: And as an object similar to one of these is suppos'd to be immediately present in its impression, we thence presume on the existence of one similar to its usual attendant.

(Hume 1978: 89–90)

In some respects, however, this did not seem to go far enough. Universal laws were regarded as exactly that: universal both in time and place applying to the past, the present *and* the future. Hume's reasonings though, by making causal generalisations the result of sensory experience, could provide no guarantee that the generalisations would hold in the future since they were based on evidence which could only be gathered in the past and the present: they applied to events *so far*. By definition, constant conjunction could not now be observed for future occurrences, and water might, in the future, boil at 80° rather than 100° centigrade. Hume's reply to this would be that, indeed, there could be no guarantee that such generalisations, even the best established ones of science, would continue to hold in the future. Nevertheless, we only have past experience on which to base future expectations, so all we can do is extrapolate these into the future. Accordingly, knowledge of empirical connections, of causes and their effects, is never fully certain but only probable; that is, we can never have absolute confidence in their repeated connection in the future.

A general causal statement, on this view, was a summary of our sensations of two sets of phenomena and constituted what is normally called an empirical generalisation. To determine causes we formulate categories of objects or events on the basis of their respective similarities. The relationship between them is observed, naturally or experimentally, and the sequence noted. If we find that in a large enough number of cases there is a constant conjunction of the putative cause followed by its corresponding effect, then we expect that this association will hold for the future, though there is no guarantee that it will. Thus we have our causal generalisation.

Later, John Stuart Mill was to provide further arguments for the empiricist interpretation of laws. He defined concepts as referring to classes of objects which demonstrate a likeness with respect to some property. Man, woman, cow, girl, temperature, energy, Catholic, and so on, would all be concepts in Mill's terms because each word stands for a group of objects having similar characteristics. The method of relating concepts within synthetic propositions, (that is, propositions which are empirical as opposed to *a priori*) – and the only ones relevant to science as far as Mill was concerned – he called 'induction', that is, 'that operation of the mind by which we infer that what we know to be true in a particular case or cases, will be true in all cases which resemble the former in certain assignable respects' (Mill 1961: 188).

Whereas Hume justified generalising from particular instances on the pragmatic grounds that the future will not, likely as not, be unlike the past, Mill argued that the inductive inference could be made that the knowledge we have of some cases will be true of all cases at all times, past, present *and* future. This he justified by an appeal to the uniformity of nature, itself arrived at through an inductive process of reasoning in which the accumulations of inductions of individual uniformities in nature are the basis of the all-encompassing induction that nature is uniform. Induction was justified by induction.

Mill did, however, recognise that life was not quite so simple. In nature things did not appear related to each other in simple fashion. Small empirical regularities would overlap and give the appearance of irregularity, some would appear regular only because they were commonly produced by another not-so-visible causal agent, and so on. The various absolute causal regularities could only be found by systematically sorting out one uniformity from another using experimental methods of manipulation. According to Mill, the end result of the application of these methods would be absolute causal generalisations.

However, even to the thoroughgoing empiricist this interpretation of the nature of laws had its weaknesses. Mill's methods were firmly based on the supposition that nature is uniform, lawful and causally interrelated and, therefore, the language to describe it had to be a causal one. There was little need to speak of theories. Although there are hierarchies of laws – those of Newton standing at the pinnacle – the most general laws are just empirical generalisations which are discovered, like more restricted generalisations, by application of empirical methods of inquiry. The source of all scientific law is empirical generalisation, a conclusion built upon the presupposition that nature is lawful and uniform. Lawfulness being, in other words, a characteristic of nature itself.

Modern positivistic and empirical thinking, however, holds that the interpretation of causal laws typified by Mill's philosophy of science is just naive. Knowledge in science is certain, not probable. Accordingly, while admitting of the essentially empirical nature of laws, it was argued that their certainty derives from the employment of the rigorous, necessary connections made by deductive inference in mathematics and logic, rather than from induction. Thus, 'all swans are white', if interpreted as an empirical generalisation, has to be tested again and again on each new observation of swans. Such an inference cannot license inferences to the future, just as the statement, 'All British prime ministers are male' merely reports on past experience up and until Mrs Thatcher became prime minister, and could not have said anything about the future as a scientific law should. Pure empiricism cannot generate the universal laws of science. These, it was argued, can only be provided by logic where the determinativeness, the necessity, is a consequence of the deductive structure. The conclusion of a logical argument must follow from the general premises if the deductive rules are followed. This interpretation of scientific explanation, as a marriage between empirical propositions and the certainties of deductive logic, became known as the 'hypothetico-deductive model' of scientific explanation.

The hypothetico-deductive model of explanation

On this view a scientific theory consisted of a set of statements connected by logical rules. The law was expressed as a universal statement of the form 'Whenever A, then B'. When these generalities are conjoined with other statements which give 'initial conditions' (that is, which state the empirical circumstances to which the law is applied) then a hypothesis can be deduced which can be tested against empirical observation.[14] The conception of 'giving an explanation' of an event came to mean, for the positivists, that an event can be predicted as a logical consequence of the theoretical statements together, of course, with the specification of 'initial conditions'. This interpretation seemed to solve a number of problems, not least those deficiencies of the idea of induction as the basis for the universality of scientific laws. While statements of the form 'Whenever A, then B' cannot logically be conclusively proved or verified, they can be falsified by one counter-instance in which A is not followed by B. It is the all-embracing nature of the 'universal generalisation', that is, *whenever* A occurs it is *always* followed by B that ensures its possible vulnerability to falsification. Given what the generalisation says, then it is only necessary for it once to be the case that A occurs without being followed by B for the claim that whenever A occurs so does B to be falsified. Karl Popper, who dissociated himself from the positivists even though others numbered him along with them, throughout his career denied the pos-sibility of validly using inductive reasoning to arrive at a general law and, instead, proposed the falsificationist interpretation of the nature of scientific laws, as we shall see in the following chapter.

The universality of the law cannot be a matter of probability either, since this would, in effect, say that the law was sometimes true, some-times not. Nonetheless, scientific laws are subject to empirical confirma-tion, and involved in the method of testing is deduction. Scientific explanation is causal explanation in which 'the explanation of an event means to deduce a statement which describes it, using as premises of the deduction one or more universal laws; together with certain singular statements, the initial conditions'.[15] Scientific laws are causal state-ments describing events in nature and are capable of being true or false, their truth or falsity being determined by observation.

Another issue the combination of empiricism and logic seemed to resolve was one discussed earlier in connection with the observability, or lack of it, of social wholes. A theory, interpreted in the way just discussed, was clearly more complex than 'whenever A then B' would seem to imply. The theory may contain postulates and concepts which are themselves not subject to observational testing. Such concepts served a heuristic purpose within the theoretical language. So, although the-ories were still given an empirical interpretation, more room came to be allowed for nonobservables, concepts not directly depending for their truth on a correspondence with the world. The formal structure of a theory was so complex and detailed that 'theoretical concepts' were often necessary for the convenience of logical and mathematical mani-pulation. It was no longer considered necessary for all concepts in a theory to have empirical meaning. One way of expressing this was to speak of a theoretical language and an observational language linked together by correspondence rules which interpreted some of the the-oretical concepts empirically.[16] In this way the theory was still subject to empirical test through hypotheses deductively derived from it.

These moves away from the rather naive empiricist interpretation of theoretical explanation as propounded by Mill and his followers did not, however, destroy the empiricist spirit: reinterpretation merely amended it to conform more closely with what was seen as scientific practice. For the social sciences this was a helpful development in that it licensed what are now orthodox research methods. The distinction between a theoretical and an observational language was crucial. So, too, was the account of the supposed certainty of science. The empiricist interpretation of scientific laws had claimed that they were only probable in the sense of being tentative and open to revision. How, then, could the certainty be accounted for? According to the hypothetico-deductive account of scientific explanation it was the combination of mathematics-cum-logic and the essentially empirical interpretation of laws that gave laws their 'certainty'. This 'certainty' was a fiction, a convenient and helpful one to be sure, but a fiction nonetheless in that it could not conceal the provisional nature of scientific discovery. After all, it was a matter of historical record that scientific laws had been found wanting only to be replaced by newer and more effective ones. The history of science is a history of wrong theories. For the social sciences this was encouraging since their lack of success in formulating laws of even moderate probability could be blamed on the far greater complexity of social phenomena compared with those of inanimate nature. Social phenomena were also more difficult to measure with the kind of precision achieved in the natural sciences. All of which was taken as a sign that positivistic social science was at least on the right track by emphasising the development of more and more sophisticated *methods* of research and paying less attention to the questions of the theoretical basis of disciplines.

The correlational account of generalisations

In this connection it is worth noting that Karl Pearson, a pioneer of mathematical biology and one of the founders of modern inductive statistics at the beginning of the twentieth century, argued that the precise, pristine laws of science are idealisations: the products of averaging and not descriptions of the real universe where all kinds of 'contaminations' are present (Pearson 1911). Even in the most advanced of the natural sciences, all kinds of factors are present which affect the causal relationship of interest. The result is that data are prone to variability due to errors of all kinds. Accordingly, the distinction between a causal relationship as expressed in a law and an empirical correlation among variables is a spurious one. A universal statement of a causal connection is simply the conceptual limit of correlation, but in the messy world in which investigations are done we would not expect to reach this limit due to the fact that it is impossible to exclude everything that might affect the causal connection of interest. Instead what we expect are strong but less than perfect correlations. In which case and on this argument, one distinction between natural and social science – that the former deals with causal relationships, the latter with correlations – falls down since all that this reflects are the conditions in which errors can be estimated. Indeed, such an interpretation also seemed accommodating to the fact that, unlike most of the natural sciences though by no means all, it was difficult to set up experimental conditions in social research and for good practical and ethical reasons. Social research had, for the most part, to be conducted in the 'messy' world in which it was extremely difficult to separate out all the potentially interacting factors and, accordingly, be able to specify the scope of any putative generalisation. That is, we would not be able to determine what cases would be covered by the generalisation and which by other generalisations. There are many factors which have a bearing on educational attainment, for example, but identifying which of these are the more important ones, what the interactive effects among the various factors might be, how other unknown factors might affect the relationship, under what circumstances the generalisation applies, are all difficult to achieve in the absence of effective controls. All we can hope for, in Pearson's terms, are reasonably strong correlations among the more important factors.

Other problems remained. Earlier it was pointed out that the hypothetico-deductive model of explanation required that theory be related to the world through transformation rules translating some of the concepts in the theory into observational concepts. The theory was dependent for its truth or falsity, irrespective of a verificationist or a Popperian falsificationist position, on the facts of the world. The world was 'external' to the theory; the theory did not shape the world but could only be responsive to it. The importance of a neutral observation language was precisely in this, despite the fact that the idea of such a language proved troublesome. The transformation rules also proved equally refractory and boiled down to what came to be known as the 'measurement problem'.[17]

Nomological and empirical generalisations

Among the positivist solutions to this were various measurement models presumed to apply to social research data and the contexts in which they were gathered, as we have discussed previously in connection with variables and indices. One influential doctrine was 'operationalism' which was based on the assumption that the categories used in empirical research were best defined in terms of the operations used to measure them (see Bridgeman 1927, Campbell 1957). Thus, on this doctrine, the concept of IQ is defined as that property measured by IQ tests; similarly concepts such as class, status, power, authority, and so on, would be defined by the indicators used to measure them. The concept of class, for example, could be measured by occupation or by respondents' self-report of the class to which they think they belong, or by level of education, and so on. Such measures could be, and indeed are, used in statistical analyses of data. Once again, operationalism embodied an empiricist conception of the nature of concepts which did not meet the hopes invested in it. One difficulty was that, as strictly conceived, operationalism created acute problems of validity. Though, strictly speaking, one could not ask what a test *really* measured since the measure *was* the concept, questions of validity did arise. For one thing, different measures of phenomena, such as IQ, could be said to be measuring different things since they were different measures. Similarly, different measures of social class or social status would be measuring different things. Clearly this was not a satisfactory situation since often measures had to be different for very good practical reasons and yet researchers still wanted to generalise to all instances of the phenomenon, whatever it might be, despite having to use different measures. After all, physicists, for example, measure temperature in a variety of ways using a variety of instruments but all are seen as measures of the single property. Also, even a weak operationalism, that is, one which did not claim that concepts were the measurement operations themselves but, instead, took the doctrine as a useful imperative to guide social research, still led to the problem of relating empirical concepts to theoretical ones.[18]

While measurement procedures in a number of the social sciences are extremely sophisticated, as are those methods of quantitative data analysis, there remains relevant the important question about the theoretical relevance of such techniques.[19] Most have been designed to exploit the principle of association or correlation very much in the tradition of discovering empirical generalisations, the aim being to measure concepts at a sufficiently high level to meet the assumptions of correlational techniques first developed in genetics at the beginning of the twentieth century. While the use of such techniques have resulted in any number of empirical generalisations, none has so far been offered as a causal law. Social science has produced a catalogue of associations between any number of variables: between, for instance, class and educational attainment, educational attainment and mobility, class and voting choice, class and mental illness, religion and voting choice, the degree of industrialisation and domestic political violence, and so on, almost too numerous to recount.[20] All range from weak to strong, none is perfect, a fact attributed to various kinds of measurement error and the difficulty of controlling for all possible factors. However, what do such generalisations amount to? Are they 'proto-laws' from young and immature disciplines which, nonetheless, could serve as a basis for sounder laws? Or are they merely empirical generalisations describing local and temporally restricted relationships?

Let us first take the question of the nature of such generalisations. Such associations are normally derived from a sample of some population, the measures of association summarising the relationships among the variables in that sample. In any sample any number of such associations could be produced between all kinds of disparate phenomena that we would not normally consider to be of much interest. Accordingly, the associations summarise relationships among those variables felt to be important enough to be considered. So, how is the decision reached as to what to include within a study, given that it is impossible to include everything? The hypothetico-deductive model would suggest that the theory dictates what should be included, what variables should be examined, what variables should be controlled, and so on. Mill himself, although as thoroughgoing an empiricist as one is ever likely to find, did not dismiss the importance of hypotheses as necessary if one was to apply any of his methods of inquiry and derive verifiable consequences of the laws themselves. But for Mill, all hypotheses were suggested by experience and capable of being true or false. If we accept this it is still not quite clear how associations between variables could be said to be theoretically relevant. What are we to do about a less than perfect association or correlation? Does it prove or disprove a theory? Alternatively, should we want to say something a little weaker: that it 'lends support to' or 'is not entirely consistent with'? In fact, the interpretation of such associations is usually a *post hoc* affair in spite of the obeisance made to the hypothetico-deductive model's espousal of the test of prediction. All kinds of rationalisations, some more plausible than others but many still plausible enough, are entered into to make the associations theoretically interesting. That classic of positivistic social science, Durkheim's study of suicide, contains many generalisations summarising the correlations between marriage and suicide, religion and suicide, urban living and suicide, and more, while the remainder of the analysis consists of interpretations and arguments, many of them shrewd, ingenious and insightful, elaborating *post hoc* rationales to explain what it is about the correlated phenomena that leads to suicide. What is clear is that associations between variables do not speak for themselves.

Can such associations be regarded as proto-laws? An affirmative answer to this question looks remote since what has been said so far points to the conclusion that no empirical generalisation can ever logically entail a law. The fact that A has always hitherto been followed by B does not imply that it will always be followed by B. Indeed, not all statements of the logical form 'Whenever A, then B' can be treated as lawlike in the sense required by science. 'Nomological generalisations', for example, support subjunctive and counterfactual conditional statements whereas 'empirical generalisations' do not. For example, the law concerning the effects of dissolved solids on the boiling point of a liquid entitles a subjunctive conditional such as, 'If this solid salt were dissolved in this pan of boiling water, then the boiling point would be raised.' The law, along with statements about the initial conditions stating that the law is applicable in this particular case, entitles us to make such a statement. Similarly, it lends support to counterfactuals such as, 'If this piece of solid salt had been dissolved in water – though in fact it had not been – the boiling point of the water would have been raised.' In short, 'nomological generalisations' or laws allow us to make inferences about cases that do not now occur, have not occurred in the past and may not occur in the future. They state hypothetical relationships of invariable connection irrespective of whether or not the relationships is actually exemplified.

None of these characteristics applies to empirical generalisations. The generalisation that all the people in the room are under six feet tall does not entitle the inference that any future incomer to the room will be under six feet tall. Although a number of such generalisations may have always held in fact, at all times and places, this will still be, as Brown puts it, 'a happy accident and not a consequence of there being a law-like connection between the properties in question or, more basically, of there being a scientific theory from which the generalisation can be derived'.[21] That is, in the absence of any scientific theory to preclude the appearance of anyone over six feet tall entering this room, we have no basis for the kind of inferences we can make using nomological generalisations. The question is, however, whether empirical generalisations or nomological ones are the kind of generalisations produced by the Lazarsfeldian-type methods of social science.

Suppose, for example, after intensive studies of samples of individuals we find a high positive correlation between the number of siblings in a family and poor educational performance. What kind of generalisation would this be? An 'accidental' one or an empirical one, or what? It is hard to say since the case could be made for both. This, however, is not really the issue. If we wanted to use the generalisation to *explain* why little Johnny down the road with 12 brothers and sisters is not doing very well at school, it might indeed be offered as an explanation. But is this good enough? What about other factors which may play a part? How do we know that it is the number of siblings that causes the poor performance rather than, say, the poor school, little Johnny's passion for fishing, his dyslexia, or whatever else might characterise little Johnny's life and circumstance? Could, to be brief, little Johnny's poor educational performance be deduced from the generalisation? The answer is no, and for two major reasons. First, unlike the laws offered in natural science, the *ceteris paribus* conditions under which the applicability of the law is judged, in this example and in most real-life social science examples, have not been determined – to say the least. Second, the lack of a theory from which to derive the generalisation and, importantly, along with some statement of the conditions under which the theory will apply, means that any application will have to be determined *post hoc*. Though the mechanisms involved here have intuitive plausibility – for example, large families means less time for study, less parental attention for any one child, sibling rivalry, and so on – this *ad hocing* process is not quite what is to be expected from a scientific theory and the observations that might be deduced from it. Moreover, there are, in fact, any number of theories that could explain little Johnny's poor educational performance, some consistent with the generalisation but many not so, and for which the empirical connection between number of siblings and educational performance is an irrelevance. Third, since the generalisation is drawn from samples, all we have is a statistical generalisation stating that a property (number

of siblings) is associated with another property (educational performance) in a particular direction and size. From this, nothing follows
about any *particular* instance.[22] A deductive conclusion cannot be found,
only an inductive one. Premises made up of such generalisations cannot
logically imply a conclusion, only lend support.

In this respect Lieberson offers an illuminating example.[23] He asks:
how might social researchers, using their methods and ways of thinking, go about studying the question of why objects fall? He visualises
a study, based on an analogy with the typical type of social research
study in which the characteristic objective is to explain the variance in
the behaviour of different instances of the phenomena (such as the
differences in individual's or classes of individual's educational attain-
ments). Thus, in the natural science analogy a variety of objects is
dropped from a height without benefit of strong controls such as a
vacuum: a condition, to repeat, which parallels most circumstances in
social research where controls, such as they are, enter *post hoc* at the
data analysis stage. If the objects differ in the time they take to reach
the ground, the question becomes: what characteristics of the objects
determines this difference? Air resistance in the absence of a vacuum,
and the size and density of the objects, will, on the face of it, affect the
speed of the fall. Assume that these factors, even including others,
taken together account for all the differences in velocities of fall
between the objects.[24] In a social research context, likely as not, it would
be concluded that a complete understanding of the phenomenon had
been achieved since all the differences had been accounted for. But, of
course, the point of the example is that we would not have come up
with the idea of gravity. What is wrong here? As Lieberson puts it, data
on the *phenomenon* of interest are not necessarily relevant to the *question* of interest. So, an analysis of the rate of fall of various objects
might tell us why they differ in the rate of their fall, but not why they
fall. What we would not have available is the power of the theory of
gravity and its statement of the constancy of the rate of acceleration
of falling objects to deal with many of the applications for which it
is employed.

An important consideration here, one we have met before in our
discussion of Pearson's ideas and one also fully acknowledged by
Lazarsfeld in pursuing the ideas of variable analysis, is the nonexperimental character of social research. Without the ability effectively
to make *ceteris paribus* assumptions about the effects of unwanted
factors, identifying causal relationships where 'contamination' by multifarious influences is ever present, is likely to present fundamental difficulties to positivistic researchers. As said earlier, in variable analysis
controls are normally employed at the data analysis stage – through,
for example, the matching of units in the statistics on some characteristics to see how, given those characteristics are the same, they differ
on other characteristics – with the aim being to see how much of the
variability of the values of the dependent variable is accounted for by
one or more of the independent variables. Again, as indicated earlier,

for such as Pearson this is entirely what the problem is, namely, finding those variables which account for *most* but not *all* of the variance. For him there is simply no point in trying to add causes together until all the variation has been explained. The complete elimination of variability in real world observation is a chimera. It is only highly correlated variables that matter.[25]

Positivism and theory

The positivist conception of scientific knowledge with its emphasis on observation and empirical method to the relative neglect of theory turns out to be a poor characterisation of the logic of natural science which it supposedly extolled. This is not to say that observation and empirical method are unimportant in natural or any other science though positivism perhaps tended to fetishise these. The problem was positivism's treatment of theory and theoretical generalisations and their connection to the empirical. On the positivistic account the foundations of scientific knowledge are to be found in the systematic and persistent relationship of observable to observable.[26] It is a system of trial and error and no less effective for that. By contrast, rationalism emphasises the logical connection of idea to idea as is characteristic of logic, mathematics and some metaphysical systems of thought. Science shares characteristics of both but in a very different way to that proposed by positivism. Science is indeed primarily concerned with producing theoretical explanations of empirical connections but not, at least in any simple way, as a relationship of observable to observable. Its theoretical explanations are, we might say, more rationalistic than empiricist and in the most advanced of the natural sciences consist almost entirely of mathematical formulations. The concepts of the theories are given empirical import through abstraction by means of which properties of empirical objects are selected out and rationally connected together within a theoretical framework. The force of the earlier example from Lieberson is that social science methods cannot simplify their problems sufficiently to be able to formulate definite laws. Cannot, to use the example again, abstract out the relevant properties of 'falling bodies' by making assumptions about, in this case, a perfect vacuum in which objects are falling and so providing the conditions for the mathematisation of the theory.[27]

A scientific explanation uses determinative theoretical connections, not connections interpreted as general causal statements as positivist thought had it. But this is the determinativeness of rational connection. To illustrate (Willer and Willer 1973: 16). A relationship between cold weather and cracked car radiators can easily be established using empirical methods. In such a case the connection is made as a result of repeated observations and, Hume would add, habit. Such an explanation, making use of the empirical connection between cracked radiators and freezing weather, can be adequate for its purpose, especially if the aim is to avoid cracked car radiators. A scientific explanation, on the other hand, might begin with the idea that under perfect elasticity, stress is equal to strain. Then an attempt would be made to determine a value for the limit of elasticity for radiators by measuring the amount of force applied before the radiator cracks. By measuring air temperature and that of the water at night the point at which the water freezes to produce enough ice to apply the stress that would bring the radiator to its strain limit can be determined. A stress greater than the strain limit would break the radiator. In this case a law is being used in which stress is equal to strain under conditions of perfect elasticity. The purpose of the law is to derive a measure for the strain limit by applying stress, and to compare the calculated stress at the time of breakage with that limit. In so far as the value of the strain limit was determined from a calculation of stress, it is difficult to see how the laws could be proved false in such an application. The exact calculation of a limit could not have been arrived at empirically. Even though temperature could have been measured as precisely as possible using empirical methods, and the generalisation offered that the colder it gets the more likely the radiator is to break, this could not result in the calculation of a limit. It may result in a probability distribution, but this will not tell us whether or not the radiator will crack. The scientific law can point to a measurable condition under which breaking will occur, an empirical generalisation only that it will break with a certain probability.

Earlier it was remarked that the positivist account of the ways in which particular instances were transcended was faulty. In effect, it proposes a process of applying a name to a set of similar properties so forming a particular category: a Ford Mondeo belongs to the general category 'car', John Hughes to the category 'male', Charis Hughes to the category 'daughter', and so on. These are then related to other empirical categories by means of such methods as correlations. Science, on the other hand, transcends particular cases, as said earlier, by abstraction; that is, by a process of selection and not by the summation of similar characteristics. Indeed, observational phenomena abstracted in this way may bear little obvious similarity to each other. Pool balls are not like rockets but both may be abstractively connected to the concepts of the same laws of motion.

The meaning of abstracted concepts is derived not from the similar appearance of objects but from their relationship to other concepts within the theory. The process of abstraction is, in effect, one of conceptualising observations so that they may be deterministically related to other concepts. At once an infinite universe is provided as a conceptual framework for the theory. The rational connection between the concepts in the theory is not like a causal connection at all. We may well use the relationship $d = vt$ ('distance' equals 'velocity' multiplied by 'time'), and use it to build speedometers, measure distance travelled, work out how long it will take us to travel to Scunthorpe, and so on, but we do not observe distance to discover if it is, in fact, velocity multiplied by time; vt *tells us* what distance is in terms of time and velocity.

Abstraction in science moves back and forth between the empirical and the theoretical, expounding and sharpening the scope of application of the theory and its explanatory power: a matter of establishing an isomorphism between theoretical terms and empirical observables. This may be aided by manipulation under laboratory conditions, constructing models to fit particular cases, changing empirical conditions and varying models, and so on. As far as the abstraction process is concerned, and unlike in the case of generalisations, there is no problem about how similar is similar since the theory and its model(s) are deliberate constructions, even inventions, to fit and translate the theory to apply to particular cases. Indeed, theories may be applied to a large number of cases, as the law of falling bodies applies to anything that falls or flies. This is not the case with empirical generalisations. Lack of success in the case of a theory does not mean that the theory was false: it may instead indicate a limit to its scope, or mean that an abstractive error has been made.[28]

A very different conception of measurement is embodied in this view of scientific explanation. For the positivist, measurement is effectively a matter divorced from theory. Accordingly, the so-called 'measurement problem' in social science has largely been seen as an effort to scale all kinds of variables, from the macro structural variables to the affective, trying to give them the kind of precision and exactness felt to be characteristic of measurement in science.[29] Energy was devoted to constructing 'indices' for theoretical concepts, the aim being to connect the theory to the empirical world of observables by the use of essentially empirical techniques. However, on the abstractive view of the connection of theory to empirical observables, it is measurement which gives a theoretical concept empirical interpretation. Measurement orders data, not the other way around, and is very much a consequence of theory. 'Length', for example, in a scientific theory has a purely theoretical meaning determined by the postulates and laws of the theory. The concepts that are measured are chosen as a consequence of these postulates and laws and can be empirically interpreted in many different ways according to circumstances. The application of a theory to a broad range of phenomena gives rise to very different empirical interpretations. As Pawson points out, in science:

> the objective of measurement is to incorporate and embody within an instrument, principles derived from theoretical science. Instrumentation is thus seen as a branch of engineering and engineering is nothing other than the application of the laws, theories, hypotheses and principles of theoretical physics . . . the incorporation of theory into the observational domain is seen not as the problem, but as the true justification of measurement.
>
> (Pawson 1989: 106–7)

Temperature can be measured, for example, using an ordinary mercury thermometer or, with very cold objects, by means of the resistance to an electric current. In both cases, the measurement is the direct result of the laws of thermodynamics applied to different domains, the expansion of liquids in the one case and electrical conductivity in the other. Measurement of a rigorous scientific character is impossible without a strict theory specifying the strict mathematical relationship between concepts.

If the views just summarised are correct then the positivist conception of scientific knowledge must go by the board. It emphasised some aspects of science, particularly its empirical character, at the expense of failing to see the significance of others, especially that of theory. Science is empirical but it is also profoundly theoretical; indeed, perhaps a more convincing case could be made that science is more interested in theory than it is in the empirical. Laws, the aim both of positivism and science, are not causal empirical generalisations but rationally connected statements. True enough, in their infancy, some sciences may well proceed in a more empirical manner by correlating observables with other observables, but matters do not end there if it is to progress. Positivism did suspect that rational connection might be more important than some of its adherents would allow and the hypothetico-deductive model of explanation, for example, was an attempt to rationalise the importance of logic and mathematics, but firmly within the empiricist framework.

However, although it may well be accepted that the positivist view of science was misconceived, this is not to say that the methods it authorised as the methods of social science are also entirely useless. It may be that they are not scientific, either in the way that positivism understood or, indeed, in terms of the view just outlined, but this does not imply that they are pointless as a form of knowledge. It does, however, imply that we cannot get away so easily by according the methods a paragon scientific status they do not have.

It has been argued, and from diverse approaches, that the effort to emulate natural science, and the most advanced of the natural sciences at that, is premature given the current development of the social sciences. The use of the hypothetico-deductive model of explanation, for example, may well not be a useful one given the special conditions on which it depends – well-grounded knowledge, an ability to hold constant factors extraneous to the relationship of interest, clear deductive connections to the overarching theory, and so on, and, accordingly, at the present time the social sciences must remain content with 'lesser' forms of explanation. After all, history works well with 'genetic explanations' which are concerned to show how certain events came about and without any explicit reference to laws as such but by the deployment of an explanatory narrative.[30]

It is also possible to take the tack that there are more ways of being scientific than the one posivitism allows and that the social sciences cannot be treated as if they were immature natural sciences but are distinctively different and, hence, must needs follow a different logic of explanation. This was, broadly speaking and as we shall see in Chapter 5, the focus of the debates in Germany beginning in the late nineteenth century.

These are, obviously, large questions, some of which will be taken up more directly in subsequent chapters. For now, one or two preliminary conclusions are in order. One implication is that the positivistic account of the intellectual authority of social science methods is flawed as are some of the claims made on behalf of those methods. In so far as such methods produce empirical generalisations they will be subject to the kind of logical constraints discussed earlier. But, and to reiterate, this is not to say that such generalisations are of no interest.

There are also implications for interpretations of the nature of social scientific theory, most of which become less than scientific. Even within a positivistic framework the relationship of theory to data was a troublesome one. Theory was supposed to be dependent for its truth on the 'facts' of the world which were external to the theory itself. The theory did not shape the world, but was responsive to it. The importance placed on developing a theory-neutral observation language lay precisely in this. However, many of the candidates for theory in social science were, and still are, rejected on extra-empirical grounds. In the 1960s, for example, the great theoretical debate in sociology was between conflict theories and functionalism. Functionalism was attacked because it seemed to ignore the fact of conflict in social life, whereas one of its major aims was to examine the causes and consequences of conflict within a set of concepts stressing the systemic nature of society. Each side of the debate, however, effectively talked past each other. Something other than the scientific status of the respective theoretical positions was at issue, having much to do with what the connotations of concepts like 'conflict', 'stability' and so on, carried with them about familiar events and processes in historical societies. Such debates might better be seen as quarrels about how the social world ought to be looked at and less to do with the scientific value of such theories. This brings us to another general point about social scientific theory and one which will be discussed more fully in the next chapter.

Positivism, with its stress on the idea of a neutral observation language, empirical generalisation, and so forth, was disinclined to concern itself with the origin and source of theories. This is illustrated by the relative lack of interest shown in the matter of scientific discovery which was relegated to a sideshow beyond serious philosophical concern. Of much greater importance was the matter of verifying theories once formulated. The discovery of theories was a matter of conjecture on the part of scientists and their imagination, fancy, even induction and speculation, but certainly beyond formal logical description. What could be described as a logical process, it was argued, was the confirmation and testing of theories. To this extent theories had to conform to certain formal criteria in order to be capable of test against the 'facts' of the world. However, although this emphasis might have seemed excusable or justifiable in connection with natural science theories, it is less so with reference to the social sciences. The very notion of a domain of inquiry, whether it be sociology, economics, physics, chemistry, history or whatever, presupposes some conceptual schema ordering the world as a prelude to the observation of the relevant facts. This is what Durkheim, for example, was insistent on establishing, namely, the conceptual distinctiveness of sociology as an autonomous discipline with its own domain of facts, facts which gain their importance and significance because they are distinctively social. In other words, the conceptual ordering necessary to identifying a species of facts begins to challenge the idea that observation is entirely a theoretically neutral affair. It suggests that the knower is an active constituent in the construction of knowledge. On this view scientific theories become like inventions actively engaged in creating a reality, not passively waiting for their substantiation by the facts of the external world. Indeed, much of social scientific theory is underdetermined by the facts of the social world in the sense that no 'strategic experiment' is conceivable that could decide between them. Rather, such theories are better seen as conceptual schemes stipulating, even legislating, what the domain of fact might be.

One final point. Although the positivist conception of science has been shown to be seriously flawed, this is not the same as saying that the social sciences cannot be scientific within another interpretation of science. This issue will have to be dealt with, but before doing so it is necessary to bring some of the debates about the nature of science up to date.

Notes

1. Carnap (1967, first appeared in German, 1928), for example, gives an account of the whole apparatus of empirical discourse in terms of remembered similarity among sense impressions. These are the basic elements out of which are constructed, with the help of logic, the concepts of material things, other minds and social institutions. The topics of thought stand in various levels each reducible to the one preceding it. Higher level statements are justified by induction from statements of the levels below; the basic lowest level statements need, and can have, no inferential justification. At this point the system of statements makes contact, through observation, with the world of 'brute' empirical fact.
2. Many members of the Vienna Circle, as it was known, went to the United States prior to the Second World War and had a major impact on the philosophy of science there as well as on philosophy generally. See, for example, Ayer (1959) and Achinstein and Barker (1969).
3. This is taken from Ayer (1990: 114). The selection is taken from Ayer (1946); who cites the British Hegelian, F.H. Bradley, as the source of the example.
4. As we shall see later in Chapter 6, the relationship of 'facts' to theoretical frameworks became a salient issue in the work of Kuhn and the social constructionists.
5. As Smelser some years ago wrote of the language of science: '. . . the language of the ingredients of science; independent variables, dependent variables, theoretical frameworks, and research methods' (1968: 43). However, this betrays the extent to which social science empirical research was

captivated at the time by variable analysis since in physical science talk of variables is extremely rare. Another example from about the same time is the advice one textbook on methods gives: 'it is necessary to translate your ideas . . . into the language of variables . . . The experienced sociologist develops the habit of routinely translating the English he reads and hears into variables, just as a bilingual person can read one language while thinking in another' (Davis 1971: 16). It would be hard these days to find anyone expressing such sentiments with this kind of enthusiasm.

6. Lazarsfeld and Rosenberg (1955: 15). This whole collection, despite its age, is a testament to the vigorous enthusiasm of variable analysis in its early days.

7. See Ackroyd and Hughes (1991). There are also many others which deal with these techniques.

8. There can be little doubt that Lazarsfeld's thinking owed much to his commitment to survey research.

9. This is evident in the work of Blalock, perhaps the foremost exponent of causal modelling in sociology. See, for example, Blalock (1984).

10. Collective concepts, for Weber, 'have a meaning in the minds of individual persons, partly as of something actually existing, partly as something with normative authority . . . Thus, for instance, one of the important aspects of the existence of a modern state . . . consists in the fact that the action of various individuals is oriented to the belief that it exists or should exist, thus that its acts and laws are valid in the legal sense' (Weber 1978: 14).

11. Structuralist sociologies, sometimes derived from interpretations of Marx combined with ideas taken from linguistics, take this further and see the individual as the 'bearer' of larger relational structures in such a way that these structures act through the individual. See, for example, Althusser (1969). These ideas will be taken up in Chapter 8.

12. See Lazarsfeld and Menzel (1969) for an attempt to resolve such questions within the variable analytic framework.

13. By the seventeenth century the idea of 'laws of nature' began to lose its theological overtones and, hence, the idea that these were somehow expressions of God's will. See Outhwaite (1987).

14. If, for example, the law states that 'whenever sulphur is dropped into a candle flame', the flame turns yellow, then the initial conditions could state 'sulphur has been dropped into this candle flame', thus licensing the conclusion-prediction that this candle flame will turn yellow.

15. Popper (1959: 59). For Popper it was the possibility of a theory being falsified by empirical evidence that formed the distinction between scientific theories and nonscientific theories. Many of social science theories would, on his criterion, be rendered unscientific.

16. See Nagel (1961) for a discussion of 'theoretical' and 'observational' languages of science. It was also a conception used by Lazarsfeld.

17. This is how, for example, it appears in the work of Blalock. See, for example, Blalock (1982).

18. For a useful review see Pawson (1989).

19. Such questions are not only raised by philosophers but also by practitioners. See, for example, Blalock (1982) and Lieberson (1985).

20. See, for example, the compendium of 'findings' offered in Berelson and Steiner (1967). It is perhaps a sign of the times that no one since has tried to repeat this exercise.

21. Brown (1973: 93). In the 1997 British general election, pollsters were much agitated that this time they got their predictions of the results correct after having failed in the previous election. They succeeded after making

various adjustments in their methods to take account of changing rates of the disclosure of voting intentions and other social changes. This time they predicted the election result extremely well, but they are still dealing with empirical generalisations rather than theoretical ones.

22. Robinson (1950) is a classic paper which identifies a number of 'ecological fallacies' involved in inferring about individuals from aggregated data.

23. Lieberson (1985: 99–101). It is also important to note that he understands social research to be mainly survey research and quantitative data analysis.

24. This assumes that one could account for all of what is known as the variance, statistically defined, in social research. Such a state of affairs would be unprecedented. Lieberson draws some devastating conclusions about the ability of nonexperimental social research to realise its ambitions of producing theoretically relevant explanations.

25. Unfortunately for this kind of conception there are serious technical flaws, quite apart from the ones suggested by Lieberson's example. Turner (1987) points out, for example, that both the metaphysics underlying this conception of social research and the statistical techniques used to implement it, fail to realise that theories remain underdetermined. Not only is there no attainable goal of the complete elimination of variability, there is usually more than one way of adding or combining variables to the point of redundancy, assuming that this is capable of plausible definition, irrespective of the further fact that there is more than one choice about the way in which the variables can be measured. Turner points out that no logical relationship can hold between theoretical claims and generalisations based on statistical data, largely because of the assumptions about the order of variables, their completeness, their linearity, or otherwise, and their independence: all essential to the mathematics of statistical modelling, and which always make the generalisations assumption-relative. This is not, however, the same as stating the conditions of a law. Newton's laws, for example, apply in a vacuum at low speed, without significant light pressure, and so on. But these are known and measurable factors not assumptions that have to be made in order to use statistical models.

26. This is one of the distinguishing features of most forms of empiricism and is to be found in many diverse activities from primitive magic to modern technology. See Willer and Willer (1973: 16).

27. The process is, of course, more complicated that this and does not take into account the years of patient working which laid the basis for the idea. But, remember, the discussion here is about the logic of scientific explanation, not the practice of science. 'Falling bodies' were known about before Newton proposed the theory of gravity. The issue for him was to explain why bodies fall.

28. The advent of Einstein's relativity theory and quantum mechanics in physics, for example, have not so much rendered Newton's theory false as indicated its scope, that is, its restriction to low light speed and relatively short distances.

29. Duncan (1984) has much to say on the so-called exactness of measurement in the physical sciences and, at even greater length, on the efforts of the human sciences to emulate this. In the 1930s and 1940s, considerable effort was devoted, mainly by psychologists, to what was known as the 'theory of measurement' which treated measurement as if it were a 'free-standing' logic independent of theoretical considerations. See, for example, Torgerson (1958); Stouffer (1962) contains writings by one of the main initiators of this movement.

30. But see Nagel (1961) for an alternative view of historical explanation.

CHAPTER 4

Positivism and the conception of science

This chapter takes a rather wider perspective on issues in the philosophy of science, but one which continues some of the themes raised in the previous chapter; once again reflecting on that perennial ambition to be scientific in the fashion of the natural sciences which was bequeathed to the twentieth century social sciences by nineteenth century positivism. As mentioned previously, the vision of science was very much philosophically inspired and philosophically controversial. We will first review once again the hypothetico-deductive model of explanation.

The hypothetico-deductive model of explanation again

The hypothetico-deductive model represented a scientific theory as a set of statements connected by logical rules. The law was expressed as a universal statement of the form 'Whenever A, then B'. From this and other statements of 'initial conditions' a hypothesis about what should happen could be deduced which could then be tested against empirical observation; that is, checked to see if what should happen did happen. An event was considered to be explained if it could be shown to be a logical consequence of the theoretical statements. In other words, the truth of the explanandum (i.e. the statement which says what has occurred or which specifies the event which is to be predicted), is, in crucial part, guaranteed by logic, as long as the explanandum is logically deducible from empirically true statements about the initial conditions and the general laws – the 'explanans' as these are called. If the scheme is used retrospectively it gives explanations; used prospectively it provides predictions. If the universal law is true then the prediction will be confirmed; if not, then the prediction will fail and, ideally, the universal law will be falsified.

As we have seen, this interpretation seemed to solve a number of problems, not least those involved in proposing induction as the basis for the universality of scientific laws. Scientific laws are empirical laws subject to empirical confirmation, and involved in the method of testing is deduction. Scientific explanation is causal explanation in which the 'explanation of an event means to deduce a statement which describes it, using as premises of the deduction one or more universal laws; together with certain singular statements, the initial conditions' (Popper 1959: 59). Scientific laws are causal statements describing events in nature and are capable of being true or false, their truth or falsity being determined by observation. There is no need for any inductive process or, indeed, for any metaphysical refuge in appeals to the uniformity of nature.

The hypothetico-deductive model seemed to offer a characterisation of scientific reasoning that social science could live with and emulate. Further, the adoption of such a mode of reasoning, even at the modest levels the social sciences could realistically achieve, would place the social sciences firmly within the camp of science. In other words, the schema served as a criterion definitive of scientific forms of knowledge. However, in the hands of Karl Popper, matters did not turn out quite so straightforwardly.

Popper's falsificationism and the road to the sociology of science

In the previous chapter attention was drawn to the failure of inductivism as a justification for theoretical generalisations. Popper agreed. The classical model of induction could not logically escape the uncertainty that succeeding observations posed. Scientific knowledge cannot proceed by the verification of theories by means of empirical testing but, instead, has to rely on a critical method of 'bold conjectures' and attempts at refutation. Popper's philosophy of science, however, is more than just a criticism of inductivism; he was also vitally interested in looking for what was distinctive about the scientific method. Not all forms of knowledge are scientific and, like logical positivism, he was interested in developing a demarcation criterion that could distinguish 'science' from, in the first instance, metaphysics which could disguise itself in some of the forms of science, but actually comprise only a 'pseudo-science'. Inductivism failed to distinguish science from pseudo-science since many activities laying claim to scientific status, but whose claims to scientific status Popper dismissed, relied upon induction. Not only had inductivism failed to provide an adequate justification for the truth of scientific generalisations, it had also run the risk of allowing into the collection of scientific disciplines such endeavours as astrology, psychoanalysis and Marxism, to mention but three which Popper denied were genuinely scientific, the latter two being metaphysical in nature. Popper wanted to demarcate science from metaphysics and, in the course of this demonstration, to show that Freudianism and Marxism, though they thought they were scientific, were pseudo-sciences because they were really metaphysics.

The 'demarcation criterion' Popper offered was that of falsifiability. No amount of observations could ever finally confirm a generalisation of the form 'Whenever A, then B'. The most it could confirm were claims of the order of 'Very often, when A, then B' or 'In all cases observed to date, when A, then B' which fall short of universality. Universal claims such as laws subsume all events of the appropriate kind, including those which will occur in the future and, as Hume had argued, there can be no certainty that what has happened every time up until now must happen next time. There is an asymmetry between confirmation and falsification. One counter-instance of an A not being followed by a B would conclusively disconfirm the universal generalisation and this, Popper argued, indicates the true method of science; that is, to seek the disconfirmation of a theory's predictions. Bona fide scientific theories expose themselves to the risk of falsification by unequivocally stating, in their predictions, what must be the case in specific circumstances if they are true. Thus, they exhibit the condition for their failure as theories, whereas the theories of pseudo-science do not. These latter have, as it were, escape clauses for explaining away any failures of their predictions and, as a consequence, cannot be falsified. Astrological theories, for example, are unfalsifiable and, therefore, not scientific as, on the same basis and much more importantly in Popper's view, are Marxism, Freudianism and even Darwinism.

In this way Popper revised the orthodox positivist conception of science and considered that in doing so he had done enough to dissociate himself from the positivists. The object of science is not to infer from specific instances to generalisations but to search for ways of rejecting what he calls 'conjectural hypotheses'. Science is not a body of accumulated and accumulating true theories but a collection of conjectures which have yet to be refuted: science is a 'system of guesses or anticipations which in principle cannot be justified, but which can only be claimed to be valid in this sense: up to this time, they have withstood the toughest tests that scientists have been able to set them' (Popper 1959: 317). Further, it is those theories which make very precise predictions, and accordingly are more likely to fail with one crucial experiment or test, which are the best.[1] The ability of theories to withstand tests, their 'corroboration', is related to the improbability of their predictions. They state things, that is, which *prima facie*, and independent of the theory, would seem implausible, as initially did Einstein's prediction that light would bend in the vicinity of the sun. The best theories, like Einstein's general theory of relativity, provide for very precise predictions across a range of tests and, therefore, have a high empirical content which, for Popper, means that they can rule out a great many possibilities by saying, if they are true, what must occur and what could not possibly do so. It is those theories, which are unfalsifiable in principle, which are virtually devoid of empirical content; they cannot rule out anything since they never say unequivocally what must happen. Science is, as a consequence, above all a critical pursuit, one which is ruthlessly competitive, forever seeking to destroy or refute its conjectures, even its best ones. It is by critical trial and error that science proceeds, discarding those theories that fail to match up to the tests and trying to intensify the tests of those, at least for the time being, that have passed the best tests that can be currently devised for them. It is only through the rejection of theories that our knowledge can progress for, given the nature of Popper's argument about universal generalisations, we can never have the certainty that any of these are true. All we can ever be fully certain of is that some such generalisations have been shown to be false. As long as 'we admit that there is no authority beyond the reach of criticism to be found within the whole province of our knowledge . . . then we can retain . . . the idea that truth is beyond human authority' (Popper 1965: 29–30). This 'evolutionary epistemology' is no different, for Popper, to the way that all forms of life adapt and it is really only an extension of the trial and error mode of learning. Of course, there is always the risk of holding on to an unsound theory or, for that matter, abandoning prematurely a good one. But these risks science has no choice but to live with since, as Popper admits, there are nonlogical criteria involved in the selection and promotion of scientific theories. As studies in the sociology and the history of science have shown, there are many reasons why theories are often held on to, or thrown over, other than for strictly scientific criteria, including such prosaic matters as personal preference, career advancement or religious conviction. But, for Popper, although such things are an ineradicable feature of the social history of science, they are not part of its logic, and it is this with which Popper sees himself as primarily concerned. The only defensible concern of epistemology as the theory of scientific knowledge is with regard to the actual procedures and products of science. Science aims at truth in the sense of correspondence with reality, yet we can never conclusively demonstrate that our conjectures are true. Rather truth is tested by eliminating falsehood; 'we are seekers of truth but we are not its possessors' (Popper 1972: 59).

Nonetheless, though Popper's criterion of falsifiability is intended as a logical one, reservations have to be expressed as to whether its point is descriptive or prescriptive. If the former, then as an account of how science works it is clearly deficient. Scientists are not critical all the time, do not necessarily search out the most rigorous testing grounds for theories, cannot always fulfil the conditions for strict falsification. If the latter, then falsificationism does not only rule out well-known and well-respected theories in the human sciences, it has the same effect on a number of natural scientific theories including, for example, Darwin's theory of evolution. As far as Popper is concerned, theories must be predictivist: it is the predictions that open theories to falsification. Heuristic theories are not allowable. Further, no notice is taken of the immense amount of taxonomic work fundamental in many sciences. These issues apart, even as an account of the logic of science, Popper's is idealised, paying little attention to the other than strictly logical reasons scientists might have for accepting and rejecting hypotheses. This matters if Popper's criterion is invoked prescriptively since it no longer just describes the difference between 'proper' science and pseudo-science, but begins to stipulate how science ought to be done.

In Popper's defence, however, we need to note that, in the main, he insists that he is not trying to describe how all science is done, but only that science which can contribute to the growth of our knowledge; science which casts itself in such a form that it runs the risk of falsification. Popper does not give a generalised account of how scientists all behave: many scientists operate in a bureaucratic spirit, are cautious and evasive of intellectual risk, and conspicuously devoid of the relentless critical spirit that Popper commends. What he sees himself as describing is how *successful* science is done, how the great scientists have brought about great leaps in our knowledge by completely revising our ways of thinking. Scientists such as Newton and Einstein exhibited a proclivity for intellectual risk taking. Popper would also allow 'heuristic theories' so long as they were used to work toward theories which were falsifiable. In the end, however, for Popper it does not matter how theories are arrived at, only that they should lead to 'bold conjectures' and be open to refutation since it is in this that scientific progress lies.

As far as the social sciences were concerned, the first impact of Popper's work was devastating. The requirements of falsification effectively ruled out of the court of science many tried and trusted social science theories because they could not articulate theories in a form which would expose them to the possibility of refutation. They were more like Freudianism and Marxism, indeed were often derivatives of these, than they were like Newtonian and Einsteinian theories. As far as Popper was concerned, all they offered was ways of looking at, or points of view on, social life; they were not *scientific* theories. This aspect of his work was developed in his vehement arguments against collectivist views of society, such as those of Marxism, as inviting not more freedom for the individual but less. Any attempt to impose equality as a major social organising principle – or, indeed, to undertake any kind of comprehensive reconstruction of society in the name of some social science or general principle – would, likely as not, produce tyranny (see Popper 1945, Sharrock 1987). The arguments are connected, and strongly so, to Popper's sense of the limitations of human knowledge and, in this respect, his suspicions of those inspirations of social science, of which Comte was a precursor, which see it as a way of enhancing the rational intervention in the wholesale reorganisation of human society to ameliorate its evils. For Popper such an ambition, if conceived holistically, is inevitably to invite tyranny for it would require the subjection of the whole society to one central, controlling and planning authority and that, in turn, would result in the suppression of all alternatives to the commanding point of view. Scientific knowledge is a matter or trial and error conducted through testing and criticism, and this can only be institutionally realised in an 'open' society where a plurality of points of view can exist and compete with each other. Such a process requires that criticism flower, argument thrive, dissent flourish, and these cannot do so in 'closed' societies. The social sciences are not, however, denied all possibility of useful social intervention, but this can only be successful on a modest scale, what Popper termed, 'piecemeal social engineering'.

Thus Popper's doctrine of falsificationism gave one strong reason as to why the hypothetico-deductive schema was so important to philosophy of science in being a format which imposed the demand for expression in falsifiable form on a scientific theory. Whether interpreted in verificationist or Popper's falsificationist terms, the hypothetico-deductive scheme has been a powerful idea in the philosophy of science, though, as with everything else, it has not been without its critics. It was intended to avoid the philosophical difficulties of inductivism but also, sometimes inadvertently, while concerned to maintain the rationality of the *method* of science did, at the same time, highlight the importance of the history and sociology of science if only, to put it in Popperian terms, to understand which theories entered the evolutionary race.

The Kuhnian turn

Popper's intervention, however, raised a number of issues which transformed the debate on the nature of science and the scientific method. Though Popper himself rejected the charge of relativism, the claim that science could only, at best, obtain 'successive approximations' to truth along with the view that observations are invariably theory impregnated, do invite relativist conclusions. Popper made two important claims: first, that the logical method of science is falsification; second, that science progresses through trial and error, by an evolutionary epistemology incorporating a logic of criticism. Kuhn (1996), however, claimed that neither of these assertions is supported by the history of science. Far from the history of science displaying a steady continuity in which theories, subjected to steady but unrelenting criticism, are weeded out leaving only the best conjectures holding the field, conformity and conservatism seem to rule. For most of the time scientists exhibit a strong attachment to general frameworks, or 'paradigms', within which 'normal science' proceeds its uneventful and cautious way. Such prolonged periods are punctuated by upheavals in which 'revolutionary science' overthrows the orthodoxy only to establish itself as a new orthodoxy. Upheavals such as these are relatively rare, however, and it is in many ways only reluctantly that scientists contemplate the need for radical theoretical change.

Here Kuhn is drawing upon sociological ideas and using them against philosophical conceptions of science, including those of positivism. In brief, science is a social institution, and in a mature science, newcomers are socialised into conformity with a received frame of reference: learning to be a scientist is learning how to accept, work and think within the idioms already established in their particular scientific discipline. In doing so they become committed to a 'paradigm' which, though it is not always clear just what Kuhn means by this, contains, first, a constellation of values and beliefs, cognitions, rules of order and techniques of procedure shared by a given scientific community, and, second, a collection of exemplary work within a discipline that serve as recipes for problem-solving activity. Paradigms involve a shared set of symbols, metaphysical commitments and values, as well as criteria of judgement and the worth of work done. So, becoming a member of a scientific community involves enculturation into the reigning paradigm. 'Normal science' characterises the kind of attitudes and practices that exist within a paradigm-based discipline for most of the time, in which scientists patiently and undramatically work to elaborate the established theories and accumulate findings shaped by the orthodox framework. However, such a process always creates puzzles and problems – reported phenomena which do not fit the expectations of established theories – which, though for a time they can be put on one side, eventually accumulate until they become so serious that the orthodox paradigm is increasingly seen as inadequate. The search for a new paradigm starts: a search best done by younger scientists with reputations and careers to establish. Out of this turmoil a new paradigm emerges.

For some, Kuhn's version of the development of science overemphasises the irrational and nonrational factors. The change in paradigms amounts to a *gestalt* switch in which things can never be the same as before. A new paradigm is a new way of seeing the 'same' things differently, and the kind of phenomena with which a discipline deals change fundamentally. Paradigms are incommensurable. They cannot be jointly compared against an independent, neutrally observed reality since part of the disagreement about what reality consists in includes, naturally, disagreement over how it is to be correctly described. When the phlogiston theory of combustion was refuted and Lavoisier discovered oxygen, the universe was different for science (Anderson *et al.* 1987: 252). In which case, if Kuhn is right there can be no theory-independent view of the world and if a change from one paradigm to another is a movement between incommensurables, then it can be made to sound as if scientific change is merely a history of changes and science unequivocally a social process and the selection of competing theories dependent on this context. Moreover, such a view seemed to reject a correspondence theory of scientific truth. Theories are radically underdetermined by the facts of the world. The world, to put it slightly differently, is capable of bearing a very wide variety of theories, none of which could be said to be absolutely superior to another on the basis of just one single, unequivocal criterion. Kuhn himself claimed that he was not a relativist, and expressed unease at the apparent abandonment of the idea that sensory experience was fixed and neutral, but he also despaired of securing the objectivity of science through persistence with the positivist idea of a neutral observation language against which the hypotheses of rival theories could each, objectively, be compared (Kuhn 1996: 126, 1974).

The dispute between the Popperian and Kuhnian views is over the character of scientific logic and its place in understanding the development of science, in particular as to whether it is possible, or sensible, to describe science's development as a progress towards truth (see Lakatos and Musgrave 1970). It is often but wrongly thought that Popper wants to say that despite local vagaries and perturbations, the choice between theories, between paradigms even, is, or can be, made on rational scientific criteria and that Kuhn wants to deny that science is our most rational mode of operating. Popper is apt to be viewed as holding that it is the effort to falsify theories through the trial and error of criticism that results in the slow progress towards truth as weaker offerings are discarded. Kuhn, on the other hand, is understood to suggest that such choices between one scientific theory and its successors are *not* rational because the choice of the theory is the outcome of nonrational, extrascientific considerations and factors, such as the distribution of power and reputation within disciplines, within society itself, personal commitments, wider cultural and political circumstances, and so on. The 'facts' cannot decide the matter because what the 'facts' are is dependent upon the particular paradigm they belong to, as are the standards in force for judging which theories are better than others. Facts, methods and standards are internal to paradigms and there is no independent position from which to judge them – least of all by an appeal to a world independent of any theoretical position whatsoever. Such a thing is a chimera.

However, such a characterisation of the difference between Popper and Kuhn neglects the extent to which Popper also, and long before Kuhn, adopts a 'sociological' view of science as a basis for its objectivity as well as emphasising the nonrational sources of scientific motivation.[2] Popper insists that the objectivity of science depends upon criticism, and this is only possible in social arrangements within which criticism is institutionalised. The fact that individual scientists are human like the rest of us, have their own opinions, prejudices, blind spots, extrascientific beliefs, and so forth, is not to be regretted but welcomed. It is the diversity of scientists' convictions which provides the motor for vigorous criticism. If they did not have strong, even passionate, convictions, why should they be motivated to make the effort to criticise other views? But the fact that scientists are as much 'irrationally' motivated as they are 'rational' does not detract from Popper's view for, as noted, with regard to the problem which concerns him, that is, the growth of knowledge, it does not matter in the slightest how scientific conjectures are arrived at: only that, when they are produced, they are testable. A testable conjecture could be generated in the most irrational way. The rationality and objectivity of science lies in the process of criticism within which prejudices and biases can, so to speak, cancel each other out. However Popper and Kuhn do differ, if not with respect to the existence of 'irrational' motivations within the scientific community, then over the essential nature of scientific activity as critical and conformist.

Although Kuhn's views provoked no little excitement in social science, it is not clear just what their implications might be, except as a way of writing the history of social science in terms of paradigm changes (Urry 1973). In other words, it is not clear just what philosophical or methodological consequences would flow from Kuhn's conception. Are the social sciences at a preparadigmatic phase, or do they exhibit a plurality of paradigms which, though incommensurable, can be ignored until a better paradigm emerges? But what follows from any answer to these and other questions of this order? As far as the sociology of science was concerned, however, Kuhn's work proved to be a liberation.

The impact on the sociology of science

Hitherto a relatively minor branch of sociology concerned with studies on, for example, the background of scientists, the social history of science, the rise of science as an institution, and so on, the sociology of science began to see itself as able to make inquiries into the cognitive aspects of science, scientific knowledge itself, and so encroach, it was claimed, upon territory hitherto reserved for philosophy.[3] For some, it meant that philosophical questions about knowledge were at last open to empirical solution. The 'strong programme' in the sociology of knowledge, for example, saw itself as banishing forever the philosophy of science and all the epistemological and ontological questions that went with it. Science was through and through a social construction and, therefore, a concern of sociology rather than philosophy (see e.g. Bloor 1976, 1981, Shapin 1982, Woolgar 1981, Law and Lodge 1984). It is social and political as well as wider moral attitudes that determine the theories which are held and sustained and those which are rejected. Boyle's atomic theory of matter, for example, crucial to the origins of modern chemistry, had a strong affinity with the corpuscular philosophy that shaped the political opinions of the 'establishment' groups to which Boyle belonged in post-Civil War England. Corpuscular philosophy was the ideology of an establishment class and corresponded with the requirements of their social, political and economic interests.

The claim is that all knowledge, including scientific knowledge, is social. Although knowledge can be analysed and studied as if it were asocial, that is, independent of the social circumstances which produced it, this is a very limited conception and one which will not be able to explain why some theories, some beliefs, are held and others not. If one looks at the history of science one can find many theories, including some that were just as plausible in terms of the evidence available, but which were not accepted while others were. This cannot be explained purely in terms of rational criteria. A proper footing for the examination of knowledge is the sociology of knowledge rather than philosophy. According to the strong programme in the sociology of science, what such an examination should seek to do is specify the causal connections between social conditions and knowledge, irrespective of whether or not these bodies of knowledge are true or false. In other words, it should not simply seek to explain why false beliefs are held, for example, why some people still believe that the Earth is flat, but also try to explain why true beliefs are accepted since the fact that they are true does not itself explain why people believe them. Nor is the sociology of knowledge to be exempted from its own strictures; it, too, is capable of explanation in terms of its causal social conditions. One implication of such a view is to render meaningless the quest for intellectual authority, as positivism did, for example, through a philosophically secure conception of the foundations of human knowledge. Philosophy, too, as a body of knowledge is socially caused and, hence, dependent on the social conditions which produced it. It is social conditions which determine what will be accepted as knowledge, even that which is accepted as true, not any absolute principles or criteria independent of social determination. Accordingly, there are no secure foundations for human knowledge: all knowledge is relative.

However, what this represents is a mistake traceable back to some interpretations of Kuhn, of confusing the history and the sociology of science with the philosophy of science. For, even accepting that the boundaries between disciplines are not always clear, it can be argued that history, sociology and philosophy involve very different kinds of problems, to be approached by quite different methods and, as such, are incommensurable in respect of their problems and procedures. A philosophical question cannot be answered, if it can be answered at all, by an empirical scientific method. In which case, the claims of the strong programme, for example, to answer philosophical questions empirically must be simply mistaken, for philosophical problems are not of the kind to be resolved empirically. Its interest in the world is independent of whatever empirical conclusions history or sociology might provide. This is an issue that will surface again; but as far as Kuhn's work is concerned, if he was doing no more, as suggested earlier, than describe the development of natural science in a particular period of European history, then it is debatable as to whether his analysis has any methodological consequences for the social sciences as to how they might meet the requirements of scientificity.[4]

However, Kuhn did argue against the kind of view which, under positivist influence, prevailed in sociology, that the way to turn a 'prescientific' discipline into a fully scientific one was to place great emphasis on measurement. While it was true that the most successful natural sciences were fully quantitative, they did not become so by adopting the dictat: 'Go forth and quantify'. Their capacity to quantify arose only slowly from their accumulation of an immense empirical, qualitative familiarity with their phenomena so that they then understood things well enough to be able to work out meaningful and effective forms of measurement. The positivists' policy of 'go forth and quantify' in the social sciences was likely, therefore, to be fruitless without developing the corresponding familiarity with their phenomena. In the long run qualitative research, which they so vituperatively decried, might prove a more effective route toward meaningful quantification.

Scientific progress and scientific method

Rightly or wrongly, however, one of the implications that has been drawn is that Kuhn's arguments deny the possibility of scientific progress.

Science does not grow, it simply changes. As Laudan points out with respect to Kuhn's conception, 'scientific revolutions are regarded as progressive because the ' "victors" write the history . . .' (Laudan 1977: 10). This, as said earlier, for many is an absurd conclusion but it is not one which Kuhn himself endorses. Kuhn did not deny that scientific progress took place. It did. Modern sciences are much more empirically well based, have more powerful and more general theories, and just know a great deal more than their predecessors. What Kuhn did criticise was the idea that progress could be measured on some continuous scale when, in fact, it is judged in terms of a number of criteria which themselves change over time and which interact among themselves. Whatever scientific discipline we choose to take, be it physics, chemistry, biology, mathematics, history, even any of the social sciences, our knowledge has not merely changed but grown, though not always in a straight linear fashion. However, this is not quite the problem. We could still accept that scientific knowledge has grown and still deny that this is solely the result of the rational accumulation of knowledge. Lakatos turned to this in an effort to reconcile some of Kuhn's insights into the historical development of science with the view that science is a rational activity or, more correctly, with Lakatos' own notion of what 'rationality' ought to mean (Lakatos 1978 and 1984, Anderson *et al.* 1986). Falsificationism, as far as Lakatos was concerned, failed as a demarcation criterion between science and nonscience because it underestimated, even ignored, the tenacity with which theories were clung to despite disconfirmation; a point which Kuhn dwells upon. However, Kuhn's own conclusions about the incommensurability of theories was far too relativistic for Lakatos' taste. Science, for him, is a rationally accumulating body of knowledge; but it does not progress, as Popper claimed, through trial and error. The key notion for Lakatos is not, as it is for both Popper and Kuhn, the theory but the 'research programme'.

Newton's theory of gravitation, Einstein's relativity theory, Marxism, Freudianism, among many more, would qualify as 'research programmes' in Lakatos's sense. They are characterised by a 'hard core' of definitive propositions protected by a belt of auxiliary theories and hypotheses which connect the 'core' to the domain of facts to which they pertain. Thus, for Marxism, the theory of value formation and the creation of surplus value would be the core, and the theories of alienation, diminishing return to capital and of revolution, would be the auxiliary theories. However, a 'research programme', as its name is meant to imply, is not some dead, fixed collection of ideas but a living thing directed by scholars working within it at the problems it poses, suggesting ways in which they can be tackled, exploring its ideas, indicating problems that are best avoided, and so on. It is the last kind of problems wherein lie the dynamics of 'research programmes' since, by eventually confronting them, progress can be achieved. Of course, the problem is knowing which problems are likely to prove promising and which not. For Lakatos, as for Popper, the important criterion is the ability of a research programme to predict novel facts or facts ruled out to be impossible by other research programmes. So, if a theory is running ahead of the facts, or is predicting new facts, then it is a progressive one. If, on the other hand, the theory constantly needs repair and patching up to stay in business, then it is degenerating or, at best, static.

Lakatos's 'rationalist history' of science tries to merge the philosophy of science's traditional concerns for the logic of the scientific method with those of the history of science. The tendency of science to persist with disconfirmed theories is rational in that it delays judgement until a research programme has matured. However, whatever the merits of the views just discussed, there is no doubt that bringing historical and social considerations to bear upon discussions on the logic of science has cast serious doubts on the traditional view that science is a paragon of rational-cum-empirical knowledge.

This is most pronounced in the work of Paul Feyerabend, who argues that scientific change and progress is really a conversion from one myth to another. Rejecting the distinction between observation and theory, as well as philosophical rumination, as having any relevance for the operation of science, he regards science as a social institution located within a specific set of cultural, political and social concerns, just like any other institution in society. Thus, scientific changes do not simply arise from the application of a scientific method, but from the influences of 'interests, forces, propaganda brainwashing techniques' of 'professional socialization' (Feyerabend 1975). In this respect, science is no different to any other form of knowledge; it is part and parcel of 'forms of life'. The conclusion that Feyerabend draws from this familiar relativist argument is that 'anything goes' in science. There is no scientific method. There is certainly no superiority attaching to scientific knowledge. For Western society, science has become an idol, a dogma, and its conception as a progressive rational activity little more than an obsession without foundation. In this he is not claiming the need to 'correct' the actual practices of science, but to bring its ideology more into accord with these practices.

His own examination of the Copernican revolution in astronomy during the sixteenth and seventeenth centuries suggests that Copernicus's theory did not succeed because it was 'obviously' more rational and more progressive than Ptolemaic astronomy, a point that Kuhn also made. Indeed, Copernicus's theory did not fit many of the widely accepted astronomical 'facts' and made use of some of Aristotle's theories about the harmony of the universe. It was not until the use of the telescope that the majority were eventually persuaded to accept Copernicus's heliocentric theory of the solar system. Other aspects of the theory depended upon Galileo's new theory of motion. But Feyerabend's point is that conversions such as these are not the products of reason, evidence or method, but have much to do with self-interest, ideology and wider cultural beliefs. Although Feyerabend's anarchism is well known and fits well with his rejection of the notion that there is any superiority to the method of science, he is not against science, only against its pretensions and idolisation, more a critic of 'scientism', that is, an unquestioning faith in the 'cure all' capacity of science, than anything else.

Popper, Kuhn, Lakatos and Feyerabend represent, although in different ways, a response to the epistemological problems posed by induction as the basis of scientific knowledge. Popper revised the scope of the problem by proposing that it was the scientific method that was rational, not necessarily any particular scientific theory. Science is a human activity and, consequently, prone to mistakes, confusion and error. Nonetheless, the rationality of science and the cut and thrust of scientific debate ensures that, in the end, better but never finally true theories will prevail. This apart, Popper's reflections on science had the further consequence of making science's history and its social context highly visible, eventually leading to the prominence of views which gave science little credence as the epitome of reason. Science did not progress rationally. As Feyerabend would put it, change in science is simply the replacement of one myth by another. Relativism is loosed, a theme we will take up in Chapters 5 and 6.

Although the social and historical nature of science, indeed of any form of knowledge, is well accepted by most, what are less palatable are precisely the kind of relativist conclusions that seem to follow. For one thing, although it might be accepted that observation is theory-laden and there is no theory-independent way of observing the external world, and that theories might well be incommensurable, surely nature must play some role in determining which particular theories, categories, methods, and so on are the right ones? Surely we cannot just determine what the world is like in whatever way we choose? If we cannot then a fundamental requirement is the independent existence of an external world which has a character independent of human conceptions of it. It was questions such as these which provoked a rethink of empiricism in an effort to avoid the problems of positivism.

Redefining empiricism

However, positing the above requirements for an adequate philosophical empiricism is one thing; demonstrating it, as we have seen in the discussion of positivism, is quite another, especially after the forceful attacks made by arguments concerning the social construction of knowledge and, importantly as a consequence, varying standards of truth and validity. If science is a social construct, then any claims it might have to a unique accessibility to the nature of the external world has to go. Our conception of science, its methods, and its findings, are a contingent consequence of our history, our society, and not the result of some privileged method for describing and explaining the nature of reality. Science becomes, at best, simply another way in which the world may be described. As Willard Van Orman Quine argues, our experience of the world, of facts, does not impose any single theory on us. Theories are underdetermined by facts, and the factuality of the external world, to call it that, is capable of sustaining many different interpretations of it.

This, as just indicated, Quine accepts with equanimity, but does not conclude thereby that we should abandon science. While we can have no firmer knowledge than science can give us, this knowledge is always revisable and contingent. What has to be abandoned is the epistemological goal of trying to discover those principles which would guarantee certain knowledge. Such an endeavour is futile. Epistemology is really an inquiry into how we come to know the world in the way in which we do, and not an inquiry into whether we can acquire certain knowledge. Indeed, Quine is prepared to consign epistemology to psychology: that is, as part of an empirical rather than a philosophical discipline.[5] For his own part, his interests are ontological rather than epistemological and begin from the position that there is nothing that can be more certain than science and therefore no philosophy that can be foundational to it. This is not, as said earlier, to claim that science is certain. Quine is trying to reverse the view that science depends upon philosophy and, instead, holds that philosophy depends upon science for it is science which gives the best guide as to what kinds of things there are in the world which, for Quine, is what philosophy wants to establish in the most general form. So what Quine is offering is a limited scepticism about science unlike, say, that offered on some interpretations of Feyerabend's remarks. We do not have to accept or reject science *in toto*, but we should recognise that some of the theories and the findings of science will be wrong, as they have been in the past. This is the best we can hope for (Quine 1969). For Quine, science and philosophy, though not the same, are joint endeavours distinguished by the generality of their respective concerns. Nevertheless, philosophy must take its lead from science. What Quine seeks to provide is an economical, not to say austere, account of what there is: an ontology that postulates as few entities as possible. There is one important difference between science and philosophy, however. Philosophy does not investigate the world directly, but through language invoking what Quine calls the principle of 'semantic ascent'. Instead of examining 'things' as science does, philosophy investigates how things are talked about and, through this, investigates the nature of the world.[6] Quine is a relativist to the extent that he claims that although the aim of both philosophy and science is to discover what there is, neither can claim to do this in any theory-independent way.

However, instead of regarding this as the conclusive result of philosophical rumination, Quine, in effect, comes at the issue from another direction. The answer to the question 'what exists?' can only receive the answer 'what exists is what theories posit'. Since there are different theories, these will posit different things. Accordingly, Quine is happy to accept some of the implications of the Kuhnian type of view, which argues that different theories postulate different existents and that there is an incommensurability involved in this. But, for Quine, this is to take an 'externalist' view of theories. However, we look at the world *through* theories and though we can accept, from an external point of view, that there can be alternative accounts of the world and what exists, we judge their adequacy from the point of view of our 'home' theory and that is, for us, science.

Quine is claiming that certainty cannot be sought from the places philosophy has traditionally looked for it; that is, what we can know independently of all experience, the *a priori*, or that which is certain because it arises directly from experience, the *a posteriori*. These are, for Quine, the two 'dogmas' of empiricism (Quine 1953, see also Anderson *et al.* 1986: 153–4). What he intends is nothing less than eroding the distinction, that has long been central to philosophy, between analytic and synthetic statements. Philosophers have tended to regard the truth of sentences as a matter to be settled for each sentence separately when, in actuality, sentences are part of whole languages. The same is true of sentences within theories. It is language, or the theory, which is the unit of meaning and, accordingly, the truth and the meaning of any one sentence in that language, or in that theory, has to be answered in terms of its relationship within the whole. The sentences that make up theories, for example, are like a spider's web, anchored at some points, but connected by filaments of thread such that perturbations at one point will affect others. Thus, at some points there will be sentences that are directly related to our experience, others will be more remote. Some we may be readily prepared to abandon, others less so. Still, all sentences are linked together and it is this organisation which has much to do with our conception of the world rather than only those points anchored to a more direct experience of the world.

The structure can be revised, of course, though there will be some statements we might be more reluctant to give up than others. However, Quine insists that there are no statements which we could not give up if we saw sufficient point in doing so. There are no statements, however well entrenched in our lives, which we ultimately have to hold true. Some will have more consequence than others and their abandonment would involve major revisions to the structure, while others might have only minor effects. The reason, therefore, why the analytic–synthetic distinction cannot be sustained is that questions of meaning and those of fact are thoroughly intertwined within the structure. The discovery of black swans does not suddenly render the statement 'all swans are white' synthetic, for we could choose not to regard black 'swans' as swans at all (Anderson *et al.* 1986: 156). In other words, the facts do not necessarily impose either solution on us. The configuration of the web of our beliefs, theories, sentences can be altered to cope in various ways with any changes we might be forced to make: 'a statement about the world does not always or usually have a separable fund of empirical consequences that it can call its own' (Quine 1969: 82). Thus, and this is the important point, our experience of the world does not impose any single theory on us, nor any particular response we need to make in adjusting theories to meet new facts. It is this which sets limits to the certainty of our knowledge: theories are radically underdetermined by evidence.

Accordingly, the hope of positivist empiricism that certain knowledge of the world could be provided by sensory experience is rejected by Quine. Even the sentences which report on our direct sensory experiences are also part of the web of sentences and, as a result, revisable as necessary. Quine is not here rejecting the idea that the evidence of our senses is the evidence for the theories we have: indeed, this is the only evidence we have. But theories go beyond that evidence and cannot be limited by it. There will always be more than one logically equivalent theory (note, not *any* theory) consistent with the evidence we have. This is not because that evidence may be insufficient, but because the same facts can be accommodated in different ways by alterations in the configuration of the theory. Of course, there may be lots of good reasons why we should prefer one theory or another logically and evidentially equivalent theory, but these cannot be on the grounds of evidence alone.

Similar problems emerge in translating one language, or a theory, into another. As Kuhn seems to have suggested, theories are incommensurable and, as a result, changes in scientific theories represent fundamental changes in our conception of the world and, indeed, in the ontology of the world. For Quine, translation between two theories is a matter of aligning two systems, not simply trying to match up the meaning of separate words, concepts or sentences. So, attempts to match, say, separate sentences between two systems will involve making assumptions about how the bits fit into separate but respective wholes; and, as before, we can provide different solutions for particular sentences depending upon the adjustments and compensations we wish to make. Translating involves guesswork, assumptions about the ontologies referred to by the respective theories and, for Quine, there is no right way of deciding which translation might be the correct one. There is logical room for doubt that even the speakers of a common language hold the same ontology. This, however, makes no practical difference to social relationships. It is the pattern of behavioural dispositions that is crucial and there is no way of telling from these, with absolute certainty, whether a person has the same ontology as we do. In logic there is no compelling reason why our ontology should be chosen over another.[7]

The sort of revisions Quine, and others, envisage for empiricism are major revisions against positivism, modifications to it in the light of powerful objections to some of its main features. In trying to obtain an ontology for science, what we cannot do, as positivism did, is to look to the nature of the world independently of our theories, our language. As one philosopher of science expresses it, it is 'generally agreed . . . that the idea of a descriptive vocabulary which is applicable to observations, but which is entirely innocent of theoretical influences, is unrealizable' (Harré 1972: 25). But looking towards theories simply brings us up against their incompatibility and incommensurability, and their indeterminacy, and the spectre of relativism. Once again, we seem to lose any possibility of justifying scientific knowledge over other forms.

Others, however, such as Putnam, while agreeing with Quine that we can have no knowledge stronger than science, nevertheless want to reintroduce the notion of 'essence' through a theory of 'direct reference'. Thus, although an object might manifest all kinds of appearances, what is essential to this is the nature of 'the stuff'. Gold, for example, can vary in appearance in relation to light, heat, etc., but its physiochemical constitution cannot vary, cannot become, say, like that of water and still remain gold (Anderson *et al.* 1986: 169, Putnam 1975, 1978). What links a word and an object is an act of 'dubbing', and what the name is linked to is whatever it is that makes it the kind of stuff that it is. So, when scientists discover 'essences', what kind of stuff a thing is, then they discover necessary relations: that is, discover what it is that makes something what it is. Such a theory is intended to avoid Kuhn's and Feyerabend's claims that there is no continuity between theories. Even though, before and after a scientific revolution, beliefs about the things theorised may have changed, this is irrelevant since these do not 'fix the reference' of the terms.

One further consequence of these efforts to revise empiricism is embodied in Hacking's recommendation that philosophy turn its attention to the ways in which scientists intervene in the world to produce their theories in order to see what ontologies their methods of experimentation, observation and measurement are committed to (Hacking 1983, see also Hacking 1981). In other words, philosophical interests in science should have less concern with the question of how scientific theories *represent* the world, and more with how they *intervene* in the world in order to investigate it. Such a conception does not require that science has a single unified ontology. Realism for theories only causes us problems when we try to imagine that we can effect a match between the theory and the world independent of the theory. Without theories we have no idea what the external world is like. Realism belongs *within* our theories: what Putnam later (1978) refers to as 'internal realism'. Propositions are true within a theory, or within a given language, but we can cope with the diversity of the conceptions of the world implied if we regard ontologies as allowing us to make experiments, observations, and so on, to give organised and systematic descriptions of what is found, rather than requiring us to match theories with how the external world *really is* organised. In this there is no need for a unified theory, a unified method, or a unified ontology. The theories of the various scientific disciplines are descriptions of what is observed, measured, experimented on, counted, and so on. The 'phenomenological laws' of physics, as Cartwright (1983) calls them, are the outcome of many different premises, assumptions, interests, exigencies, and problems that are peculiar to particular disciplines. These laws are correct within their respective domains but do not add up to a theoretical or ontological unity. Any attempt at unification by connecting them to more 'fundamental laws' is bound to distort them since they can only be approximations to the concepts deployed in the original theories. Various orders of observations, measurements and the phenomena displayed in the investigations of different disciplines cannot be reduced to each other without 'lying'. In which case, science has to be committed to multiple ontologies, multiple realities, rather than the myth propounded by the likes of positivism of a single, unified description of the ontology of the external world.

The implications for social research

The implications of the new philosophy of science for the social sciences are radical in some ways, inconsequential in others. What is rejected is positivism's effort to build a view of science stressing the unity of its method, its search for laws, and so on, which the social sciences, if they were to become scientific, would have to emulate. However, the views reviewed here cast doubt, in various ways, on the idea that there could be a unified science committed to a single ontology of the external world. The work of Kuhn, and the sociologists of science, as well as the arguments of Feyerabend, showed that scientific change has little to do with the shape science obtains through the application of a general rational method, and has more to do with the fact that it is a social institution. Arguments about the incommensurability of theories raised questions about the truth of theories and provoked damaging doubts about the correspondence theory of truth espoused by positivism. Nevertheless, rather than abandon science to anarchy, as Feyerabend is alleged to want, contemporary realists and empiricists, such as Quine, Putnam and Hacking, have revised the conception of science and knowledge in light of the arguments raised against positivist conceptions of science. What was rejected was not science, or indeed its eminence as a form of knowledge, but the view of science as requiring epistemological and ontological unity. What is emphasised is the diversity and the disunity of science. After all, scientists do not worry about epistemology and ontology but about the particular problems they confront from their theories and investigations. And, indeed, as Pawson (1989: 32) reminds us, the theory-laden nature of observation is a feature of scientific work that natural scientists find unremarkable and obvious.

A further implication of this kind of view is that the intellectual authority of philosophy is eroded. If all that matters is that scientists go about their business in the ways that they are taught, learn and acquire, using methods appropriate to the problems they have to deal with, then philosophical worries about ontology and epistemology are an irrelevance. Quine, for example, argued for the 'naturalisation' of epistemology by reducing it to one of the sciences of knowledge, such as behavioural psychology or brain physiology, to discover those laws of cognition which determine why we accept and hold the theories and the beliefs that we do. Ontology, too, becomes the business of the respective sciences and their investigations. In which case, as far as the social sciences are concerned, if they want to emulate the natural sciences what they should do, like them, is disregard philosophical versions of science and get on with tackling their problems as they see fit. There is certainly no reason to feel bound by stipulations about a unified method or a unified ontology for science, for on these arguments no such creature exists.

For some realists, especially those concerned with the social sciences, this kind of conclusion is unsatisfactory. While recognising that positivism has been found wanting, they still want to assert that science is concerned to describe real structures, entities and processes which constitute the external world. In this, the regularity that is required by the orthodox notion of laws is less important than identifying and describing the real, operative causal mechanisms which have real effects. It is not required that these operating mechanisms and their entities be observable, *contra* positivism, but by isolating their causal effects in suitably designed studies, their existence can be plausibly postulated. Many of the more powerful mechanisms postulated by natural science theories, as said before, are not directly observable, though their effects can be. Laws need not be universal in the sense required by positivism but should represent recognisable tendencies (Outhwaite 1987, Keat and Urry 1975, Bhaskar 1978). As Bhaskar says:

> The citation of a law presupposes a claim about the activity of some mechanism but not about the conditions under which the mechanism operates and hence not about the results of its activity, i.e. the actual outcome on any particular occasion.
>
> (Bhaskar 1978: 95)

The consequences stated by laws happen only in special circumstances, that is, when their operation is not 'impeded' by complicating tendencies and the *ceteris paribus* conditions are in place. All objects heavier than air fall, for a simple example, unless 'impeded' by things that do not allow them to 'realise' the law of falling bodies, so to speak. In the natural sciences, the ability to set up 'closed systems' often, but not always, experimentally, allows for the more detailed specification of the *ceteris paribus* conditions for a law. This is the major difference between the natural and the social sciences. Accordingly, it should not be expected that the degrees of precision attainable in most of the natural sciences should be found in the causal statements of the social sciences. In addition, the view also stresses realism for theories in that entities have their meaning and significance from the theories of which they are a part.

This realist conception of the nature of social science is in many ways in accord with much of the new philosophy of science and, in this sense at least, tries to avoid many of the problems of earlier positivist and empiricist philosophies of science. However, it contains little of direct guidance to social research itself. It is still a language of causation and in this respect attractive to materialists. But, in addition, it represents a serious relaxation of the criteria for determining causal relationships as exhibited in natural science. Others, however, recognise that any realist social science would have to take into account the fact that social actors themselves have their own theories about the way in which the world operates, and taking this seriously raises the question of whether any causalist conception of the business of social science can be sustained. This is one of the issues to be taken up in the next and subsequent chapters.

Notes

1. For a fuller treatment see Anderson *et al.* (1986: 236–43).
2. See his critique of the sociology of knowledge in Popper (1945: Vol. 2).
3. See, on the earlier work in the sociology of science, Storer (1973).
4. As history, Kuhn's views have been subjected to some criticism. See also Kuhn (1977).
5. Quine is a materialist and the kind of psychology he has in mind is a behaviourist one.
6. Quine would reject the view that what such studies investigate is language alone. No sharp line can be drawn between examining meanings and examining facts.
7. Davidson (1984) further explores Quine's remarks on translation as does Chapter 8 of this book.

CHAPTER 5

The interpretative alternative

In the previous chapters a distinction has surfaced, in many guises, which, historically speaking, is fundamentally important in Western thought, namely that between mind and matter. The whole history of Western philosophy could perhaps be written as describing a contest between the various ways of formulating just what, philosophically speaking, this distinction is. Some materialists, for example, aim to reduce mental phenomena to epiphenomena of the material. The mind, its activities and its contents, are the outcome of the material processes of the brain and the nervous system. In the extreme materialist case, the mind *is* the brain. At the opposite extreme, idealists argue that the so-called material world is really only a set of ideas in the mind.[1] Materialist and idealist thinkers, of course, hold more detailed and more sophisticated views than these summaries might indicate. For our immediate purposes in this chapter, what is important is that the distinction of mind from matter raises the question that there are different orders of phenomena in the world which, accordingly, would have to be known in different ways. In this and the next chapters we intend to explore some of the philosophical doctrines and their implications around this dualism and, in so doing, revisit some of the issues discussed in the previous chapters.

Some intellectual forerunners

For the social sciences the distinction between mind and matter became a prominent issue through the debates in Germany in the late nineteenth century. These had as their forerunners the ideas of the Italian Giovanni Batista Vico (1660–1744) and the Swiss-French Jean-Jacques Rousseau (1712–1778) who had offered radical alternatives to the Enlightenment conception of people and society (Manicas 1987). In brief, they rejected the conception of the rational, almost asocial, individual in favour of a conception of the individual as belonging to a wider social and cultural entity, namely, the moral and political association of society. In French and English thought these beginnings failed to flourish in quite the way they did in Germany (Manicas 1987: 73). In Germany they established a strong tradition, through Johann Gottfried Herder

(1744–1803), Georg W.F. Hegel (1770–1831) and Karl Marx (1818–1883), which culminated in the debates over the nature of humanity as material or 'spiritual' beings just referred to. Again in brief, the tradition was one which tried to develop theories of history, considered as the distinctively human science and its unifying discipline. In important respects, the disputes were about historical method and, in particular, whether the study of history could be a natural science or whether it had to develop its own distinctive methods as a distinctively human inquiry: a debate which, almost inevitably, spread over into the social sciences more generally. In rejecting the philosophical route to a science of history, hence rejecting Hegel, the question was how to turn history into a soundly founded empirical discipline given that its object of study was not inanimate nature but the human life in all its manifestations? How to come to terms with the fact that history involved, in short, the understanding and self-understanding on the part of those human beings under study?

Important to this nineteenth century phase of the debate, known as the *Methodenstreit* (the 'dispute over methods') were considerations arising from biblical philology.[2] Translating texts which had themselves gone through a number of different translations and modifications from their original language did not simply involve linguistic considerations, but also required them to be related, in order to discover their original meaning, to the wider social context in which they were originally produced. So, making sense of textual materials required a union of philology and history and, one might add, sociology and anthropology. It was this which provided what has become known as hermeneutics – a term originally used to identify biblical interpretation but coming to be used for the general process of cultural interpretation – with its abiding question: how is an understanding of the past to be gained through its texts and other remains (Anderson *et al.* 1986: ch. 3, Bauman 1978)? Friedrich D.E. Schleiermacher (1768–1834) who, in the early years of the nineteenth century, was responsible for drawing hermeneutics away from its original home in philology and applying it to the problems of historical knowledge, took this as *the* problem of history.[3] To understand the past one has to identify with it. By complementing grammatical interpretation with psychological identification, hermeneutics was introduced into the study of human activities more generally, more particularly elevating interpretative understanding to a prominent position in the methodology of the social sciences. Wilhelm Dilthey (1833–1911), building on Schleiermacher and as part of a widespread romantic reaction against positivism, held that the positivist methodology of the natural sciences was inadequate to the understanding of human phenomena except in so far as human beings were natural objects. Positivism left no room for the idea that history and society were human creations and that this free creativity constituted the essence of all social forms. The study of human history has to be based on the fact that humans were purposive creators who lived within a world which has meaning for them. The duality of the subjective and the objective was irreducible. That is, there was no way of making the study of history the exclusive property of the natural, material, sciences for the reality of history consisted predominantly in mental, or spiritual, phenomena as exemplified in social institutions, law, literature, government, morality, and values.

Investigating this 'mental reality' required a wholly different method to that of natural science, but one which should be no less philosophically well justified. The method had to recognise the actions, events and artifacts from *within* human life in the terms in which they were experienced and known by those living among and through them and not through the observation of them as though they were some distantly perceived external reality. Knowledge of persons could only be gained through an interpretative procedure grounded in the imaginative recreation of the experiences of others to grasp the meaning which things in their world have for them. History, society, art, indeed all human products, were the objectifications of the human mind and not at all like material things. Accordingly, understanding such phenomena required that the lived experiences of others be grasped through the apprehension of the thoughts and understandings that had gone into their production. The sociohistorical world cannot be understood as simply a relationship of material things which exist in themselves, for the material things which play a part in human life often have a symbolic character: they express some content of the human mind.

So for Dilthey and others of like mind, culture and the social were by their essential nature different from the world of natural science and required different methods of study. Science, conceived mainly in positivistic terms, studied the objective, inanimate, nonhuman world. For Dilthey, though, society, a product of the human mind, was subjective, emotive as well as intellectual. What we would refer to as causal, mechanistic and measurement-oriented models of explanation were inappropriate, since human consciousness was not determined by natural forces. Human social behaviour was always imbued with values, and reliable knowledge of a culture could only be gained by isolating the common ideas, the feelings, or the goals of a particular historical society. It was in terms of these that the actions and achievements of individuals were formed. The observer, as a human being studying other human beings, has access to the cultural world of others through some form of 'imaginative reconstruction' or 'empathy'.

Others, notably Heinrich Rickert (1863–1936), did not accept Dilthey's dichotomous view of reality as split between nature and culture, but, instead, argued that reality was indivisible. However, unlike the positivists who held a similar view, this did not imply that the methods of natural science were thereby applicable to the world of society, culture and history. Differences between the natural and the social, or cultural, sciences were based on logic rather than on ontology. For Rickert, human beings could have no knowledge of the world independently of what was in their minds. They had no way of finding out whether their knowledge faithfully reproduced a reality existing outside the mind and independent of it. They could only know things as they appear as phenomena, never as things as they are as such.[4] Facts, so to speak, are constituted out of the phenomena and given both form and content by the mind. This is a volitional act and its performance an intentional activity. All human knowledge, therefore, is selective, involving abstraction according to particular interests. Objectivity, therefore, is achieved not by matching ideas to some external reality, as the positivists would have it, but by the intersubjective establishment of those facts by those who have an interest in knowing them. Accordingly, if the knowledge of laws of nature is the only knowledge that anyone wants, then the legitimate method leading to their discovery is the method of natural science. If, on the other hand, the interest is in knowing different things than the natural sciences can accommodate, then the basis of knowledge, too, is different.

In fact, according to Rickert, there are two basic principles of selection at work, each making it possible to arrive at one of two different kinds of representations of reality, namely, the nomothetic and the ideographic. The former, characteristic of natural science, is an interest in discovering general laws, while the latter, more characteristic of history, is concerned to understand the concrete and unique case. We are not interested in the unique and the specific attributes of ordinary natural phenomena, such as blades of grass or clouds in the sky, but are satisfied with knowledge of their general characteristics. We are, however, very much interested in the unique and specific attributes of other human beings, in knowing all kinds of things about particular persons. This dichotomy represents no fundamental difference in the ontology of the world; it does not mean that human beings are essentially different from blades of grass or from clouds, but implies a difference in the kind of knowledge required by different interests. Human products embody values and it is these which need to be understood by the social scientist in order to make sense of the unique constellations that make up human history. So, while natural science is interested in forming general concepts by abstracting from the concrete case those features which are in common with other cases, historical inquiry is concerned to form individual concepts by focusing on the unique combination of elements that represent a culturally significant phenomenon, such as the life and character of some great figure, say, of Napoleon. Both forms of inquiry use their own principles of selection for the purpose of isolating the elements of empirical reality which are essential to their respective cognitive purposes. The ideal of objective knowledge requires both methods, as any one of them gives only a one-sided picture of reality. The same reality, however, can be presented either as history or as natural science.

Although Dilthey and Rickert differed as to the reasons for the employment of different methodologies with respect to the natural and social worlds, they did concur that positivistic natural science types of method could not be used to gain adequate knowledge of the social and the cultural. Max Weber (1864–1920), much influenced by Rickert, accepted the distinctive character of the social sciences – that is, their interest in the individual case – but not the implication that they were, therefore, unscientific in being unable to meet the rigorous standards of objectivity in scholarship. With Dilthey, Weber accepted the importance of 'interpretative understanding' as the distinctive form of knowledge for the sociohistorical sciences but only as a means towards objective knowledge. With Rickert, he supported the view that the essential distinction between the natural and the social sciences was methodological rather than ontological. Indeed, the possibility of 'interpretative understanding' in the social sciences was, for Weber, a tremendous opportunity and not something to be apologised for. By its means human action could be studied in greater depth than a natural scientist could ever penetrate into the nature of the inanimate world (Weber 1969: 101, Bauman 1978: ch. 3). There was, however, a price to be paid in objectivity, precision and conclusiveness. For his own part Weber tried to reconcile the advantages of 'interpretative understanding' with the demands of scientific criteria.

Weber's interventions

However, to understand quite what this meant it is important to understand something of the road that led Weber to this conclusion. At the time, two general positions dominated the debate over the social scientific method: one, positivism, we have already reviewed at some length, and the other, intuitionism, that is, the notion that we can understand others through our own empathetic intuition of their minds. Weber rejected both of these. Any sociocultural science must use a method distinct from that deployed in natural science, but this is not characterised, as the intuitionists wanted, by any allegedly unique stance of empathy. Both forms of knowledge, the natural scientific and the sociocultural, are 'invariably tied to the instrument of concept formation' (Weber 1975). In other words, the problems of the logic of concept formation, that is, the way in which they are to form theoretical ideas, are the same for both the natural and the social sciences despite the fact of practical differences in the manner in which intellectual inquiry is pursued. The crucial difference lies in the 'theoretic interest' or 'purpose' of understanding which, for the sociocultural sciences, is understanding subjectively meaningful phenomena. Thus, we understand and expect the historical, the sociocultural, sciences to be distinctive in their objective of interpreting meaning because of our own historically shaped, and theoretically informed interests. It is the values in our own culture which determine the kinds of interests that we take in history and in the social world as subjectively meaningful. By the same token, we take the 'theoretic interest' of the natural sciences to be in the production of universal-general concepts and propositions, or laws. But each of these different kinds of theoretic interests cannot be reduced to the other. This is not for ontological reasons, as the intuitionists argued, but because of differences in the axiological or theoretical purpose of the enquiry, and this does have methodological consequences for the socio-cultural sciences. A different method of inquiry is called for, given the theoretic interest of understanding or interpreting meaningfulness, and this is the method of *verstehen*, that is, attempting to reconstruct the subjective experience of social actors.

To this end Weber advanced two major methodological principles, both of which are still part of the contemporary language of social science, namely, value neutrality and the method of ideal types. So far as the first is concerned, preserving the same distinction that positivists made between fact and value, Weber held that social scientists should never abuse their scientific authority by passing off their value judgements as scientific truths. About conflicting values scientists can have nothing to say as to which is to be preferred, but can only review the likely outcome of the various value alternatives. Science deals only with the rational, and is a technically oriented, instrumental activity (Weber 1949). The second methodological device, the ideal type, which involves building abstractions which simplify and exaggerate traits found in reality into a more logically coherent pattern than can ever be found in the world, was offered as a means of grasping subjectively held meanings more objectively. By drawing out as clearly as possible certain relations found in reality, the 'ideal type' provided a means of structuring and focusing the scholar's inquiry by highlighting features of empirical phenomena. Thus, for Weber, all irrational and emotive aspects of human behaviour are to be seen as deviations from a conceptually pure type of rational action, one which worked out how people would behave if they were, so to speak, entirely logical, so allowing us better to appreciate why they behaved in other than logical ways; how, for example, emotion or thoughtless habit figured in forming their course of action. Understanding, then, was transformed by Weber into the construction of rational models. Weber felt that the natural science method, transplanted to the study of social behaviour, would produce valid knowledge but of largely irrelevant and unimportant activities, at least as far as the subjective perspective was concerned. The contrast between the natural and the social sciences occurs because, in the latter, human beings are both the subject and the object of inquiry, which means that knowledge of society is a form of self-knowledge. *Verstehen*, or interpretative understanding, gives social observers a method of investigating social phenomena in a way that does not distort the social world of those being studied. Since the essence of social interaction lies in the meanings agents give to their actions and environment, all valid social analysis must refer back to these. However, the insights gleaned in this manner must be supported by data of a scientific and statistical kind. All phenomena, no matter how unique and particular, are the products of antecedent, causally related conditions. By this Weber does not mean that social acts are to be reduced to single all-embracing laws, but rather that, from the complex whole of social reality, limited and unique antecedents and consequences are abstracted and related to observed phenomena. Such 'adequate causation' provides probabilistic explanations.

This tradition of thought reacting against positivist conceptions of science and their importation into social science had a powerful impact especially in Europe but, while not ignored, less so in the United Kingdom and the United States, at least until recently.[5] For our purposes one feature above all stands out, namely, the view that the social sciences involve radically different methods from those of the natural sciences. Admittedly, the arguments for this did not always take on an ontological form but pointed instead to the different kinds of knowledge required by the respective disciplines. Either way, different methodologies were involved. It is to an examination of some of the issues here that we now turn.

Social action and meaning

In part, the 'humanistic' stance is a reaction against the 'scientised' conception of the social actor which is seen as embodied in orthodox social science of a positivist persuasion. The accusation is that those features which make social life a distinctively *human* product are misrepresented when analysed out and reduced to the interaction of variables.[6] Of course, at times such accusations are excessive. Indeed, however we might end up judging Lazarsfeld's initiative in establishing variable analysis as a research method in social science, one of his intentions was to develop a mode of analysis which allowed for the fact that most of the more important concepts of interest were qualitative and, yet, amenable at least to a modest level of measurement. As we say, variable analysis might not, in the end, turn out to be a successful attempt decisively to transform things in a much more 'scientific' direction, but its motive was not to eliminate, to use our earlier phrase, the 'distinctively human' from social scientific analysis. Nevertheless, exactly what positivistic social science had left out was a matter of some debate; was it freewill and choice, moral and political concerns, a regard for human fate, values, the self, the subjective dimension, or what?

The argument is about the object of social scientific inquiry and the means by which this is to be understood. Even if it were readily possible to describe empirically patterns of social activities by using all the elegant correlational apparatus of positivist social science, this would fail, it is argued, to get at the proper subject-matter of social science. It would fail to provide adequate knowledge of why the patterns occurred as they did as the social product of acting human beings. At best, such accounts would be only partial; at worst, the very methods distort the reality of social life in profound ways.

The manifold issues here are encapsulated in Weber's famous definition of 'social action': an action is social when a social actor assigns a certain meaning to his or her conduct and, by this meaning, is related to the behaviour of other persons (Weber 1969: 88). Social interaction occurs when a person's actions are oriented towards the actions of others. Actions are oriented not in any mechanistic fashion of stimulus and response, but because actors *interpret* and give meaning both to their own and to others' behaviour. Weber himself devoted considerable efforts to elucidating the implications of this formulation of the central tenet or, for Weber, the objective of sociology. The important point has to do with the idea of meaning and its relationship to the kind of knowledge we require in order to understand and explain social phenomena. To speak of meaning is to begin to point to that most important fact, that human beings have a rich and highly varied mental life reflected in all the artifacts by which, and institutions in which, they live. In modern sociological and anthropological terms this is referred to as 'culture' and includes all that social actors can talk about, explain, describe to others, excuse or justify, believe in, assert, theorise about, agree and disagree over, pray to, create, build, and so on. In other words, the world of social actors is a world which is intelligible to and for them.[7]

One way of regarding meaning is to see it as a subjective or internal component of behaviour. This would be to draw a contrast between the objective features of social action and its subjective elements. Then, the regularities we discover by studying society are only the external appearances of what the members of a society understand and, thereby, act upon. This point can be illustrated using Hart's famous example of traffic behaviour (Hart 1961, Ryan 1970: 140–1). A stream of traffic controlled by traffic lights displays regularity. If it were to be regarded purely as the product of causal factors, then to explain the patterns we would have to specify the necessary and sufficient conditions which produce a given pattern, and go on to formulate a theory linking the traffic signals to the movement of the traffic stream. We would have to postulate the causal mechanism involved in effecting the connection between the different coloured lights and the movement of the vehicular units. However, as it happens, we know that there are regulations governing traffic lights which the drivers of the cars and other vehicles are expected to obey and, in doing so, produce the traffic patterns in response to the patterns of the signals. Thus, the connection between the lights and the movement of traffic is one which can be explained in terms of the *meaning* the lights have, that is, they stand for the injunctions 'Stop!' and 'Go!' for example, within the culture.

An important issue arising from this example is whether an explanation in terms of meaning is compatible with a causal explanation. If the answer is negative then this would seem to indicate a fundamental difference between the social and the physical sciences. The claim would be that the relationships between the traffic lights and the behaviour of the road vehicles is not of the same logical order as, say, that between sunlight and plant growth, between thunder and lightning, or between colliding billiard balls. Though classically regarded causal elements are involved in the traffic lights and the behaviours they produce – for example, in the mechanisms which activate the lights and in the control systems of the vehicles – these are irrelevant to understanding the relationship between the lights and the patterns of traffic. The relationship is composed of a meaningful connection. Motorists stopping and starting their cars are obeying a series of instructions signalled by the traffic lights, and what we have uncovered is a custom- or rule-regulated practice rather than a causal law. The drivers could give *reasons* why they stopped when the light shone red, moved on when it changed to green. In short, they themselves could explain why they did what they did: 'because the red light signalled "stop"', 'The green light allowed me to proceed', 'If you don't stop at a red light you can get in trouble with the police', 'You have to obey traffic lights otherwise the roads would be in chaos', and so on. Such reasons would invoke intentions, purposes, justifications, rules, conventions, and the like, rather than impersonal causal mechanisms.

There are a number of problems here to do with the ontological status of reasons and rules, and with the status of social science theories in relation to those accounts offered by the members of society, the nature of social action and its description, among others, all intertwined in complex ways. However, in this chapter let us try to establish some preliminary positions.

One predominant way of characterising the task of the social scientist is to see it as attempting to provide a theoretical account of social life. This requires empirical research in order to bring data to bear on the theory. These data must derive in some way from the lives of the social actors being studied, but unlike physical phenomena, social actors give meaning to themselves, to others and to the social environments in which they live. They can describe what they do, explain and justify it, give reasons, declare their motives, decide upon appropriate courses of action, try to fit means to ends, and so on. As Schutz expresses it:

> It is up to the natural scientist and him alone to define, in accordance with the procedural rules of his science, his observational field, and to determine the facts, data, and events within it which are relevant for the problems or scientific purposes at hand . . . The world of nature, as explored by the natural scientist, does not 'mean' anything to the molecules, atoms, and electrons therein. The observational field of the social scientist, however, namely the social reality, has a specific meaning and relevance structure for the human beings living, acting, and thinking therein. By a series of commonsense constructs they have preselected and preinterpreted this world they experience as the reality of their daily lives.
>
> (Schutz 1963: 234)

The social scientist, then, must come to terms with these meanings for, as we shall see later, in a fundamental sense the origins of the researcher's data, whatever the research method used, lies in these meanings. The starting point for empirical social science research is the observation of what the members of society do or have done, say or have said. These observations may be in the form of records, statistical rates, tape-recordings, writings, questionnaires or interviews, archeological remains, diaries, and so on. An essential aspect of observation is the description of the phenomenon. Actions and behaviours must be classified and categorised. Decisions must be made, for example, about whether a man carving a piece of wood is doing something economic, religious, political, artistic, or whatever. What is also certain is that the man himself would have a sense of what he is doing. What, then, is the relationship between his account and any that the social scientist might offer? What, if any, should the link be? More generally, what difference does the fact that social actors assign meaning to their social reality make for the study of social life?

Since positivistically inspired social science has not exactly ignored what might loosely be termed, the 'meaningful components' of social behaviour, and since the philosophical positions being discussed in this chapter involve a critique of the positivist's treatment of this, it is as well, perhaps, to begin with some statement of the traditional ways in which 'components' such as reasons, motives, intentions, rules and conventions have been regarded in traditional social scientific theorising.

Rules, motives and the description of social action

In the traffic light example used earlier two sorts of phenomena were identified as important in a 'meaningful' account of behaviour: the rules regulating traffic at stop lights and dispositional concepts such as reasons, intentions, or motives. The latter especially point to the 'internal' character of the relationship between the lights and driver behaviour; that is, to the subjective meaning which leads to the sequence of actions we would describe as 'obeying the rules of traffic signals'. The idea that social action is rule-governed is not, of course, new or surprising. Some of the basic concepts of social science, such as norms, institutions, deviance, rationality, authority, profit-seeking, exchange, legitimacy, and many more, all pay more than just passing homage to the idea that social behaviour, whatever else it consists in, involves rules. Typically, rules are invoked as an explanation of social conduct. Durkheim's insistence that society is a moral entity, for example, stresses this aspect of social life, as does Weber's interest in the nature of social action and, building upon this, the centrality of the notion of authority in his conceptions of how social organisation is produced and reproduced. Both feature rules as distinctive to social organisation.

The typical mode of explanation is predicated on the notion that interaction is both rule-governed and motivated. Patterns of action are explained by reference to two groups of factors: dispositional ones, such as attitudes, motives, feelings, beliefs, personality; and sanctioned expectations, or normative rules, to which the actor is subject. These latter are sometimes referred to as 'role expectations' attaching to the incumbent of a particular position within a network of social relationships. The occupants of managerial positions, for example, are expected by others to behave in particular ways as are, though in different ways, mothers, fathers, prime ministers, ministers of religion, bank clerks, and so on. These expectations can be seen as rules guiding or even dictating the appropriate mode of behaviour for someone in one of these positions. A newly employed teacher, for illustration, has to learn the rules, both official and unofficial, that shape what others with whom he or she comes into contact will expect. Moreover, the incumbent of any particular position will be expected to occupy that position authentically by having the right motivations to perform the role properly.

These expectations or rules are, as it were, 'external' to the individual. They exist prior to whomever occupies a position and, moreover, can act as coercive elements producing appropriate behaviour. In Durkheim's terms they have a 'thing-like' quality to them. Their 'externality' in this sense produces social patterning because similar rules apply to similar positions; managers are all subject to much the same kinds of expectations, as are mothers, fathers, and all the rest. This is much of what is meant by the idea of a normative order and, as a consequence, a major source of the aggregative patterning which is characteristic of much of social life. There is presumed to be a more or less stable linkage between the role performance expected of position occupants and the situations in which they find themselves because of the normative rules governing behaviour in that situation. It is further presumed that actors have been socialised into a common culture so that there is some substantive cognitive consensus among them enabling them to identify situations, actions and rules in more or less the same way (Wilson 1974, Weider 1974). The regularly and routinely occurring patterns of social life enable social scientists to speak of such stable societal elements as 'social structure', 'institutions', 'the political', or the 'economic system'.

For the sake of completeness, it is important to make the point that there may be significant subgroup differences within a society in terms of the expectations and normative definitions attaching to particular positions, but these do not modify the general picture. Indeed, such differences pose problems of some interest as the studies of such phenomena as role conflict, marginality, social change, and deviance illustrate.

In a similar vein to rules, motives, reasons, intentions, and so on, are seen as causal antecedents and, therefore, external to action, which impinge upon or coerce persons into certain behaviours. Behaviour, in short, has a motivated character. To ascribe a motive to someone, on this view, is to identify an 'inner' causal mechanism that produces an 'outward' display of behaviour. To say that workers strike because they have antimanagement dispositions or attitudes is to say that the 'inner' picture of their working world produces, or causes, their intransigence *vis-à-vis* management. It is to give their striking behaviour a purpose or goal, and offers an explanation in terms of the ends the action is designed to meet. Weber's (1960) analysis of the economically innovative behaviour of ascetic Protestants ascribes a particular set of religious motivations which caused the persons holding such beliefs to work harder, be thrifty in their ways, endeavour to succeed in all that they did, and so on. Of course, motives, though regarded as 'internal' and private states, are not considered to be randomly distributed among the population. As with rules, socialisation into a common culture means that motives are patterned, typical to particular socially defined persons and, in this way, produced by the social structure. Thus, occupancy of a particular social position 'leads to' the development of certain socially relevant and consequential dispositions which, in their turn, result in conduct or behaviour of a particular kind. The motivated character of such actions are often said to arise from the interests embodied in the occupancy of particular positions; voting for reasons of class advantage, joining certain associations in order to improve one's career prospects, or striking to improve the earning position of oneself and fellow workers are such examples.

This, then, is the basic model of social scientific accounts using those elements of meaning we have referred to as rules and dispositions. Although we have relied on sociology for the lineaments of this account, it is by no means restricted to that discipline. The assumption of *homo economicus* in economic theory is to postulate an actor with the disposition to act rationally (Anderson *et al.* 1988): historical explanation is provided in substantial part by imputing motives to personages acting within specified historical circumstances; political science accounts of why people vote for particular parties see them as being, at least in part, motivated by their assessments of their social and economic interests, and so on.

From a positivistic point of view there are some additional elements which it is necessary to add to this model. First, that the explanation must be couched in a deductive form showing how the observed behaviour can be deduced from a set of premises containing the theory plus stated empirical conditions. The theory must, of course, contain reference to the rules and dispositions which are hypothesised as causing the observed behaviour. Second, and as a consequence of the first condition, the behaviour to be explained must be definable independently of the rules or dispositions which are said to cause it otherwise we cannot claim that what we are examining is the causal relationship between two, or more, distinct entities. Third, descriptions of the empirical conditions, the facts to be explained, and the rules and dispositions of the theory must have stable meanings and not be dependent on circumstances and occasion (Wilson 1974: 71, Quine 1960).

Given that the mode of explanation outlined earlier satisfies these conditions, then the framework is coherent. The job of empirical research is to discover precisely the pattern of the contingent relationships between rules, motives, situations, social relationships and behaviour and formulate them as regularities, bringing them under a theory which explains why they have the form that they do. To see just how far this is justified, let us examine the relationship between motives and the description of social action a little more closely.

As pointed out, in the typical form of explanation outlined above some internal and private characteristics of persons is offered as a causal antecedent that predisposes the actor to behave in a particular manner. The motive and the behaviour are regarded as independent, the internal and private state being the causal mainspring, as it were, for the external behavioural display, the action. However, this formulation of the relationship gives rise to all kinds of methodological problems for social science. Being conceived as internal and private, and therefore not open to direct inspection, the problem is to devise methods of assessing such internal states to which effect a number of techniques, such as attitude scales, questionnaires, interviews and personality inventories have been devised. The results provided by these are usually correlated with 'objective' indices, such as level of education, social class, ethnic identity, associational participation, voting, spending patterns to mention but a very few of the kinds of variables employed.

With methods such as these, which rely for attributions as to 'mental states', to use a catch-all term for the moment, from what respondents say, there has always been the problem of relating what people say to what they do (see, e.g. Deutscher 1973). During an interview, respondents might well say one thing but when faced with a corresponding 'real life' situation do quite another. They may well, for example, express strong antipathy against the government of the day but yet vote for it come polling day. In other cases motives are inferred from what people do or have done. From the fact that the earliest capitalists were members of ascetic Protestant sects it is inferred that their religious membership motivated them to engage in behaviour appropriate to capitalist accumulation.

The problem is seen as one of securing the inferences to 'mental states' from so-called outward behaviours. However, the conception of the relationship between so-called 'mental states', such as motives, intentions, and reasons, and the behaviour presupposed in the model outlined above is, we argue, fundamentally misconceived. Consider the following description of fairly mundane acts: 'He raised his arm', 'He raised the glass', 'He toasted the happy couple', 'He assuaged his thirst', 'He decided that the only thing to do was get drunk'. All these statements describe what could be said to be different actions and yet could also be said to consist of, or involve, much the same bodily movement. This one 'behavioural display' is capable, then, of being part of many different *actions* and, generalising from this, we can say that there is no necessary one-to-one matching of an action description with a behavioural display. Pitkin puts the point rather well:

> With the same physical movement, the stroke of a pen or the shake of a head, a man can break a promise or make one, renounce his birthright, insult a friend, obey a command, or commit treason. The same movement can, in various circumstances and with various intentions constitute any of these actions: so in itself it constitutes none of them.
>
> (Pitkin 1972: 167)

An observer seeing someone raise his arm and a glass of beer could describe the action in a number of ways. Any of those offered earlier could be appropriate, though 'He raised his arm' does seem singularly uninformative without the provision of some context. If we hold to the picture of intentions, motives, and so on as literally 'inner' states located in the mind (which is, on this picture, usually supposed to be contained 'in the head') then the observer cannot directly apprehend any supposed 'mental states' which bring about the observed behaviour. Nonetheless, the way in which the very action of an individual is to be identified hinges upon reference to supposed 'mental states'. But the attribution of such 'mental states' does not involve problematic inferences about events 'in the head' but, instead, involves noting the circumstances of the activity – it was a wedding, a hot day, he had just been jilted, and so on – some description could have been supplied without much trouble or anguish about what was really the case. Some of these descriptions might well impute a motive or purpose to the behaviour, such as a desire to get drunk, be sociable, wish luck to the happy couple, assuage a thirst, and so on. In such cases what the motive does is tell us more about the action that is being performed, tells us what the person was doing, 'getting drunk', 'toasting the happy couple', 'assuaging a thirst' or whatever.

In describing many actions we are unavoidably involved in imputing motives of one sort or another. The analytic force of motives and reasons lies not so much in their being 'internal' and private causal mainsprings to action or behaviour, but in their being tantamount to rules for identifying a piece of behaviour *as* action of a particular kind. Motives, reasons, and other dispositional concepts can be seen as rules, or embedded instructions, if you will, for seeing behaviour in such-and-such a way, for explicating action further, for giving an account of that action. It follows that any particular behavioural display can be described and explained in a variety of different, and often competing, ways; that is, as several kinds of motivated action. As Austin (1961, see also Anderson *et al.* 1986: ch. 9) expresses it:

It is in principle always open to us, along various lines, to describe or refer to 'what I did' in so many different ways . . . should we say, are we saying, that he took her money, or that he sank a putt? That he said 'Done', or that he accepted an offer? How far, that is, are motives, intentions, and conventions, to be part of the description of actions?

(Austin 1961: 148–9)

The issue here is, perhaps, most apparent where the motivated character of an event is equivocal as in a case reported by Atkinson (1971, see also Heritage 1978). An 83-year-old widow was found gassed in her kitchen. She had lived alone since the death of her husband. Rugs and towels had been stuffed under doors and around windows. Neighbours testified at the inquest that she had always seemed a happy and cheerful person. The coroner returned an open verdict on the grounds that there was no evidence to show why the gas taps had been turned on. In this case, the circumstances of the death, which occurred during the winter, were insufficient to lead to a definitive verdict. For example, it was difficult to establish whether the rugs and towels had been used to keep out the cold and the draughts rather than to keep the gas in, and, accordingly, to establish whether the leaving on of the gas was intentional or whether unmotivated and due to absent-mindedness. If the death had occurred in the summer, the motivated character of the events might have been less ambiguous. The fact that it happened in winter meant that the motivated character of the scene could not be clarified without recourse to circumstantial evidence regarding the widow's state of mind. Different assumptions regarding her state of mind would have instructed those responsible for reaching a verdict to compose an account for the scene in particular ways or, vice versa, assumptions about the scene would instruct them to make inferences about the victim's state of mind, and so on. It is important to emphasise that the uncertainty in this case is not due to the fact that the widow's intentions were concealed from us, 'within her head' so to speak, but because they were concealed from us *within her room*. If we had been there to observe her actions at the time, we could much more successfully have determined what her purpose was.

To presume, as the typical mode of social scientific explanation would have us do, that behaviour can be described as a kind of 'brute fact' independent of motives or reasons, is seriously to misrepresent the relationship these have to the description of action. To describe the action referred to earlier as 'raising a glass to his lips' as if this were somehow more real than other descriptions which involve imputations or inferences about motivations, leaves out those very elements which make it a *social action,* though, it must be said, for some purposes such a description may well be adequate. However, such a description, treated as a description of indisputable 'brute fact' or fundamental 'observational datum', allowing meaning or the imputation of motive, reason or intention, merely as a subjective component, is to misconceive the process of action description.[8] Further, motives can be arguable, indeterminate and doubtful as a matter of course. Conjecture as to motive does not arise out of the absence of evidence we might have but do not – as the despairing positivist spoken of earlier might have it – but is a review of a range of possibilities where the relation of behaviour to its circumstances is just ambiguous, though for those whose activities are being observed this may not be so.

As with motives, so with rules. Any piece of behaviour could be made out as consistent with a vast number of rules, though in practice only some would be deemed relevant on any occasion. Some rules are commandments to do, or not do, something we could do whether or not the rule existed. We could, for example, refrain from eating certain foods without having been enjoined to do so by some religious dietary restrictions. In this sense, rules are external to the behaviour to which they apply. The Ten Commandments, for example, forbid various kinds of behaviours which, presumably, the framer of the rules regarded as less than wholesome, such as adultery, thieving, envy, worshipping false idols, and so on. However, some rules make possible the very activities to which they apply, and can thus be said to be 'constitutive' of action in the sense they prescribe what is required in order to perform a certain action. It would be impossible, as an obvious example, to imagine playing chess without the rules of chess, for it is those rules which lay down how the game is played, what ways of moving the pieces count as moves within the game, and so on. Suspend rules like this and the activity in question ceases to exist. There would, of course, still be the behaviour of pushing pieces of wood or plastic around a chequered board, but this would hardly be playing chess.[9] In the same way 'obeying traffic lights' would make no sense outside of the notion of traffic rules.

A relevant distinction here is that between a process being in accordance with a rule and a process involving a rule; between 'action in accord with a rule' and 'action governed by a rule'.[10] Any observed agent, process or action can be brought under the auspices of many rule-like formulations, none of which is unambiguously *the* rule governing the process or event. As Coulter expresses it, the 'rules which make an action what it is are not reducible to any (set of) descriptions of physical or physiological transformations, since virtually any "action" or "activity" can be realized through *different* transformations . . . and the converse is also true . . .' (Coulter 1989: 14). An activity accords with a rule if it exhibits the regularities expressed by the rule. It involves a rule if agents actually *use* the rule to guide or assess their actions. Rules, however, do not determine their own application but have to be used, and one of their more important uses is to bring a set of events, processes, persons or conduct, or all of these together, into some scheme of interpretation. In this sense the notion of rule is tied to that of 'making a mistake' and it is the possibility of this which helps distinguish being 'rule-governed' from mere regularity. That is, it enables us to evaluate what is being done, to attribute fault, to be subject to criticism. Invoking rules is a way of depicting or describing action, of pointing out what it is we are doing, of making our actions accountable. Used in this way, rules are part of our resources for making the world understandable.

The upshot of these remarks strongly suggests a very different sort of relationship between action and its description, and the rules or the motives which could be said to govern the action, from that envisaged in the positivistic approach. For one thing it claims that actions and their descriptions are conceptually tied to reasons and motives, neither being describable as if they were separate and independent; on the contrary, they inform each other reflexively.

This discussion of rules, motives and other intentional concepts – let us call them action concepts – argues that these are resources through which we give the social world its sense and meaning. It is making the point, too, that the vocabulary of action displays very different properties to those presupposed in a causal one. Action is predicated on the idea of an agent, specifically a human agent. The vocabulary of action is used by human beings in speaking to each other about what it is they are doing. An agent differs from a causal process because he or she can be said to make a choice, be held responsible for, initiate, do something, and so on. An action can be praised or condemned, commanded or forbidden, because the person performing the action can be praised, condemned, commanded or forbidden.

The use of causal expressions in action contexts should not entice us into thinking of invariant relationships or into thinking that these are somehow more real than noncausal ones. To say something like 'The fact that it was dark caused him to trip over the stool' is to make use of a causal type relationship between the amount of available light and the ability to see, but its import is offering an excuse, suggesting that he was not just clumsy, but could not help himself and, accordingly, could not be blamed for what happened. Actions do not come along conveniently labelled as 'suicide', 'clumsiness', 'obeying traffic signals', 'walking the dog', 'voting for a party of the working class', 'being motherly', and so on, but have to be described, and doing this is itself an action. It involves more than just looking at 'concrete behaviour', if this makes any sense at all, but paying attention to circumstances, reasons, motives, rules, and so on.

Of course, it is clearly not the case that intentions, motives, rules or conventions, are necessarily imputations in action descriptions. One can kill inadvertently, deceive without intending to deceive, and so on, while in other cases matters are not so clear; can one murder without the intention to murder, promise without intending to promise, for example? Events can also be described without motive implications: 'The gun happened to be loaded, the trigger knocked, the bullet hit her and she died of wounds received.' Whether or not such a description would be deemed accurate or adequate would depend on the purposes for which the description was formulated. The description of an action is an occasioned event, is itself an action, done for some purpose, informed by some interest, done in some context. The point is, however, that action descriptions are essentially defeasible; that is, it is always possible, in principle, to argue against any particular description by bringing in other particulars about the situation, the person, the event or the object. Let us illustrate with another homespun example.

Some time ago one of the authors (JAH) was walking down a corridor and, as it happened, stopped to hold open a door for a woman following behind. The woman stopped and made the remark that what he had just done was sexist. JAH apologised in some confusion and said that holding the door to allow her to precede him was a gesture of simple courtesy which he would have done for anyone, male or female. This did not carry a great deal of weight and the argument went on for some minutes. The point of this anecdote is not the by now familiar one of the same behavioural display – opening the door, standing back, and so on – being open to different interpretations, which it is, but that it is open to different descriptions as an action. The issue is not one of fitting the right description to an event as one might have to fit round pegs into round holes or the right words into the lines of a crossword puzzle. It has to do with justifying an action, describing it in socially consequential ways. To ask whether the right description of the act JAH performed was 'a courtesy' or 'male chauvinist piggery' is to miss the point. The matter of description is bound up with justifying the action or a point of view with appropriate reasons and arguments, to do with persuading, cajoling, threatening or coercing, someone to accept that what happened was of such and such a character. The issue is not whether JAH's intention is irrelevant or whether he has the intention that he avowed. It is about whether the intention alone is enough to decide the character of the action here, or whether the very possession of that intention shows naivety about the context of male–female relationships within which such an intention cannot be 'innocent', since it is a failure to recognise that treating a women in ostensibly the same way as one would treat a man is not really treating her in the same way at all. It is, as it were, a residuum of patriarchal attitudes.

The woman and JAH could have argued each of their cases sensibly. He could have pointed to his exemplary record of courtesy in all things, while she could well have taken this as more evidence for her case, arguing that such behaviour indicated a patriarchal attitude on his part and that sexism was part and parcel of this. As in the case of motives, various arguments could be invoked, reasons adduced, in order to support the claim that the scene should be looked at in a particular way. They could only have come to some agreement if they held, as it were, a framework in common whereby such disputes could have been resolved (Ryle 1966).

However, the failure to find 'common methods', so to speak, is not some failure of our knowledge but a characteristic of our vocabulary of action. In pointing to the essential defeasibility of action descriptions it is being claimed that the vocabulary of action is part and parcel of moral discourse and, as such, is concerned with the appraisal of conduct. In this realm of discourse what we have done or are doing has no well-defined description in ways required by positivistic science, though such descriptions work well enough in the context of action. Knowing what it is you are doing, what you are going to do, what you have or have not done, cannot be fully explicated by looking at what in fact you do. To know what you are doing is to be able to elaborate the action, say why you are doing it, excuse or justify it if necessary, and so on (Pitkin 1972: ch. 7). What is at stake, in short, is what in fact was done. Was JAH's opening the door a flagrant piece of male chauvinist piggery or the last throw of knightly courtesy? And even if the 'last throw of knightly courtesy' would not this be yet more 'male chauvinist piggery', and so on? What the dispute is about is not the sort of issue that can be resolved by consulting some putative dictionary of social actions.

These arguments suggest that the description of social action is a problematic matter both for social actors and observers alike. Descriptions are, it has been pointed out, deeply sensitive to context and defeasible. Description itself is a social activity done for particular purposes and deemed adequate or inadequate, as the case may be, in terms of these purposes. This leads on to another general property of descriptions, namely, that they are always, in principle, incomplete. Whatever is included in a description is always selective and cannot exhaust all that can be said about an object, event or a person. More could always be added: a person could be described, for example, as 'dark haired', 'tall', 'selfish', 'reticent', 'a worker', 'of higher than average intelligence', and so on, but these could not exhaust all that could be said about the person. Descriptions are selections from what could possibly be said and, depending on the occasion, be perfectly adequate for that occasion and that purpose. Although descriptions have a fringe of completeness about them, or, as Frederick Waisemann puts it, an 'open-textured' quality, this does not impair their ability to do the job required since nothing like absolutely definitive completeness is ever attempted by speakers of a natural language (Wiseman 1951, Pitkin 1972: 61–2). As said before, often a single descriptor will provide an adequate description – 'this friend', 'my colleague', 'the landlord of the Plough', 'that stupid dog' – the remaining particulars being, as it were, bracketed away for present purposes or their sense 'filled in' using the specifics of the contexts in which uttered. It is always possible, however, to produce alternative descriptions of an object, event, action or person. Other properties may be added which modify the original description, or other aspects come along which provide additional elements to qualify, modify or even undercut the original. The relationship between the features of an object, an event, an act or a person and some description is not a determinate one. A speaker's selection of a descriptor from all that could be said or predicated of some phenomenon normally tells the hearer something about the practical purposes of the speaker in offering that particular description. It calls forth a host of possible elaborations, and this means that, on the occasions of its use, a description can only index what it might mean, a quality referred to by Harold Garfinkel as 'indexicality' (Garfinkel 1967, especially ch. 1).

The arguments reviewed here challenge the presumptions of the conventional explanation of action tied, as it is, to the requirements of positivism. The social science tradition from which they derive places meaning centrally in understanding social life and points to crucial differences between the 'vocabulary of action', to retain that phrase, and picture of action resident in positivistic explanations. The rather grand, and overworked, term 'meaning' more than hints at the inter-subjective character of social life and, in its way, points to the fact that human action is not as determined in its course as the inanimate subject-matter of natural science.[11] Whereas positivism might perhaps attribute this to the paucity of good measurement, good theories and the infancy of the social sciences, or to the greater complexity of the social world compared to the natural, what is being claimed here is more fundamental, namely, that human life is essentially different, and that this difference requires another methodology to that required by a positivistic conception. It might also require a different kind of knowledge. Of course, matters hang heavily on the banal observation that human beings are capable of giving accounts of their own lives and their relationships to others. However, what is also being claimed is that this ability is essential to there being a social life at all. Giving reasons, justifications, explanations, making descriptions, are themselves profoundly social activities and, consequently, make social life what it is. What we have to examine now is whether or not these considerations do imply that a social science is impossible.

Reasons versus causes

One major methodological consequence of binding reasons, motives and other dispositions to the notion of action is that it raises questions about whether social science can be concerned with the causes of action. The conceptual tie between the imputation of reason and motive and the description of action argues that one of the major criteria for identifying a causal relationship is not met: that is, the logical independence of the antecedent factor, the reason, and the effect, the action. Instead a very different relationship is claimed in which the reason (or the motive) and the description of action are mutually informing, though not in any determinate way. A further objection to the causal account arises from issues addressed in connection with the description of action itself, and is an objection to the use of the hypothetico-deductive model of explanation. It is argued that such a method can only be used if literal description is possible; that is, description not dependent for its sense or meaning on the occasion of its use (Wilson 1974: 75).

As has been pointed out, descriptions enter into the hypothetico-deductive form of explanation in at least two places: in statements about the initial conditions and in the deduced prediction that constitutes the explanandum. The burden of the argument here, however, is that literal description is possible in the social sciences only by ignoring the interpretative nature of social action and forcing categories into a framework to satisfy the requirements of literal description. '*Knowing what* people are doing (including oneself) is *knowing how* to identify what they are doing in the categories of a natural language, which requires *knowing how* to use those categories in discursive contexts . . .' (Coulter 1989: 15–16, italics in original). Thus, if one wants to describe a piece of behaviour, which may be an utterance or a bodily movement, as, say, indicative of 'mental illness', neither the utterance itself nor the movement will indicate this without the use of some schema which enables one to compose this as an instance, an indicator, of mental illness. It goes without saying that different schemas would prompt different descriptions, though not always inconsistent ones. Similarly, if I make use of someone else's descriptions of the same elements, to understand this I must use the same interpretative procedures in order to appreciate how the instances were gathered into the description used. Garfinkel (1967: 76–103) refers to this as the 'documentary method of interpretation' in which a set of appearances, which may be objects, events, persons, or symbols, is taken as evidence for some underlying pattern, while the postulated pattern serves as a guide for seeing how the appearances themselves should be read. Thus, the classification of the description of any piece of behaviour on a given occasion as an instance of a particular type of action is not based on a set of specifiable features of the behaviour and the occasion but, rather, depends on the indefinite context seen as relevant to the observer, a context that gets its meaning partly through the very action it is being used to interpret. The meaning, hence the action being performed, for example of a raised arm would depend on the context; similarly, the context itself would be partly made intelligible by the meaning or the description given to the movement. It follows that any interpretation is always both retrospectively and prospectively revisable in the light of further evidence.

These arguments, and we shall examine more in the next chapter, seriously question the idea of a social science based on the search for causes. Winch (1990), among other critics, argues that action concepts are logically incompatible with the idea of causal necessity and, thus, with natural scientific causal explanation. There have also been attempts to deny the force of this distinction between reasons and causes. MacIntyre (1977: 117), for example, bothered by the fact that agents may offer many reasons for why they do something, wants to argue that an agent's possession of a reason may be a state identifiable independently of an agent's performance of an action and, accordingly, a candidate cause. The attribution of a reason is itself a matter of relating a person to a context. To say of people that they have a reason is just to say that they are in a particular situation. In the classic detective stories the investigators find out that many characters had reasons to hate the murder victim, and they do this by discovering the relations of these people to the victim. They find out that one of the suspects was in a position to be exploited and mistreated by the victim without being able to do anything about it, and this is a reason why this person may have hated the victim enough to murder him or her. Obviously, not everyone who has a reason to do something does what they have a reason to do. It is only in Agatha Christie's *Murder on the Orient Express* that all suspects who have reasons for murder are the murderers. In the usual murder mystery only one of those with a reason to kill the victim commits the murder. Having a reason to do something does not mean that one will do it. Saying that someone has a reason is more like saying – sometimes it *is* saying – that they have a justification or entitlement to act. We say 'more like' because having a reason to murder someone is not to have a justification or entitlement to kill that person unlike, for example, the case where we might say that someone has a reason to sue, i.e. and would be justified in so doing. However, attributing a reason to do something to someone is a very long way from saying that the person will do the thing that he or she has a reason to do; it is not remotely like identifying a cause.

Of course, that people have reasons can be identified independently of their doing the action for which they have reasons. They may or may not do the relevant deed. But this is not the point that those who insist that reasons are not causes, or even like them, want to make. Their point is that the identification of a reason is logically connected to the action for which it is a reason, that the reason is identified to begin with *as a reason for a certain action*. One cannot investigate the life of an individual to see what reasons he or she would have and then, having established that the person had these reasons, conduct further inquiry to see what actions they were reasons for. In the classic detective story, establishing the reasons for murder, the reasons for murdering *this* victim, is integral to saying what action it is a reason to do. One cannot, therefore, conduct the kind of empirical investigation which seeks to find out what consequences a certain condition will cause in order to find out what kind of actions possession of a reason will give rise to. The very identification of reasons says what actions they are reasons for. Of course, it is an empirical question as to whether a person has a reason for an action and as to which, if any, of the persons with a reason to perform that action did so. There can even be investigations to establish if someone with that reason who performed that action, performed it for that reason. There might be more than one reason, for example, for someone to perform a certain action, and that person may perform it for only one of those reasons. Reasons enter as justifications, as further elaborations of actions and are not necessarily formulated as prior antecedents to the action for which the reason is relevant. Nor does the argument destroy the conceptual link between reasons and the description of action: a relationship which is not one of independence or contingent invariance.

The attachment to the idea that all phenomena, including actions, must have causes can be, in part, a manifestation of an attachment to positivist ideas about science, that is, that the mode of scientific explanation is universal and causal. If actions are to be brought under science, then they must be explained causally and, accordingly, if reasons explain actions then they must be some kind of cause. Resistance to this view holds that there is more than one kind of explanation, and that not all explanations give causes. Explanations by means of reasons are distinct from causal ones but they still explain. They explain by making clear what the point or purpose of an action was. Giving the reason why the murderer committed the murder makes clear what its point was: to stop further exploitation and ill-treatment by the victim, say, or to inherit the money left in the will. Thus, the reason elaborates the identity of the action.

The desire to retain the notion that causal explanations are the only, the only real, explanations of actions is also connected with determinism and free will, a debate which can be briefly summarised as follows. On the one hand are arguments which say that we hold people responsible for what they do, blame them when they behave badly, and so forth, and that we do so because they have free will. They did not have to do what they did, they were free to do otherwise. They had a choice.

On the other hand, if everything that people do is caused, then that means that they are made to do whatever they do, and so the idea of free will is an illusion. So, there would be no point in blaming someone for doing something beyond his or her control. What people do is the function of the supposed causal factors, such as upbringing, personality, situation, and therefore, they are merely the helpless victims of all these factors. While we may all feel free to choose and act we are, in fact, unaware of the causes of our actions.

The conflict here, while easily stated, is not so easily resolved. The notion of cause itself is used in a variety of ways, not all of them accommodated within a Humean conception of causality. The fact that we give 'reason' and 'intention' explanations for actions does not necessarily imply that we *never* give causes for actions. Peters, who takes the view that we often give other kinds of explanations for actions than causal ones, nonetheless holds that we are likely to give causal explanations when something has gone wrong, 'where there is some kind of deviation from the purposive rule-following model; when people, as it were, get it wrong' (Peters 1960: 10). In such cases doubts are raised as to whether an action was fully performed. Also, we tend to give causal explanations of action where the actor's choice or responsibility is minimal or, alternatively, has no interest for us. We might do this, as Pitkin (1972: ch. 7) illustrates, in considering how to get a third party to do something. Here causes are not incompatible with reasons, motives and intentions. In historical explanation, for example, we tend to be rather more interested in accounting for why a person did what they did than in holding him, or her, responsible or attributing blame.

One could say that this is all very well. The practices of ordinary language in respect of causal attributions versus the imputations of motives or reasons are well taken in connection with particular actions, but are not exactly relevant to social science which is concerned with the explanation of whole classes of actions. In reply, one could say that in trying to achieve explanation of this kind one runs the risk of stretching language until insoluble conceptual difficulties are created. 'Free', 'determined', 'cause', are concepts connected to many other concepts and giving up notions of 'free will' would not just mean dropping the expression 'free will' from our vocabulary, but would involve reorganising our whole way of talking about what we do and dispensing with ways of talking which are useful to us for other purposes than scientifically explaining our actions. If asked the question, 'what is a free action?' we could, with little difficulty, give many illustrations, synonyms, analogies, offer concepts roughly equivalent in meaning, which would show the notion of 'doing X freely' so thoroughly interwoven with so many of our ways of speaking. If we denied that any actions were free then we would be involved in rejecting whole categories, and relationships, denying, in effect, whole regions of our language. Terms such as 'free', 'cause', 'determined', and concepts associated with them, are used in particular contexts, used for assessing some particular action taken or contemplated. Whether a person has or has not a choice are questions partly dependent on the position adopted by a speaker in the situation at issue and has nothing to do with whether there might be causes for their actions. One might say to a close friend, 'I can't come to the cinema with you because my parents are visiting' and intend that the force of the parental obligation means that I am not 'free' to go. The acceptance of this explanation by the other would mean that they would not be offended or disappointed by our turning down their invitation. If, on the other hand, a friend wanted accompanying to the hospital, it is possible that one might override parental obligations and our parents would understand why we 'had' to neglect our obligations to them. One might not for an acquaintance, though even that might be dependent on the seriousness of the reason for the visit to the hospital. The point is that in each of these situations one is taking a position with respect to others, and it is by this that one will be judged. What is difficult is to generalise from these particular cases to distinguish criteria by which *all* actions are to be seen as causally determined.

In any event, it is difficult to see how one might *discover* whether all our actions are really causally determined or whether they are really all free. In fact, it looks as if the issue is hardly a matter about the facts of the world at all. If, as was suggested above, we seriously entertained the idea that all action was caused (or free) this would involve vast changes in the conceptual system in which and through which our lives are constituted. It would be difficult to speak of responsibility, blame, punishment, honour, achievement, generosity, valour, skill, quality, failure, conduct, and so on. We may, it is true, retain the use of these and like terms, but their point would be lost. One might still 'punish' but this would be the application of another causal mechanism designed to modify behaviour. One might still 'praise' but this would not be giving credit for some personal achievement and would only add another factor to induce a particular behaviour, one that we as 'blamer' or 'praiser' could ourselves take no credit for since, we, too, could not help ourselves. The point is that though our language and our understandings do change and are conventional they are not arbitrary. They are shaped by our conduct as human beings. The determinist might argue that the distinction between actions and causes arises because we are ignorant of the causes of some actions, but this is to miss the point.

It is also difficult not to see the very presentation of the determinist standpoint as contradicting the substance of its doctrines. Determinists try to give us reasons for thinking that the determinist case is right and require our acceptance of their case not on the basis of causes which compel us to believe determinism, but as a matter of complying with the obligations which acknowledgement of a better argument impose upon us, that is, to accept what we have been shown.

One could not get a starker opposition. The positivist kind of approach supposes that only objective observation can make possible the investigation of the true nature of things, supposing, as part of this, that such objectivity requires standing apart from the phenomena being observed. The other side of the argument is that this 'removal' from social phenomena does not bring out their true nature but distorts their character. Far from enabling us better to understand the things that we do, the positivist point of view would either misunderstand or evaporate them. The supposedly 'objective' viewpoint is hardly that if it removes the observer so far from the realities being observed that their specific and distinctive character is lost. A purely 'observational' science, in the sense that positivists intend it, might satisfy the requirements for compliance with standard scientific procedure, but it would also mean giving up the action vocabulary out of which, as argued above, so much of our existence is composed or constituted. What would the positivist be observing? Such an observer could not discern promises, wars, power, interests, worship, organisations, exploitation, deprivation, and so on, since these could not strike the action-concept-free observer. In short, such a science 'could not answer the questions we can now formulate, for they are formulated in the concepts we have' (Pitkin 1972: ch. 7).

In the next chapter we shall examine further arguments relevant to this matter.

Notes

1. Or, as Bishop Berkeley (1685–1753) would have it, ideas in the mind of God.
2. Originally the debate arose in economics but soon widened into a more general debate into which scholars from history, legal and language studies were drawn.
3. See the introduction to Mueller-Vollmer (1985) for an overview and analysis of the rise of hermeneutics.
4. See Burger (1976: ch. 1) for a discussion of the influence of Rickert.
5. The decline of academic Marxism as a dominant force in the UK has renewed interest in Weber.
6. See, for example, a nonphilosophical critique, Blumer (1956).
7. This is, of course, just what is used in the construction of questionnaires and attitude scales, for example. The issue, however, is how this meaningful dimension of social life is treated methodologically and the extent to which such treatments distort the phenomena that are the objects of social science.
8. Coulter (1979) develops this theme at some length. See also Coulter (1989).
9. On 'constitutive rules' see Searle (1969).
10. See Coulter (1973: 141), Rawls (1955). The distinction is owed to Wittgenstien (1958: paras. 199–202).
11. That people's actions are not causally determined does not mean that social life is therefore disorderly or inexplicable. Social life is immensely routine and predictable most of the time. The issue is about the basis on which it is so orderly.

CHAPTER 6

Lay versus scientific conceptions

In the previous chapter we discussed a number of problems for positivistic versions of social science arising from the nature of the vocabulary we use in our ordinary lives to talk about, and perform, actions. What we have tried to bring out is the tension between the 'vocabulary of action', to remain with this phrase for the time being, and the attempts to develop a vocabulary more in keeping with the observational requirements of a positivistic science. As we have tried to make clear, the issues here are not simply about 'vocabulary' in the sense of a collection of words by which ordinary people talk about their affairs in one way, while scientists talk about them in another. As we have tried to show, as far as the social sciences are concerned, the fact that their subject matters live within an already preinterpreted world has very serious implications for the nature of these disciplines. That is, the issues are much more than about words but about the ways in which the very phenomena, the very stuff, of social life are constituted in and through language-as-an-activity.

In this and subsequent chapters we want to consider what follows from the attempt at a deep critique of positivist methods. Although we have looked at arguments which show that the positivist picture of science is seriously flawed, this does not necessarily mean, as we pointed out in the introductory chapter, that the research techniques putatively associated with the viewpoint are entirely useless. They may be unpromising in their capacity to achieve the ambitions assigned to them in the positivist scheme of things, but their merits as a means of data collection do not entirely depend on authorisation from the positivist project. They can still serve a purpose in social research. The criticisms which are directed at the positivist project arise from the supposition that the project had a seriously mistaken idea about the nature of social life and the means most suitable to its study. Such critiques, of course, also carry implications as to how, in their view, social life may be better understood and what means are appropriate to its study. Many of the criticisms we have reviewed take exception to positivism's inclination to take the concepts and findings of science as the principal measure of knowledge and to regard concepts as unsuitable for proper understanding unless they have been formed as, or transformed into, supposedly scientific ones. Whereas positivism sought to transmute lay conceptions into scientific ones, the approaches we will be discussing in this and the following chapter sought to examine the general implications of the fact that the social sciences study phenomena which are significantly the product of the meanings produced and used by the members of society.

In this chapter we are mainly concerned with the potential methodological importance of giving the notion of 'meaning' a more prominent role in defining the possibilities for a social science, bearing in mind that in using the term 'social science' we are simply using it for convenience and are not committed to any particular view of science in this connection or, indeed, whether the social sciences can be sciences at all. The criticisms of the positivist project which result from giving meaning a more central role are ones which raise fundamental doubts about the project on the grounds of the alleged inability of the methods modelled on the natural sciences to capture and characterise the meaningful nature of social phenomena, of its failure to understand the degree to which the nature of these phenomena are constituted by meanings and, finally, with misunderstanding the way on which 'commonsense concepts' of ordinary language, the primary vehicles of meaning in social life, articulate with the technical concepts of science. The result of this latter failing, it is argued, is that positions such as those of positivism will be confused and ambiguous over the extent to which their supposedly 'scientific' concepts and findings depend upon and involve common-sense concepts. We go on to the presentation of some attempts to formulate alternatives to positivism beginning with Max Weber, who played such a key role in bringing the notion of 'the meaning of social action' into twentieth century social science. We then outline two ways in which attempts have been made to move away from Weber, both giving even more thorough emphasis to the idea of meaning than Weber did.

The first of these is the hermeneutic tradition which attempts to treat social inquiry as a distinctive process of 'understanding' from that of science. On this view, 'understanding' is the business end of social inquiry and not, as in Weber, a means toward empirical ends. The second is the work of Alfred Schutz who, though approving of Weber's emphasis on social action as a meaningful matter, was critical of the clarity and consistency with which Weber had tried to work through his own project. Schutz sought to rethink Weber's project in terms of 'phenomenological philosophy' and, in so doing, came to argue that 'understanding' was a constituent feature of the relations between members of society and, therefore, the examination of the possibility and nature of such understanding should be part of social inquiry and not merely take-for-granted as a means of doing social research.

The chapter begins with illustrations of the ways in which purportedly 'scientific' studies can be described as unwittingly, or unreflectively, incorporating common-sense understandings in their data collection and analysis.

Positivist methods and common-sense meanings

As we have discussed earlier, it is not as if positivistic methods have ignored actors' meanings in their inquiries. As we have seen, a considerable amount of effort was devoted to finding ways in which instruments could be devised to measure the rich 'inner life' of social actors, their beliefs, values, ideologies, attitudes, opinions, and so on. Accordingly, one of the main modes of explanation using positivist methods is to correlate observable acts, events and attributes with data about the 'inner life' of beliefs, values, attitudes, and so on. The former are generally treated as 'objective' facts while the latter are treated as 'subjective states'. Although 'subjective states' can be measured objectively, as we have described in Chapter 3, by using instruments, such as questionnaires or interviews which allow a researcher to *report* the values or the beliefs which people hold, they are 'subjective' in the sense that they are not attributes of 'objective' social reality but versions of them. The aim of explanation is to show how patterns of 'subjective states' are correlated with features of 'objective' social reality. Thus, and for example, explaining why people hold different political beliefs involves showing how particular beliefs are associated with 'objective' features of the social lives of various categories of people, such as their occupation, their level of education, their age, and so on. Of course, and as we have tried to make clear throughout, this is not simply a matter of research techniques but is also about the theoretical picture that is being deployed: a picture which sees persons as living within a social environment which has an 'objective' status, and which is causally related to the 'subjective' versions that people have about the society in which they live and their place within it. The fact that people have beliefs – attribute meaning to their world – is itself a fact about that world. However, the world which is the object of these beliefs, versions, meanings, can only be made up of 'objective' factors which have a causal influence. In short, meanings are only allowed into the discourse of positivistic social science if 'placed in quotes and attributed to individuals as their opinion, belief, attitude' (Taylor 1978: 172). What are being referred to as 'subjective states' are allowable into social scientific explanation provided that they conform to the canons of positivistic description.

This conception, if we accept the arguments of the preceding chapter, seriously misconstrues the nature of social action and, importantly, the part that so-called 'subject states' play in the construction of social action. It does so by relegating these to a status as versions of social reality and, in so doing, introduces a confusion between 'objectivity' and 'subjectivity' as, briefly, 'inner' and 'outer' features of social actors, and 'objective' and 'subjective' as standards to do with the appraisal of some claim as being impartial or partial. When, for example, we describe someone's opinion as 'subjective' we are not commenting on the ontological status of the opinion, that is, identifying it as an expression of a person's 'inner state', but, in the latter of the above two senses, invidiously characterising it *vis-à-vis* another position the person might have chosen and which might have been deemed more 'objective'. Thus, condemning a statement as 'subjective' is asserting that the view the person expresses has been formed without scrupulously weighing up the pros and cons, is unreasonably blind to some crucial facts, is not sufficiently detached, and so on. Confusions such as these rampage through the objective–subjective dichotomy. In addition, what may also be implied is that 'there is a social reality which can be discovered in each society independently of the vocabulary of that society, or indeed any vocabulary, as the heavens could exist whether men theorised about them or not' (Taylor 1978: 174).

As discussed in connection with the correspondence theory of truth for scientific theory proposed by positivism, there is no theory-independent way of looking at the world. What the above ideas do is add an additional, and highly significant, twist to this, namely, that the phenomena of social science cannot be studied independently of the meanings, beliefs, values, the language, the 'subjective states' as, following a widespread pattern of usage, we have called them, of the members of society. In other words, social reality is constructed in and through meanings and cannot be identified in abstraction from the language in which they are embedded. However, 'meaning' in the sense in which social researchers tend to talk about this, does not involve only the meaning of words in the language, but also the meaning of the expressions of the things the members of society say and do. Meaning is profoundly to do with language considered not as a system of words and grammatical rules but as social interaction. To adapt a statement from Austin: language does not merely report on the world but is itself performative of action in the world (Austin 1961: 66–7). The language and the practices, things and events in the world are inseparable.

We need to be as clear as we can about what the view just outlined involves. At this stage we will assert two of its main presuppositions and elaborate on them later in this chapter and the next. First, it claims that reality, whether natural or social, cannot be conceived of or known independently of the concepts in language. Second, it asserts that as far as *social* reality is concerned, this is constituted through meanings; that is, that the very phenomena which make up social life consists in nothing other than the meaningful relations between persons. The language we have is not something which we can use *only* to describe our activities and relations with others with the implication that these activities and relations can be conducted without recourse to language. Our activities and relationships are carried out in relation to the language we have; that is, we relate to others in greatest part through talking to them or employing other forms of language-mediated exchange. So, although we might happily concur that the natural world exists independently of language – though not independently of the ways in which we know it – this cannot be the case with the social world. The relationships we have with others are not independent of the language we use to describe and perform them.

According to the presuppositions just outlined, in studying social life we are not dealing with a reality made up of 'brute fact' but one which is constituted through the practices identified and given meaning by the language used to describe, invoke and carry them out. Proponents of this kind of view argue that social life cannot be studied using the methods and presuppositions of positivistic science since they are predicated on an ontology which cannot be supported. Some of the arguments for this have already been discussed in the previous chapter. The argument can, however, go further than this by pointing out the paradox that despite the kind of criticisms we have reviewed, positivist methods 'work' in at least the sense that such research produces findings and results which are intelligible. They are not, that is, obviously nonsensical. However, they 'work', to the extent that they do, because they rely, despite their positivistic rhetoric, upon just those features outlined. The use of the methods is embedded in the sense of social life conveyed in language. But this would have serious consequences for the intellectual authority of positivistic explanations of social life. They 'work' *despite* their own epistemological justifications and, in the end, have no more intellectual warrant *as science* than any other institutionalised social practice.

Let us examine some of the issues here and bring out some of the implications of the remarks made earlier in this and the preceding chapter to bear more directly on positivist methods of social research.

The social embeddedness of positivist methods

Whatever serves as 'data' in social science research begins its life, though not always in an obvious way, constituted by what are termed the 'first order' constructs used by members of society.[1] However, for precisely those qualities discussed earlier in relation to the 'vocabulary of action' and its alleged inadequacies as a vehicle for the acquisition and expression of objective, scientific knowledge, these 'first order' constructs are deemed inadequate candidates for inclusion in the vocabulary of a positivistic social science. Often vague by comparison with the precisely defined technical terms of the advanced sciences, often imbued with emotional overtones, often opinionated, often value laden, often ambiguous in meaning, they are held to be hopelessly inappropriate as precise scientific concepts. The spirit of this objection is well captured in Durkheim's remarks on the official statistical categories he used in his study of suicide. He dismisses the official statistics on the motives of the recorded suicides on the grounds that they are 'actually the statistics of the opinions concerning such motives of officials, often of lower officials, in charge of this information service' (Durkheim 1952: 148). He goes on: 'These are known to be defective even when applied to obvious material facts comprehensible to any conscientious observer'. The conclusion is that such conceptions must be repaired in some way, made more objective, or scientific one substituted. The issue is precisely the nature of such a transformation.

Take the example of a scaling procedure. These are used in the measurement of attitudes and in personality assessment mainly, though they are sometimes used to measure phenomena other than psychological dispositions. Such scales are normally constructed by selecting items from a series of statements, with which the respondent has to agree or disagree, or select one of a number of alternatives, presumed to reflect the relevant attitude or disposition. The response is scored so that it reflects more or less of the attitude or disposition. The following example is taken from a Faith in People scale (Rosenberg 1955: 160):

1. Some people say that most people can be trusted. Others say you can't be too careful in dealing with people. How do you feel about it?
2. Would you say that most people are more inclined to help others, or more inclined to look after themselves?
3. If you don't watch yourself people will take advantage of you.
4. No one is going to care much what happens to you, when you get right down to it.
5. Human nature is fundamentally co-operative.

On the basis of the pattern of responses to these items respondents are scored and, on this basis, judged to have 'high', 'medium' or 'low' faith in people'. Each of these subgroups was shown, by correlation with other scales, to have different attitudes towards success in life.

As is typical of such scales, the statements which comprise the scale are phrased in recognisably ordinary language, as they must be given that they are intended to be administered to ordinary members of society and not people well-versed in the technical language of social science. They reflect the inevitable fact that 'data collection' of all kinds involves an interfacing with the ordinary languages in use in the society. As statements the items in the 'Faith in People' scale are ordinary enough so that they could have been uttered in a variety of familiar situations, in a bar, on a bus, a conversation between friends, and so on. On such occasions the responses might have ranged from grunts of assent, or dissent, to more extended replies; they might have been uttered ironically, jokingly, fleetingly, and so on. In interviewing, however, respondents are normally limited to making one of a restricted choice of answers already provided: 'yes' or 'no' or from a set of alternatives expressing the degree of agreement or disagreement with the statement. It is this feature which allows the researcher to assign a numerical weighting to the response. Thus, and for example, an 'agree' response to item 5 might well be weighted as 1 to indicate a greater degree of faith in people. The overall score is an accumulation of these separate weightings for the individual items.[2] However, if the numbers are to conform to the requirements of counting, then we need to be able to assume that person A's score of 3 is equivalent to person B's score of 3, and that both these scores reflect, measure that is, a greater quantity of the property being measured than does person C's score of 2. In other words, it has to be assumed that the meaning each item has for each respondent is equivalent in terms of the meaning that it conveys and thus in the 'strength' with which the sentiment it expresses is held, in order for the scale to work as a numerical measure of the attitude.

The open-textured quality of ordinary language, out of which the scale items are constructed, makes it tricky to use in the expectation that it can be used to formulate questions and generate answers which can satisfy the assumptions that must be in place if the results of the survey are to comprise 'measurement'. The investigator seeks to remedy, in part at least, these problematic aspects of the exercise by the provision of forced-choice answers, and suchlike, but this places a question mark against the assumption that the respondents who answer the question in the same way thereby give vent to opinions of identical strength, and the assumption that respondent and researcher do, indeed, share 'the same community of subjective meaning structures for assigning cultural significance' to the items.[3] If this assumption of meaning equivalence cannot be upheld then it is not clear in what sense it can be said that the attitude measure is a quantitative measure at all, since the assignment of numerical weightings becomes a more or less arbitrary exercise. It means that we cannot sensibly use the scores in any arithmetic operation, such as averaging, since we cannot be sure that the same numbers reflect the same quantity of the property, in this case the attitude.

If we do take seriously the arguments about the open-textured quality of ordinary language, then it is not clear that in providing an answer a respondent understands either the item itself or the response to it in the same way as another respondent, let alone the investigator, or indeed that any respondent would understand an item on another occasion in the same way that it was understood on a previous occasion. This is not to say that a respondent cannot give an answer. After all, such instruments are widely used on almost a daily basis. The issue has to do with the meaning of that answer and whether or not it is adequately conveyed by assuming that it reflects an underlying property, an attitude say, such that it can be quantitatively weighted. What can we infer, for example, about a respondent who affirms item 3, say, and also affirms item 5? Is the respondent being inconsistent, irrational, or just not thinking? He or she may be all of these things, and more, but it is difficult to judge without asking for further elaborations from the respondent. It is possible to give perfectly good and rationally connected reasons for agreeing with both of these apparently 'inconsistent' statements. Moreover, the circumstances in which the question or statement is offered may make a difference to the kind of answer it elicits. Item 5 would, we suspect, receive a very different response if it appeared on an examination paper. Item 3, too, if offered by someone who looks like an extra from *Reservoir Dogs* and who sidles up to one in an alley late at night!

Such observations, obvious though they may be, are relevant to understanding why, on occasions, respondents have difficulty responding to such items since they lack any specification of a context which might give the statements a point. Including items such as these on a questionnaire or an interview schedule gives them a disembodied, decontextualised character such that respondents want to ask 'in what circumstances?', or answer with a qualifying phrase such as, 'it all depends'.

The questions just raised are concerned with the sorts of inferences that might validly be drawn from the results of such a method. As we have shown, these are not always clear. What implications could we draw, to give another example, from the fact that a respondent received a high score on such a scale? Do we infer that he or she will always be trusting, will lend money to anyone, will be a sucker for any sales pitch, will join any group? We could infer all these things and more, but what conclusion would we draw if a high scorer did not in fact lend money to her closest friend? Say that she cheated on the scale, had a momentary lapse, had no money to lend, or what? Without knowledge of the person, the particularities of the occasion itself along with any elaborations or justifications that the person herself might offer, we would not know what to conclude.

Nevertheless, the Faith in People notion does have a common-sense meaning. We understand the sorts of things it could refer to, stand for, when it could be used, and so on. Immersed as we are in our language and culture we understand its meaning and it is this which gives the scale itself some plausibility as a device to be used in research seeking to understand social action. If the researcher had called the property being measured 'XZ' we would still want to know how this related to our concepts for talking about action. In other words, ordinary usage is a resource essential to our understanding the supposedly scientific concept and the items presumed to measure it; a resource used by both the researcher in designing the scale and the respondent in answering it. However, it can be argued that the properties of this resource, a resource used to construct the very phenomena of social action, are distorted by the process of trying to transform them into instruments to satisfy the requirements of measurement and scientific concepts in a positivistic mode.

The above comments are of wider import than attitude measurement. The coding of questionnaires, for example, depends for its validity on a presumed equivalence between what items the respondent has responded to or checked on the questionnaire and the intention of the researcher in asking the question. There are, as we have already suggested, strong grounds for questioning whether such an equivalence can be so easily assumed. As Cicourel points out in respect of his own work on fertility, 'having children' does not necessarily have the same meaning for the researcher or the interviewer as it does for the respondents (Cicourel 1973, Phillips 1971). As he puts it, meanings can alter even during a single interview. 'Having children' means one thing to virgins, another to a pregnant woman, yet another when giving birth and, more than likely, still another when talking to a research interviewer. Nor is it possible for the coder to go back to the respondent to ask for an elaboration of an answer that might be unclear or ambiguous. Even if this were possible it would be unlikely to help very much since it would multiply the problems of coding as more and more detail was added.

The criticism of the social scientific use of official statistics is well documented, especially as they arise from Durkheim's pioneering use of them in his study of suicide. As has already been pointed out, Durkheim himself voiced many doubts about their accuracy. However, as others have pointed out, those responsible for the compilation of such statistics, such as officials, police, coroners, have themselves to decide upon the appropriate categorisation of the death before them. As studies have shown, such personnel 'rely on background expectancies, commonsense theorising and typifications which enable them to make sense of and objectify the phenomena with which they are faced' (Atkinson 1978: 45, see also Cicourel 1968, Eglin 1987). In short, and as we discussed in the previous chapter, they have to assemble the particularities before them in order to achieve a description of *this* event so as to be able to classify it along with other 'similar' events. The so-called 'objective facts' measured by official statistics are the outcome of the practices relevant individuals use to make sense of, and decide the identity of, the events they are confronted with. The official record is the product of the practices and negotiations among relevant officials even though it does not, could not, capture, record or reflect the process which produce them. What the record cannot do is stand for any 'objective reality' in the way proposed by positivistic social scientists.

The points just discussed are not solely concerned with the technical validity of methods, but also have to do with more general questions arising from the attempt to transform 'first order' constructs into concepts appropriate for a deductive or generalising social science in the positivist mould. The conduct of interviewing, for example, is based on procedures intended to enable the interviewer to obtain 'clear' and 'unambiguous' responses which can be coded for machine processing and statistical analysis. Unfortunately, as has been suggested, these procedures do not necessarily reflect the ways in which respondents ordinarily talk about their social lives. Transforming such talk into abstract entities called 'attitudes', 'beliefs', 'values', 'actions', and so on is presumed to provide an adequate scientific description of what people say and do. Yet the interview is detached from the circumstances in which persons act. The coding and manipulation of such data further removes and abstracts them from the circumstances of the social lives of those who are the objects of study. The open-textured, or indexical, properties of ordinary language ensure that the things said in that language only have conclusive sense against a background or context of the occasion on which they are said. Words, utterances, indeed any symbolic form, has to be 'filled in' on each occasion of its use, and this is a major stumbling block to efforts to construct a mathematical-type language for social science. Positivist methods, on these arguments, decontextualise 'first order' constructs and so distort the phenomena they are intended to investigate. They impose, by fiat, a version which is insensitive to the ways in which the social world is a meaningful one and constructed by those who live within it. To put it another way: positivist methods produce a version of the social reality they investigate as a discovering science through the methods themselves, methods which do not so much discover facts about social life as construct a version of that life by its methods. The methods do not so much explore the nature of social phenomena, such as, in the example used, the nature of 'faith in people' or 'trust', but force them into constrictions of the format which must be applied if the research is even to look as though it involves measurement.

Yet, as we pointed out earlier, the fact remains that positivistic style social researchers do produce findings and analyses of social life which, to put it no stronger, have some plausibility. We have already indicated in the earlier discussion one way in which we might understand why this is so. Social scientific concepts, whatever else is done with them by way of research operations, are parasitic for their sense on concepts available from within the culture and the language, concepts, that is, in everyday use. Researchers trade on these same resources as a condition for doing their social research in the first place. They make use of knowledge of the typical situations, motives, reasons, situations, rules, conventions, and so on; in short, they make use of their own knowledge of the cultural practices of the society in which they live and work as in the case of the reliance on 'official statistics' of those members of society, acting as officials, deploying their own grasp of typical motives, and so on. Indeed, as already indicated, without the use of such knowledge it is impossible to conceive how their data collection could be done at all. Harold Garfinkel argues that any attempt to say with any definiteness 'what happened' in any particular instance must depend upon the individual's invocation of socially shared understandings of more standardised patterns of life in society which are known and sanctioned as part of what he calls, after Alfred Schutz, the 'commonsense knowledge of social structures' (Garfinkel 1967). This claim applies both to ordinary members of society and those who act as social science researchers. In which case, social science depends for its authenticity on meanings and understandings available within the culture (Baccus 1986).

There is another aspect to this which, as we shall see, gives rise to anxieties in the shape of concerns about the relativity of social scientific knowledge and knowledge more generally. If we accept that scientific research is an activity done in accord with rules – and the idea of a scientific method, whatever else we might say about it, has to consist in at least rules of procedure by which the method is done – then we have also to face up to the fact that no rule dictates its own application but must be *applied*. And applying a rule is a practical activity done in particular circumstances. The interview, for example, involves rules of procedure designed to develop rapport between the interviewer and the respondent in order to maximise the validity of the replies as well as rules intended to make sure that the interview conforms to the ethics of social research. As we have seen, one of the problems here is drawing a distinction between talk in different contexts, one of which, the interview, becomes talk-as-scientific-data. Positivist methods seem to draw this distinction mainly in terms of the extent to which that talk conforms to certain criteria, such as clarity, consistency, lack of ambiguity, and so forth, which tend to be formulated in logical terms. Interview talk becomes indicative of the properties of social actors. Again as we have seen, as an aide to this fixed-choice responses may be provided, tests of consistency used, questionnaires rejected if they contain too many 'don't know' responses or inconsistent ones, and so on. Such procedures, of course, have to be applied in each and every case. Was *this* respondent really paying attention in the interview? Does *this* attitude scale really represent the respondent's attitude or is it a response set? Is *this* answer compatible with the previous answer or was the respondent bored? Answers to these and similar questions cannot be provided by the rules alone but must be judged as to whether they do or do not conform to the procedures in each particular case, and making such judgements is a matter, as we have suggested, of using knowledge of the society as a resource in order to apply the procedures.

The extent to which a researcher's solution is acceptable is, in part, a matter for other accredited members of the relevant research community. Scientific activity is, like many other activities, an enforceable matter in which results, conclusions, findings, theories, and so on, are subject to the legitimate scrutiny of others: a feature which, let us remind ourselves, Popper insists upon as a condition for scientific progress. It is this public scrutiny which gives the rules of scientific procedures their voice, their warrant and their force. 'Objectivity', 'truth', 'following the procedures', and more, are activities dependent for their utility on the very practices used to practically achieve them. While, on occasion, we may want to talk about the rules of scientific procedure, the scientific method even, as abstract formulations defining the ways to obtain objective knowledge of the world, in practice this devolves onto practitioners making judgements and performing activities which are deemed to be consistent with such formulations. Like all rules they have to be applied within the particularities in which scientists find themselves. Scientific theories, scientific findings – irrespective of what we understand science to be – are the products of the activities carried out by accredited members of a scientific community and consist in the application of such rules of procedure provided for and understood by those adjudged to be competent members of that community. This is the basis for the understandings which are the resource for seeing any research as 'objective', 'consistent with the evidence', 'provisional', 'confirming', or whatever quality it may happen to possess.

The positivist programme saw itself as operating according to an epistemology based on observation. Efforts to formulate a neutral

observation language were crucial to establishing the scientific authority of a discipline since this secured objectivity. The external world
described in terms of the neutral observation language was regarded as
the arbiter of the truth of scientific theories. An observation language
referring to real phenomena and operating according to a strict logical
calculus would provide knowledge of the laws of nature including,
eventually, those of social life. The view just discussed, however,
postulates that social scientific knowledge, far from being a passive
product of the empirical world, is an active constituent in the reconstruction of the social world. It does this, first, by arguing that efforts to
construct scientific 'second order' constructs out of 'first order' ones
characteristically involves tampering with the 'first order' concepts
used by persons in their daily lives to constitute that life in order to
render them suitable for scientific use. Since these 'first order' constructs
are constitutive of the phenomena of social life, that is, are used to
carry on social affairs, then such tampering destroys the very reality
that is the object of investigation and substitutes for the 'real world'
of social actors a 'scientised' version. The trouble is that the sense
and significance of such supposedly neutral and scientifically defined
theoretical terms in social science as 'power', 'profit', 'integration',
'social system', 'deviance', and so on, in large measure derive from
the everyday language used within social action. Second, the critique
draws attention to the fact that science itself, whether natural or social,
is another human social activity. Its procedures work because there is
a strong element of agreement about their application institutionalised
as the social practices of scientific activity. 'Objectivity', 'knowledge',
'truth', and other such concepts, have a conventional quality firmly
based on the social practices which constitute scientific disciplines.

These kinds of argument have important implications for the status
of scientific knowledge *vis-à-vis* other claims to knowledge. It raises,
too, the spectre of relativism. If scientific practice is conventional one
cannot appeal to the superior ability of science to explain the world
since, on this view, the world itself is constructed out of the practices
that constitute a discipline so the world itself cannot be an independent
witness. One cannot, as the positivists tried to do with the notion of a
neutral observation language, judge the relative merits of different and
competing claims to knowledge in terms of how well they describe and
explain the nature of the external world. All we are left with are various
kinds of activities, science, art, religion, literary criticism, poetry, and
so on, each internally justified by its own conventions and standards.
There can be no absolute justification based upon an appeal to the
neutrally observed external world.

There are a number of issues arising from the foregoing that we want
to discuss at some length. Before doing so, however, we want to have
a brief look at some of the alternative methodological approaches within
social science which accord a central place to meaning in understanding
the phenomena of social life.

Alternative conceptions of social science

It would be fair to say that the alternatives in terms of method to the positivist approach lack the confident clarity that positivism once possessed. Some of them represent a theme running parallel to positivism in the history of social thought. A common idiom is a rejection of social science as a positivistically styled science and the central placing of meaning in the conception both of social life and as the focal phenomenon of social investigation, sometimes accompanied by a willingness to surrender all claims to status as a scientific inquiry. Within this general posture, however, there are particular slants. The objection to science, for example, can be less than comprehensive and can be an objection against specific versions of science, such as positivism, rather than the abandonment of all scientific ambition for the so-called social sciences. As we briefly saw in connection with the debates in Germany in the latter part of the nineteenth century, many scholars argued for an alternative conception of social science, Weber for one.

Once doubts are cast upon what has been called here a 'neutral observation language' as the bedrock and foundation of science, the positivistic ambitions for science begin to look illusory. The social sciences, however they may try to emulate the natural sciences, have forever to face the difficulties posed by the fact that their subject matter, the members of society, also have a voice. Moreover, though this voice may be shaped by social position and social processes, it is not alone in this. The social scientist, too, is a member of society, has a position within a collectivity of colleagues and, as with the ordinary member of society, these may well shape how he or she is likely to see the world. This, to recall, is an important plank in Kuhn's arguments about the nature of scientific progress.

The ways of coming to terms with this have been various. Some, such as Mannheim, and to a degree Marx, suggested that objective standpoints could only be attained by those in a specially privileged position of detachment, 'intellectuals' being, more or less, the candidates for such positions.[4] These were people who could develop a more comprehensive, more objective point of view from which to locate the real processes at work within society. For Weber, however, that social inquiry is always from within a particular society and culture is a virtue rather than a disability. As he says:

There is no absolutely 'objective' analysis of culture – or perhaps more narrowly but certainly not essentially different for our purposes – of 'social phenomena' independent of special and 'one-sided' viewpoints according to which – expressly or tacitly, consciously or subconsciously – they are selected, analysed and organised for expository purposes . . . All knowledge of cultural reality, as may be seen, is always knowledge from particular points of view.

(Weber 1949: 72)

There is, in short, no Archimedian, no neutral, point from which to stand back and perceive social reality 'objectively'. It is by virtue of the fact that the social scientist is a member of culture that provides him or her with the resources to begin to understand what 'being social' means. It is such membership which enables the social scientist to identify problems of interest, issues worth investigating, as well as providing the capacity to understand the social world of others. As we have already seen, Weber offered two notions, the 'ideal type' and *verstehen*, as ways in which we might begin to understand meaningful social forms. The latter required that the researcher empathise with the point of view of those under investigation so that the ways in which the world made sense for them could be formulated. Using data from a number of sources about the values and beliefs of ascetic Protestants, Weber presented a portrait of how such people in their situation in the seventeenth century in Europe, with the motivations deriving from their religious values, unintentionally played a significant part in the development of capitalistic economic organisation. The bare conjunction between religious affiliation and capitalist business practice cannot be understood as a causal relationship of relevance to social science unless we can also understand the connection from the point of view of those involved in it, in this case, see it in terms of the way in which it made sense to the ascetic Protestants.

The 'ideal type' was a device essentially concerned with aiding the construction of rational, simplified and deliberately one-sided representations of social forms formulated as systems of meaning arising from a central value (Weber 1949: 72–81). Thus, the 'ideal type' of bureaucratic organisation is a model of what organisation would look like if the principle of rational and calculative efficiency, *and only that*, were to be the organising principle. Of course, no 'real world' organisation is ever likely to be shaped by just this one principle. The ideal type's primary use is as a structuring device for organising historical inquiry into what Weber believed to be the intrinsically disorderly real world; disorderly relative, at least, to the categories of logical thought which we humans use to comprehend the real world. The risk is that unless investigations are conducted around some coherent intellectual issue, these inquiries will be unfocused and unstructured. The ideal type provides such a coherent centre for inquiry enabling investigators to gauge how far actual organisations – to stay with the example of bureaucracy – conform to the model. The aim is to focus attention on establishing what empirical factors inhibit or displace the purely logical interdependencies in forming the shape that real organisations take. 'Ideal types' serve both to clarify a 'shapeless' empirical world and to isolate some of the elements of interest to the researcher by providing a method for organising the historian's investigation by encouraging and enabling the formation of focused questions. Ideal types, therefore, and this is an important point, were not the end of inquiry but very much, for Weber, a means of beginning such inquiries by simplifying and isolating features of interest.

Weber's view was that the conduct of inquiry through logical thought involved, essentially, an imposition of structure on a real world which did not possess it in its own right, and recognised that the organising principles which structured any scheme of understanding originated with the investigator and not in the phenomena being investigated. Therefore, there could potentially be as many structured schemes with different organising principles as there were investigators.[5] Hence, as there could be no absolutist position for the analysis of society and culture there was little point in worrying about relativistic implications. Knowledge was inevitably socially grounded, in that the investigators' problems and schemes of analysis arose out of their own life situations, and under the influence of the culture within which they worked, and always involved partial, highly selective perspectives. But this did not imply the abandonment of the standards of scholarship. Indeed, though someone who only reluctantly engaged in methodological discussion, Weber insisted that rigour, careful weighing of the evidence, scholarly scruple, detachment, and so on, should be standards governing intellectual inquiry.[6] The fact that social science investigations require 'understanding' or an 'interpretative' methodology distinguishes them from the natural sciences but this does not imply that they are less than rigorous or demanding in their standards. Explanation in terms of meaning does not remove the need for rigorous empirical proof.

The general notion that social science, however in the end this might be conceived, has to begin with the world as understood by the members of society is the cornerstone of hermeneutics. For H-G. Gadamer, for example, the 'historicity', as he terms it, of human life is an ontological condition of understanding (Gadamer 1975, Dallmyr and McCarthy 1977). It is because of our historical and social position that we can engage in interpretative understanding; our present understandings, conceptions of life, open up the past so that we can have knowledge of it. Our social and historical position is the 'given' which shapes our experience and our understanding of that experience. Our own historical position has already been shaped by the past, and it is this which provides the tradition, the ground upon which we, as interpreters, stand. In which case, interpretative understanding is not so much reconstructing the past in and for the present, but is 'mediating' the past in and for the present since it involves attention to the continuity of heritage and tradition as 'dialogue' and a 'collision of horizons' in which our own deep-seated assumptions and historicity are revealed. The circle of hermeneutic interpretation is a process of hypothesis and revision as understanding develops. There can be no absolute account, only an endless conversation with the past. Hermeneutics, for Gadamer, is the original form of 'being-in-the-world', a universal principle of human thought and life. There is no definite meaning to attain and no standards of objectivity independent of the 'fusion of horizons' reached in the dialogue of interpretation.

Underpinning all of this is the fact that we possess language and, through this, possess and experience the world. Language is the precondition for truth and understanding, and since there is no experience of the world independently of language, this sets limits upon what we know about the world. Language has a 'disclosure power', and just as tradition is the starting point for understanding, so to know a language is to be open to dialogue with others that can transform and broaden the horizons from which we begin. Also, since there is no experience of the world apart from language, there is nowhere else to view the world from and so the question of relativity does not arise. The process of transcending our own historicity, our own partial understandings in broader and broader horizons goes on in an endless process. Tradition and language are the context of interpretation and there can be no understanding outside of these and nothing, therefore, for our understanding to be relative to.

Despite Gadamer's claims about the essential and inescapable character of interpretation within human life, for Jürgen Habermas this does not go deep enough. For him, Gadamer's claims almost celebrate the necessary impossibility of discovering independent and objective standpoints. Instead, Habermas wants to argue that the expression of our subjectivity is determined by forces that we can know objectively, that is, from without the community of social life. The methodological exemplar for Habermas is Freud who, in his view, extends and complements Marx's theory by giving a fuller account of 'distorted communication'. Psychoanalysis is essentially hermeneutic rather than scientific in character but can admit causal process into its accounts of psychopathologies. By bringing out the latent significance of the repressed parts of a patient's life history, it reveals the 'underlying' forces which generate the surface meanings. The same 'depth hermeneutics' can be used, according to Habermas, to apply the same therapeutic gaze to communication and behaviour in social life, breaking through the constraints and distortions of language which determine our experience. Accordingly, reconstituting historical materialism as a 'depth hermeneutics' gives a realisable critique of ideology and a new philosophy of liberation and emancipation. The argument explicitly appeals to a notion of nondistorted communication in which social interests are fully acknowledged and open to critical inspection. Because we know the preconditions giving rise to it, we can detect false consciousness, and so transform the conditions of human life (Habermas 1971, Held 1978).

Although that strand of the interpretative tradition represented by Weber recognised the partiality of social scientific accounts, and hermeneutics their inevitability, the phenomenological tradition did not abandon the quest for the indubitable grounds of knowledge but sought it in a different place to that of positivism. Knowledge, for phenomenology, is an act of consciousness (see Natanson 1970, Luckman 1978, Anderson *et al.* 1987). To be conscious is to be conscious of *something*. For Husserl (1859–1938), the German philosopher who founded the school of phenomenology, the 'world' means a world experienced and made meaningful by acts of consciousness. It is through these alone that the world is given and presented to us. This is as true for science as it is for any other mode of knowing. The subject matter of science, for example, is a system of constructs resulting from conceptualisations, idealisations, mathematisations, and so on, based on and derived from a 'pregiven' everyday experience. The prime task of phenomenology is to describe this everyday experience of the 'life world': the world as given in immediate experience and independent of and prior to any scientific or other interpretation. Admittedly, 'life worlds' belong to specific sociohistorical groupings. Our world, that is the everyday world of the peoples of modern societies in the late twentieth century for example, is a world seen through the lens of modern science and different, in significant respects, from the 'life worlds' of the peoples of Ancient Greece. However, no special privilege attaches to any particular 'life world' since these are shaped by sociohistorical circumstances and there can be no historically or socially independent standard by which to determine which conceptions of the world are superior to others. For Husserl, however, a 'transcendental phenomenology' could be developed as a universal theory of consciousness. Such an 'ontology of the life world' would be an *a priori* science of the universal structures of the perceptual world and would, therefore, enable us to derive any particular sociocultural product from these structures, including science and logic. If such a theory were possible, it would perform the same role that positivism envisaged for the neutral observation language; that is, a noninterpreted basis for knowledge.

For our purposes, the important figure in this tradition is Alfred Schutz who elaborated and modified Husserl's work (Schutz 1962). However, Schutz's starting point was Weber's view that it was possible to provide sociological explanations adequate at both the level of meaning and the level of causality. Schutz regarded Weber's ambition as admirable but felt that he had failed to provide the necessary philosophical premises of an interpretative social science. So, in turning to Husserl's philosophical method and his analysis of the 'life world', Schutz aimed at building the ontological framework for an interpretative social science by treating the concept of understanding as the problem which, though Weber identified, he failed to examine thoroughly enough.

Borrowing from Husserl, Schutz argued that the 'life world' of ordinary understandings is carried into the scientific world but in a manner which leaves it unexamined. The reality that the social sciences take as their topic has its origins in the 'life world', and it is this which both Weber and the positivists failed to realise. To place interpretative social science on a firmer footing, it is necessary to examine the character of daily life as the outcome of the activities of social actors. Central to Schutz's analysis is the 'postulate of subjective interpretation' which requires that social scientific accounts have to treat social actors as conscious beings whose activities have meaning for them and others. The social reality in which action takes place is the outcome of the interpretations made and courses of action undertaken by social actors. The 'objects' which this postulate makes available for study within this intersubjective 'life world' of everyday life are presented to us as an objectified system of shared designations and expressive forms. It is a world of everyday life as lived and experienced through 'common sense' and displaying the 'natural attitude', that is, the attitude of the world of everyday life. Under this attitude the world is 'taken for granted'. Social actors do not question the meaningful structure of this world, do not theorise or philosophise about it, or doubt its existence: it is a world which is 'there' and dealt with in a practical manner. For example, in the course of our daily lives we have to take so many things for granted – for instance, that the sun will rise in the morning, that the cinema we plan to go to in the evening will still be there, that the work we left to do will still be on the desk tomorrow, that the car is still in the garage, that the road to work will not suddenly have changed direction, that the letter we posted yesterday will be delivered, and so on and so on – in order to construct the daily activities that we ordinarily engage in. This does not mean that things will always go to plan or that our expectations will not sometimes be confounded. We may discover that our car is not in the garage where it was left last night. But we do not conclude by this that its nature has been changed so that a car has some intermittent existence and flickers in and out of being, sometimes being there and sometimes not. We are more likely to make the usual assumption that the car remains in continuous existence and that if it is not where it was left then it is somewhere else, that it has been stolen or, perhaps, that it was actually left somewhere else and that we had temporarily forgotten. It is not something to theorise about or something which will provoke us to raise ontological questions about the nature of reality. The meaningful structure of the 'life world' is not questioned but taken for granted. The task within the 'natural attitude' is to live in the world as practical rather than theoretical or philosophical creatures.

The world has meaning because of the intentionality of consciousness. For most of the time, what persons are doing is self-evidently meaningful. Meanings are intersubjectively shared. We make sense of our own actions and those of others through a 'stock of knowledge' that is held in common, that we inherit and learn as members of society. Though such knowledge has the tonalities of our personal biography and is continually changing, its own intersubjective structure is familiar. As Husserl emphasised, we do not experience a stream of sense data as, for example, the logical positivists would have it, but experience objects as constituted for us in consciousness, such as cars, books, TVs, houses, Jon, bicycles, curries, and so on. The structure of this 'life world' is displayed through 'typifications' constructed out of whatever relevances arise from the actor's interests and purposes 'at hand'. As used by Schutz such typifications would include the universal and relatively stable as well as the more specific and changing.

As said, the primary world in which social actors live is an intersubjective one of everyday life, a world governed by the natural attitude with its pragmatic motives and interests. In addition, actors live in other worlds of 'finite provinces of meaning', such as those of art, religious experience, dreams, childhood, and so on, each with a particular cognitive style.[7] What Schutz means by this is not that we can simply imagine the world as we choose, but that each province of meaning has its own, though not unique in all respects, structure of relevances, and that the available 'stocks of knowledge' enable us to bestow 'factuality' in different ways. The paramount reality is, however, that of daily life. Of special concern to us is the world of scientific theory. This style is that of the disinterested observer who is only

> concerned with problems and solutions valid in their own right for every-
> one, at any place, and at any time, wherever and whenever certain conditions,
> from the assumptions of which he starts, prevail. The 'leap' into theoretical
> thought involves the resolution of the individual to suspend his subjective
> point of view.
>
> (Schutz 1962: 248)

The private and pragmatic concerns of everyday life are bracketed away; that is, put on one side as irrelevant for the duration of involvement in theoretical work. Sciences, both natural and social, adopt a theoretic attitude to their subject matter. They are not primarily concerned with practical consequences except as these are theoretically given. Scientific relevances are determined by the problem at hand and the procedures of the science concerned rather than those of everyday life. In the scientific attitude, as opposed to the requirements of the 'natural attitude', anything – save the existence of the external world itself – can be doubted and, accordingly, subject to investigation and analysis.

It is in this way that Schutz faces up to what he sees as the basic epistemological problem of social science, namely, how, as sciences of subjective meanings, are they possible? Like all sciences, they seek to make objective meaning claims, but in the case of the social sciences these have to be within the context of the human activity which has created them and which cannot be understood apart from these. Schutz's resolution of the difficulty is to argue that the social sciences must recognise that difference between social actors' experience of daily life and social actors as constituted as the objects of social science. This difference is required in order to make subjectivity available under the theoretic attitude. The social scientist is concerned with 'typical' schemes of actions, using simplified, abstracted and generalised versions of social actors, models which are 'lifeless fictions', 'constructs', 'ideal types', 'puppets' or 'homunculi' created by the social scientist. These models are constructed according to the postulates of logical consistency, subjective interpretation and adequacy. The first of these proposes that the construct must conform to the requirements of formal logic, the second that it must incorporate within it a model of the human mind and its typical contents such that the observed facts can be seen as the outcome of its operation. The third postulate suggests a principle of objectivity, namely, that the construct must be formulated in such a way as to be understandable to the actor using his or her own common sense.

It is the third postulate which addresses the problem which has been a major theme of this chapter, namely, the relationship between actors' concepts and those of the social scientist. Positivism's attempt to evade the socially grounded nature of knowledge by trying to formulate a neutral observation language created tensions between actors' conceptions and those of social science. And, of course, for some, Marx and Durkheim being the classic examples, this very disjuncture between the world as understood by actors and the world as discovered by the application of social science was seen as the expected outcome of such a science. Schutz, following Weber, wants to give actors' standards and concepts a much more salient role as a yardstick for the adequacy of social scientific understanding: a point which we shall develop in the next chapter in a discussion of Winch. The social scientist's interest and purpose is to display the meanings that enter into actors' worlds. Various devices, the 'ideal type', 'homunculi', or whatever, are important to this. 'Objectivity' and 'truth' are established within 'life worlds' and their socially organised settings and there is no question of one form of knowledge being absolutely superior to any other.

The important connection between Schutz's phenomenology and social research is the influence it has had on the origins of ethnomethodology as developed by Harold Garfinkel who, as Lazarsfeld tried to with positivism, sought to turn a philosophical doctrine into a methodology for social science.[8] Although Schutz shared the aspirations of his mentor, Husserl, of constructing a 'transcendental analytic' of knowledge through philosophical inquiry, ethnomethodology is focused on the empirical analysis of the practical reasonings through which members produce the common-sense features of social life. It is interested in the properties of intersubjectivity as these are exhibited by social actors in the course of their activities in the day-to-day world (see, e.g. Button 1991, Anderson and Sharrock 1986, Garfinkel 1967).

Conclusion

What we have tried to do in this chapter is review some of the social philosophies which have tried to come to terms with the fact that the members of society themselves live within a world which has sense and meaning for them. It is recognition of this which presents the problem of the relationship between the sense of the world for social actors and social scientific concepts: a tension between the relationship between the social sciences and their subject matter. Research methods, where it might be said that philosophical conceptions get their hands dirty, as it were, reflect these tensions since their ability to do the job required of them by empirical researchers depends, in its turn, on the researcher's own commitments to one or the other of these philosophies.

As we saw in connection with the critique of positivist research methods earlier in this chapter, the argument is as much about the fundamental issue of the subject matter of social science as it is about the validity of the techniques and methods of social research itself. Though there is a case to be made that even by their own standards such methods do not work, there is also the equally important issue of the nature of the phenomena to be investigated and this will, or ought to, have a considerable bearing upon the means of investigation and the kind of knowledge that we require. Although interpretative philosophies of social science, as we have termed them, reject the positivist conception of science, not all of them by any means abandon the idea that social science needs secure foundations as well as the means of endowing intellectual rigour to inquiries. It is in this latter regard that we can understand Weber's treatment of *verstehen* and the 'ideal type', for example; that is, as ways of making the messy concreteness of the sociohistorical world amenable to rigorous empirical investigation.

As indicated earlier, a major preoccupation of the philosophies discussed in this chapter is with the grounds of social scientific knowledge and, especially in these cases, engaging with the fact that not only does it have to come to terms with a world which is already pre-interpreted but also with the fact that these interpretations are themselves subject to social and historical circumstances and change. It is this kind of conception which raises the spectre of the relativism of social scientific knowledge. If knowledge is socially determined, then on what grounds can we make the claim that social scientific knowledge is superior to that of lay social actors? What gives social science, if anything does, its privileged status as knowledge? For hermeneutics, especially in the hands of Gadamer, knowledge was irretrievably tied to tradition – this is the ontological condition which makes understanding and interpretation possible – and, accordingly, there is nothing for it to be relative to. Transcending our own horizons is an endless process of interpretation. Habermas proposes a therapeutic stance in which the presumptions of our knowledge and interpretations are exposed to critical glance and, through this, achieve a greater possibility of human emancipation. Somewhat earlier and less optimistically, Weber argued that all sciences, the natural and the social, are partial: a partiality governed by our social and investigative interests. But this does not mean that we abandon all aspirations to scholarly rigour. It is in the exercise of strict scholarly standards that we achieve objectivity rather than by slavishly following methodological recipes. Phenomenology, on the other hand, did not abandon the quest for the foundations of knowledge. Instead it sought them in the structure of consciousness, that is, the deep-seated ways in which our experience was organised and which enabled it to be shaped by social and historical conditions. By stripping these latter away it sought to uncover the basic elements which constituted the very possibility of knowledge.

It would be fair to say that much of the work within the above traditions – with the exception of ethnomethodology which, in any case, only takes selectively from phenomenology – remains philosophical rather than empirical in character.[9] The research methods typically associated with qualitative research, such as participant observation and ethnography and, more recently, discourse analysis tend to have developed independently of these particular philosophical schools. The former methods where a researcher goes 'into the field' to observe in 'real time' the social activities of a community or other group of people, arose in anthropology and came to be incorporated into sociology mainly by way of symbolic interactionism and which only later acquired philosophical credentials from the work of G.H. Mead (see e.g. Mead 1934; see also Plummer 1991).

One of the major consequences of the attempt to take seriously the fact that the members of society live in a world of meaning, is to bring language to the fore as a topic of social scientific philosophising. In the next two chapters we will address some of the issues arising from this attention to language.

Notes

1. This term is owed to Alfred Schutz (1962).
2. There are various ways in which this is done but these differences do not affect the argument being made here.
3. Cicourel (1964: 198). See also Pawson (1989) for a critique of occupational rating scales.
4. For a selection of articles on the sociology of knowledge, as this viewpoint came to be known, see Curtis and Petras (1970).
5. This is not dissimilar to the arguments about the nonexperimental character of social research as recognised by many positivists and, in Pearson's hands, the justification for correlational methods. However, generally positivists would not have given anything like the same weight that Weber did to the role of the investigator in selecting and devising structuring schemes.
6. Weber maintained that intellectual inquiry is value-relative but also insisted on ethical neutrality in scientific activities. Insisting on a distinction between fact and values, he strongly argued that there can be no question of one value being 'scientifically' shown to be superior to any other. The choice among values is a matter of decision and faith. Indeed, he complained against university teachers who pressed their political views from their academic positions as an abuse of their reputation and authority. See Lassman and Velody (1989) and Hughes et al. (1995: ch. 3).
7. Schutz never fully worked out the typology of domains, though he is clear that they shade into one another.
8. What we mean by this is a way of thinking rather than a set of techniques. Although a main concern of Lazarsfeld was to develop a collection of techniques for empirical social research, importantly this involved elaborating a way of thinking about social scientific problems so that they could be empirically investigated. For its own good reasons, ethnomethodology is uninterested in developing techniques of the kind that Lazarsfeld played a large part in developing.
9. Another exception here is Weber, of course.

CHAPTER 7

Language, reality and rationality

If, as in the previous chapter, it is argued that social phenomena are predominantly 'meaningful' in nature, and are constituted through language, then the question arises as to whether the adoption of such approaches will run the risk of falling into subjectivism, idealism and relativism? Given the conception of meaning and language as media for 'reality defining' or 'reality constituting', does this not mean that the essential connection between language and meanings, on the one hand, and an external reality, on the other, has been broken, that reality has become internal to meaning and language, and has no link to anything which exists outside of language and meaning, such as a natural world? We will examine two sets of views, those of Wittgenstein and his follower, Peter Winch on language, and those of Thomas Kuhn on the rationality of scientific progress, both of which are major sources of the anxieties just mentioned. These anxieties have also provoked counter-arguments attempting to reassert what they deem a necessary realism about the existence of an external, material or natural world and, thereby, seeking to reclaim some of the ground lost in the landslide swing against positivism while accommodating to many of the objections set against it. Roy Bhaskar's 'transcendental realism' illustrates this point of view.

One of the results of the reaction against the positivist project has been the rise to prominence of epistemological preoccupations.[1] The previous chapter has dealt with some attempts to treat the issue of meaning predominantly in methodological and sociological terms, that is, addressing the question as to how a sociology which purports to study phenomena which are meaningful in nature can come to grips with those phenomena in an intellectually rigorous but not positivistic nor necessarily scientific way. However, while such approaches may not have intended to do so, they have served, at least in part, to precipitate a movement of epistemological matters to centre stage. Such worries will be the main focus of the next two chapters. The rejection of the positivist project was inspired by, or led to, the acceptance of many different kinds of 'antipositivist' stance, in particular 'antifoundationalist' or 'antiformalist' positions.

One of the consequences of denying science a privileged position would be a rejection of the idea that science could be the bearer of certainty about the nature of reality. The necessity of certainties was part of a philosophical conception called 'foundationalism' which held that we could only have confidence in our knowledge if we could identify *some* certainties. Knowledge was like a building which could only stand if it rested on secure and unshakeable foundations. For knowledge, such foundations would be absolute certainties. Therefore, and as we sketched out in Chapter 1, a quest was launched at the very beginning of modern philosophy for a set of such certainties, a set of propositions would could not be doubted. Thus, the notion of foundations is connected to the problem of scepticism for, of course, those absolute certainties must be such as to withstand the most persistent and thoroughgoing doubtings of the sceptical challenger. As is known, the only such certainties Descartes could come up with were the existence of God and 'I think therefore I am'. However, this was enough in that from these initial certainties, he could then deduce other things and they, being logically derived, would share the truth of the premises from which they were drawn. The empiricists, with whom positivism was associated, looked for certainty in sense experience, that is, experience which we know directly. We have our sense experiences and need to make no inferences to know them so, accordingly, we do not run the risk of questionable inferences about them. When we discuss W.V.O. Quine in the following chapter, we associate him with the term 'postempiricism' partly because of the way he gives up on the possibility of certainties of the empiricist kind.

So, giving up on doctrines such as positivism could be, and was seen as, also giving up on foundationalist aspirations and, for many, adopting antifoundationalist positions. Rejecting positivism because it has a foundationalist character is often seen as implying the adoption of the opposite view that there are no foundations. However, is this a move toward scepticism? Is this not a migration to the view that there is no such thing as foundations for knowledge and, therefore, that there can never be a true, final, definitive, categorical knowledge? Must there not always be room for doubt, and must we therefore accept that our most cherished convictions might be just as misguided as those of our historical predecessors? Should we not, therefore, withdraw to a position of much greater humility and accept that our own beliefs, including the much vaunted achievements of science, are perhaps no better, no more certain or secure than those of anyone else? This, then, is another route by which relativism begins to appear as persuasive.

Another shift which has taken place in philosophy during this century, and which has risen to prominence in the latter half of it, is what has been termed the 'linguistic turn' and is reflected in all the arguments we will review in the remaining chapters. The nature and role of language has become the contentious focus for so many of the main issues in philosophy, including epistemological ones. Whether or not we can know anything becomes, in prominent part, a question as to whether the expressions in our language (in which our thought, theories and beliefs are expressed) can possibly capture the intrinsic nature of reality. Relativist positions must deny this. They must, their critics argue, at least deny that language can know any independent external reality. If different beliefs, expressed in different linguistic forms, are all equally valid, then they cannot all be identifying one and the same reality. Hence, relativism implies that language cannot be a means to knowledge of an *external* reality. Relativists may argue that the idea of 'language-independent reality' is a valid one by holding that reality is produced, constituted or constructed *through* language, and that therefore one can know reality, but it is not and can never be a *language-and-thought-independent reality*. Thus, the idea that the nature of a reality characterised by language must depend upon the structure of the reality it characterises and that therefore there must be a unique form that such a language can possibly take, is almost reversed by the claim that the nature of reality derives from language and that the language – or, more strictly, the users of the language – 'constitute' or 'construct' reality. Therefore, there can be as many different realities as there are different structures of language and belief. Talk of 'multiple realities' – though not in the same sense that Schutz identifies these – becomes possible and the relativist implications clear: what may be true in one reality is independent of and different from what is true in another.

We want to address some of these issues by an examination of the arguments contained in the work of two principal figures largely responsible for precipitating debates about relativism: Peter Winch's *The Idea of a Social Science* (Winch 1990, 1977) and Thomas Kuhn's *The Structure of Scientific Revolutions* (1996). These two books initiated debates which have been fiercely fought ever since. Both are accused of engendering relativistic positions by, in effect, undervaluing the rationality of science. We will also follow up some themes in Chapter 5 in connection with the positivist conception of the nature of social research and also relevant to problems of the relationship between lay and social scientific concepts.

First, however, we want to discuss in more detail some of the consequences of bringing language much more prominently to the fore in methodological debates.

The foregrounding of language

The idea of action as a phenomenon deeply embedded in the use of ordinary language strongly argues for a view of language as constitutive of the social world. It also implies that actions can only be identified through actors' own concepts in accordance with actors' views of the world. Further, it implies a sharp ontological distinction between the physical and the human world and, not surprisingly, this is a distinction which might well have serious epistemological consequences. In this latter regard, for example, Winch states that while both the natural and the social sciences bring systems of concepts to bear on their respective subject matters, what the natural scientist studies has

an existence independent of these concepts. There existed electrical storms and thunder long before there were human beings to form concepts of them . . . it does not make sense to suppose that human beings might have been issuing commands and obeying them before they came to form the concept of command and obedience.

(Winch 1990: 125)

As we discussed in the previous chapter, the members of society have their own conceptions of what they are doing and the 'conceptions according to which we normally think of social events . . . enter into social life itself and not merely into the observer's description of it' (Winch 1990: 95).

The thesis that the identification of actions must necessarily be in the language of the social actor is seen as having very serious consequences for the status of knowledge about the social. What is being proposed is more than simply urging social researchers to investigate the ideas and beliefs of those whom they study. The argument is about the nature of the concepts used by social science to explain its phenomena. Not only is the identification of actions dependent upon concepts employed by social actors in the course of their lives, but so too are the criteria of evidence, proof, rationality, and suchlike relevant to the making and assessment of such identifications. Thus, to be able to see that someone carving a piece of wood is engaged in a religious act requires attributing to that person the concept 'religion', the possession of which is the ability to use that concept properly and make distinctions between this and other activities.[2] Conceptions of reality and how it may be studied, while independent of any one individual's views, are dependent on the human activities concerned which, in their turn, must be defined by those who do them. This, it can be argued, is as true for science as it is for religion, for art, for raising families, for politics, and any other human activity.

These arguments have a special force in regard to the study of cultures other than our own. Such studies face the problem of categorising the behaviours that are witnessed. What, to use the previous example, is a man doing carving a piece of wood? Is it an economic activity in which he is engaged? Is it an act of worship? A political gesture? Simply a way of passing the time?[3] The problem is, as Schutz points out, that activities may look alike but have different meanings within their respective cultures.[4] Whether a pattern of activity is 'a war dance, a barter trade, the reception of a friendly ambassador, or something else' (Schutz 1963: 237) only the participants themselves can say.

It is observations such as these which have served to raise the issue of relativism. A culture different from our own can be seen as a distinctive, self-justifying realm of discourse with its own logic and standards of rationality in terms of which it must be described and judged. For some this implies an incommensurability of schemes of thought in that since our own schemes of thought, including that of science, is rooted in our culture it cannot constitute an absolutely independent position from which to understand and investigate other cultures. Such a radical relativism arises from the ideas of the linguists Edward Sapir and Benjamin Lee Whorf who have been construed as arguing that differences among languages reflect differences in metaphysics or 'world views'. This thesis is not simply about differences in the vocabulary of different languages but about the way in which vocabularies are organised by their grammars and, thus, organise the forms of thought of the speakers of the language. The grammar of a language is then seen as a theory of reality. Different ways of viewing the world are expressed in different classificatory systems which are indicated by differences in grammar and, in this way, it is grammar which determines the thought and the way in which the world is seen and constituted. There is no way of moving outside of language to determine the truth value of 'world views'. We cannot rank one 'world view', as a complete theory of reality, against another. Though it might be argued that Apache, for example, in turning nouns such as 'sun set' into verbs 'sun-set' better displays the processual nature of the event than does the English noun, this is no licence to judge Apache _in toto_ as superior to English. Grammatical structures are underdetermined by the way the world is. The world and its words can be organised in a variety of ways with no one absolutely superior to one another (see e.g. Whorf 1956, Horton and Finnegan 1973).

What we have, once again, are a number of issues which turn on the foregrounding of language in social inquiry: issues such as relativism, the nature of social science and its relationship to lay conceptions and, of course, the important issue of the nature of language itself and its relationship to reality. The work of Peter Winch is particularly apt to explore some of these issues in more depth and, as an essential part of this, to outline Ludwig Wittgenstein's treatment of the relationship between language and reality since this is important to understanding Winch's arguments.

Language and meaning

Winch's _The Idea of a Social Science_ was an attempt to bring Wittgenstein's philosophy to bear critically on the conception of social studies as science. Some of these arguments have already been reviewed in the previous chapter. Taken fully but succinctly, Wittgenstein sought to put an end to philosophy as traditionally practised, doubting whether it had any genuine, serious problems that could be considered in terms of a search for genuine, general knowledge. Thus, while he thought that the problems that philosophy addressed were often serious and deep, such as those to do with the meaning of life and of ethics, he did not think that there were any _theoretical_, and therefore philosophical, answers to such questions. Insofar as they could be answered, this could only be through spiritual or ethical, not philosophical, searching. He argued that the impression that philosophy's problems were deep, solemn and fundamental _theoretical_ questions was the result of confusions about the way in which language worked. Wittgenstein sought, therefore, to persuade philosophers to take a different view of their dependence on language.

One of the foremost traditions of philosophical thought was consideration of the question of whether and how it was possible to speak truthfully about the nature of the world, of external reality, and, in pursuing this issue Wittgenstein argued that the understanding of the nature of language became distorted in two important ways. First, language was considered exclusively in terms of the role of making factual or empirical statements. Second, as a result it was commonly thought that the heart of language was the naming relationship which provided a link between language and the world, for it represented a direct connection between a word and something nonlinguistic, external to language. So strong was this conception that it was sometimes thought that the meaning of a word was the thing the word stood for.[5]

For simplicity's sake, Wittgenstein's later work can be conceived as a fundamental reworking of the idea of how words get their meaning. He did not want to deny that words stand for things – sometimes! He did not deny that there is a difference, for example, between the dog, Fido himself, and the name of the dog, 'Fido'. Nor did he want to deny that the name 'Fido' does indeed stand for the dog Fido. But this is just another way of saying that 'Fido' is the dog's name. What he did want to question was that the dog Fido was the *meaning* of the word 'Fido' and, associatedly, deny that the naming relationship as featured in language could play the role that philosophers had traditionally wanted to assign it, that is, of ensuring a primal connection between our language and the world. Nor did he want to deny that words do talk, so to speak, 'about the world', though he did think that asking about the 'relationship between language and reality' was a very unhelpful – in fact, counterproductive – way of posing the problem.

Wittgenstein's own position can be summed up as the 'autonomy of grammar', a view which drastically undercut the more standardly accepted, and fundamental assumption, that it is the nature of reality which determines the meanings of our words. As we advance to the debate over Winch, it will be seen that Wittgenstein's critics are often reasserting precisely the view which Wittgenstein sought to undermine.

If one is concerned about the nature of the relationship between language, on the one hand, and the external world, on the other, then the naming relationship is likely to be seen to have a key role. Naming seems to be a direct point of contact between the two phenomena that need connecting, the word (the name) and a thing-in-the-world, that is, the thing that the name stands for: hence a theory that the meaning of a name is the thing that it stands for. The fact that names can be given to things suggests that if the meaning of the word is the thing that it stands for, then the meaning of the word is determined by the nature of the thing the word stands for. If the meaning of 'Fido' is the dog, Fido, then the meaning of the word 'Fido' is determined by the nature of the dog Fido himself. Thus, words are names, and their meanings determined by the nature of the reality to which they refer. The fact that we can make true statements about the world is assured by the fact that our language reflects the nature, the structure of reality.

Part of Wittgenstein's rejection of the above view – which he himself held in the first half of his intellectual career – involved pointing out some of its more transparent absurdities. If Fido, the dog, is the meaning of the name 'Fido', then we should have to say, when Fido was born, that the meaning of the word 'Fido' had been born and, when the dog died, that the meaning of the word 'Fido' had died. This, and vastly more sophisticated arguments of Wittgenstein's, challenged the view that words get their meanings from the things that they stand for. In which case, then, how do words get their meaning? They get them, Wittgenstein argued, from language itself.

The meaning of a word is its position within a complex. It is tempting to say that the meaning of a word derives from its position within a system, for it is easy and common to talk about language as a system. Wittgenstein, however, is insistent that language is not a system, certainly not in any strong sense. He likened a language to a city which had grown over many years: it makes up a whole but is composed of zones, districts, areas which are more or less independent of each other and which differ considerably in character as between old, crowded inner-city areas and neatly arranged, spacious suburbs and industrial zones, and so on. Hence, a city is a complex but not a system, and much the same applies to language according to Wittgenstein.[6] The meaning of a word is given by its position in a complex and the part that it can play in combination with other words that we use and with the things that we do.

A key move in Wittgenstein's displacement of the naming theory was a reconsideration of the naming relationship. It seems, for example, easy to understand how a point of contact between the world and language is made by naming, by the attachment of a word to a specific thing as its name. Thus, learning a language could be done just by pointing out the connection of the name to the thing. One shows, for example, a small child an apple and pronounces the name 'apple' as one does so. However, it is not quite so obvious as it seems just what connection is being made here. How, for one, is the child to grasp that when the word 'apple' is pronounced what is being done here is the giving of a name for the thing? Suppose one pointed at a picture of an apple and shouted 'Run!', would that be giving a name for a thing, would the child have learned the correct lesson?

The trouble with the view of language as made up of names for things, Wittgenstein concluded, is that it overlooked the otherwise familiar fact that a language has different kinds of words. Only some words are names. 'Run!' is an injunction, not a name. Thus, in order for people correctly to learn the name of something by having it pointed out to them and the name pronounced they must comprehend that the word being spoken is intended to function as a name. They have to be able to grasp what kind of word is being used and that, in this case, the word is a name in order to see that the object being pointed to is the kind of thing that the word names. Indeed, they have to grasp more than this. The words 'Fido' and 'dog' are both names for the creature in the corner, so the child who is being taught the words must grasp how the name is to function, whether as the name of a kind of animal or as the proper name of this particular creature. These are provided through the communicative link between the child and the teacher, through the way in which the latter sets up and carries out the teaching situation. In other words, the capacity to connect language with the world presupposes social relations between people. This, Wittgenstein intimated, shows that a grasp on the organisation of language comes prior to the making of the particular naming connections, the connections between words and the world, and that the name–object link cannot fulfil the role as the foundation to language. Naming is one kind of role that words can play, but it is only one role, and a language is a collection of different kinds of words: an arrangement which allocates them different roles. It is only if a given word already has a role as a name that we can see, when a thing is pointed out, that it is being pointed out as the thing named by the word.

To clarify the force of the argument Wittgenstein made an analogy with games, treating words as akin to pieces in a game. Thus, a chess piece such as a 'king' is what it is by virtue of the part that it plays in a complex of activities. To explain to someone what a 'king' is, is in part to teach them the game of chess. One needs to describe something of the complex of the game of chess, about squares, pieces, that it is played by two sides, that the players take turns, and so on in order that someone would have an idea of how the king fitted in with other pieces, how its capacity to move on squares is specific to it, and how it relates to other pieces. If we have no difficulty in understanding this example then why should we strain at the idea that giving someone the meaning of a word is akin to describing the part that the word plays in a complex of activities? Explaining the meaning of the word 'king' in chess involves, after all, explaining to someone that it is the name of a piece in a game, that the pieces are differentiated by the kind of moves they can make, and so on.

Wittgenstein's most decisive move was to argue that the meaning of words is their place within the language, and that their meaning derives from the role of words in people's activities, as he had done in the case of children learning words discussed earlier. Words develop in conjunction with activities and acquire their meaning because of the way in which they fit into activities. However, if this is the case then it follows that the language we have is contingent on the history we have and the activities we happen to have acquired through that history. We might, for example, never have had the game of chess, or it could have had a very different history. We could have had a very different history in all kinds of ways which would mean that our language would also have been very different. This Wittgenstein not only accepts, but insists upon. However, although we might have little difficulty in accepting such a conclusion in respect of games and other human activities that we invent ourselves – after all, throughout the world there are a huge variety of games which have their roots in specific cultures – can we so readily accept it in reference to the natural world? We may happily accept that if we did not have chess then we would have no words for the pieces or for the moves, if no soccer then no use for words such as 'striker', 'goalkeeper', 'goal', and so on. But do we want to accept the implication that if our history had been very different we might not have any word for planets, say, or for electrons, or for magnetism, or for silicon, and that, therefore, they would not have existed? Whether or not planets exist cannot depend upon whether or not we have a word for them. The nature of a planet is what it is, surely not something that results from the ways in which human beings arrange their activities? The planet Mars was up there in the sky long before we had the word 'planet' or 'Mars'. Accordingly, if Wittgenstein seems to have found his way around some of the problems in the philosophy of language, he appears to have fallen into deep trouble with his account of the connection between language and the world. If the ways in which our words name, identify and describe things entirely depends upon, and derives from, the forms of human activities, then it is at best coincidental that the ways in which we talk about things in the world relates to the way things are.

The anxiety expressed about Wittgenstein's arguments reiterated, of course, just the kind of views he was trying to reject, namely, that it is the nature of things in the world which imposes some sort of constraint on what our words can mean. It was his denial of the view that the meaning of words was imposed on them by the nature of the things they talked about which comprised his above-mentioned argument for 'the autonomy of grammar'.[7] The organisation of our language originates in the needs and requirements of our social life and its constituent activities, and is not imposed upon language by the structure of the world. But, if we accept the 'autonomy of grammar' how are we to be assured that there is any connection between language and the true nature of the world. Wittgenstein's response to this anxiety was forcefully brought to the attention of social science by Winch, though his application of Wittgenstein's arguments would stimulate rather than calm these anxieties.

Revisiting rules, reasons and causes

It was in the context of his efforts to apply Wittgenstein's arguments about the relationship of language to reality to issues in the social sciences that Winch put forward arguments about rules, causes and reasons, some of which we have met in the previous chapter. Here we want to relate these more closely to wider matters.

Following Wittgenstein, Winch argued that the meaning of words derives from their place in people's practical and social activities. Accordingly, the meaning of the philosophically troublesome word 'reality', for one crucial example, must derive from the activities within which it is used. Just as 'king' has very different meanings when used as the title of a ruler of a people and when used as the name of a chess piece, though not utterly unrelated ones, so the word 'reality' has significantly different, though again not totally unrelated, meanings when used, for example, in law, in science, and religion respectively. It makes no sense, according to Winch, to ask the question whether language relates to reality as a *general* question, for what the question asks, what the question could possibly mean, depends upon the context in which it is raised. The very idea of 'relation to reality' is different in different spheres of life. So, asking about reality in the sense of asking about what could possibly exist or be the case, and how the question of whether or not it is the case could be settled, is a quite different matter in religion than it is in science. The two sets of activities are very disparate and, for Winch, it is a regrettable fact that in our modern world, it has often come to be thought that there is only one form that questions about the nature of reality may take, namely, 'the fascination science has for us' making it 'easy for us to adopt its scientific form as a paradigm against which to measure the intellectual respectability of other modes of discourse' (Winch 1977: 18). It is Winch's dissent from this assumption that leads to his other arguments.

In social science this kind of problem looms large, though it is not only to be found in such contexts, in reference to other cultures, particularly cultures very different from our own. It is in such comparisons that we are likely to find 'strange', maybe even exotic, beliefs and social practices which we find difficult to understand. This is the nub of the anthropologist's problem: how do we come to understand an alien society? It is also a problem, as we saw in the previous chapter, for understanding historical societies which have long ago ceased to exist. In fact, the problem is a collection of problems one of which has a direct bearing on the issue of the relationship of language to reality, especially when, as in the example that Winch uses, there is a conflict between what our science says exists and the beliefs and practices of another culture.

As an illustration of his arguments Winch uses a report of an African tribe's 'witchcraft' practices by the anthropologist, E. Evans-Pritchard (1965). Winch objects to a small but important part of Evans-Pritchard's otherwise very sympathetic report in which he attempts to judge the rationality of a magical practice by invidiously using scientific criteria. For Winch this is entirely inappropriate and akin to trying to score a soccer match according to the scoring conventions of tennis. In its boldest and most basic form, the difference between Winch and Evans-Pritchard is that the latter holds that 'witchcraft' is a failed attempt at the kind of understanding claimed on behalf of science, while the former argues that religious understanding is quite different to scientific understanding and not a perverted form of it.[8]

For Winch, as we have seen, the word 'reality' and the expression 'corresponds to reality' have different meanings when employed in the comparative contexts of science and religion. It is not as if, in each context, people say things about how the world might be without any idea of how they might find out if what they say is true or not. For example, in science practitioners hold to the idea that one of the important ways of finding things out is through empirical research of the appropriate kind. Winch wants to argue that it is not as though we can, in respect of science, say that science asserts various things about the world and then ask whether using empirical methods is a good, or indeed, the best or only way of ascertaining whether the things said by science do correspond with reality. In science, the expression 'corresponds with reality' effectively equates with 'has passed experimental tests' or 'is confirmed by empirical study'.[9] Thus, when scientists claim that they have established that a certain theory or hypothesis has been 'found to correspond to reality', they mean that it has now been given empirical support, been subjected to experimental validation, and so on.

By contrast, in religion, practitioners say things about how the world is, that suffering is or is not part of God's plan, for example, or that salvation comes from good works, or that bad luck is due to witchcraft. But in making such claims the religious person is not asking whether or not these claims have passed experimental tests or other form of empirical assessment. Rather, the person seeks to determine whether this is indeed God's plan by, for example, praying for a sign, studying the scriptures, turning to guidance from a religious leader, or consulting an oracle. Accordingly, what religious people mean when they say that a particular occurrence accords with God's plan – that their conception of it accords with reality – is that it has been confirmed in the scriptures or revealed in prayer or prophesied in the teachings of a guru.

It is the failure to mark this difference in meaning which the identical words 'corresponds to reality' have when pronounced in different contexts which is, on Winch's account, the key to Evans-Pritchard's misunderstanding of Azande 'witchcraft' practices. It leads him misguidedly to talk about Azande beliefs as though their correspondence with reality was a matter of subjecting them to experimental or empirical tests of the kind used in science. The notion of 'corresponds to reality', as this is found in the tribe's way of life, means something very different. In this context it does not mean 'subject to empirical and statistical test' but, rather, 'has been confirmed by the oracle'.

Two things may be called the 'same' or 'different' only with reference to a set of criteria which lay down what is to be regarded as a relevant difference. When the 'things' in question are purely physical the criteria appealed to will of course be those of the observer. But when one is dealing with intellectual (or, indeed, any kind of social) 'things', that is not so. For their *being* intellectual or social . . . in character depends entirely upon their belonging in a certain way to a system of ideas or modes of living. It is only by reference to the criteria governing that system of ideas or mode of life that they have any existence as intellectual or social events. It follows that if the sociological investigator wants to regard them *as* social events . . . he has to take seriously the criteria which are applied for distinguishing 'different' kinds of actions and identifying the 'same' actions within the way of life he is studying. It is not open to him to arbitrarily impose his own standards from without. In so far as he does so, the events he is studying lose altogether their character as social events.

(Winch 1990: 108)

It is important to note that Winch's argument is not about the respective truth of science and religion, or any other sets of beliefs, and it does not leave him holding that witchcraft is 'just as good' or 'just as true' as science. His concern is with how we ought to 'understand' activities, in this case Azande witchcraft, rather than offering arguments about whether religious or scientific ideas are true or not. By trying to understand the tribe's witchcraft as a misguided form of science, Evans-Pritchard had, Winch alleged, misinterpreted some crucial features of the witchcraft practices.[10] This, for Winch, is a widespread misconception, and one which is at the very root of much social science, namely, the thought that science is the only basis for understanding. The inevitable result of this latter tendency is, again for Winch, not a better understanding of human sociality but a seriously distorted view of it.

As we have pointed out throughout, one of the distinctive features of science, and one of its most philosophically troublesome ideas, is its concern with regularities. For positivism, universal laws were the objective of natural scientific research and, accordingly, the longer term objective of social science. Indeed, much of the development of what here we have referred to as positivistic research methods, the social survey, the hypothetico-deductive model of explanation, measurement, and so on, was motivated by a need to build an apparatus which was capable of at least contributing to general theories. As we have seen, this turned out to be less than straightforward. For Winch, however, while certainly not denying that there are regularities in social life, the important question concerns their nature. For positivistic conceptions of science the only regularities of interest to science are causal ones. In which case what is needed is a social science which provides an account of social life in terms of a set of general, causal relationships. To give an explanation, on this view, is to identify a cause. By contrast, Winch wants to suggest that there are other kinds of regularities found in social life other than causal ones, and other kinds of explanation that can be given for social activities.[11]

As discussed in the previous chapter, one important kind of regularity to be found in social life is rule-governed regularity. Behaviour at traffic lights was the example used but the list could be extended, practically indefinitely, to include such things as timetables, queues, work activities, court procedures, conversations, games, marriage, obedience to the law, financial transactions, and many, many more. Rule-governed regularities are, again as we have seen, not like causal ones. Explaining something by reference to a rule is a very different affair to explaining something by reference to a cause.[12]

Many of the problems which provoke puzzlement about human conduct, and the possible explanations for it, do not arise from our lack of understanding as to the cause of some action, but from the unintelligibility of that action. We cannot see what action it is, or what the point of it is, or why someone would possibly think of doing it, and so on. And here is where the cogency of the 'witchcraft' example lies. The feature which puzzled Evans-Pritchard, among many others, is how these people could possibly believe in the power of witchcraft given that, from a European's point of view, it patently could not work. Accordingly, Evans-Pritchard's problem was that of trying to 'see the sense' of these practices and, whatever the pros and cons between Winch and Evans-Pritchard on this point, the nature of the issue they argue illustrates Winch's point about the kinds of problems a would-be social science would have to confront which are inappropriately approached with the manner of the scientist.

In simple terms, actions, like words, derive their sense from their location in a complex, in this case a pattern of activities. One cannot, for example, 'score a goal' without the notion of soccer, a goal, a goalkeeper, and so on; 'trade' without customers, the relationships of buying and selling; 'vote' without elections, elected offices, and so on. A word may be unintelligible to us because we are not familiar with the language of which it is a part, so too someone's action may be puzzling because we are unfamiliar with the activity complex of which it is a part. We may be puzzled about what two people are doing hunched over a table if we are ignorant of the idea of chess. Even if we are familiar with the game we may well be baffled by a player's move if the player is operating at the grandmaster level and we have only a beginner's familiarity with the game. So, for many of things which puzzle us about people's activities, clearing up our incomprehension is to describe the complex within which the puzzling action is located, laying out the connection between the action and the organised complex so as to make apparent how the activity fits into that complex, that is, how the grandmaster's move comprises, in chess terms, a fiendishly clever step. The root fact, for Winch, is that much of the work a would-be social science might actually do is more like explaining grandmaster chess to the beginner than it is like scientists trying to discover a new causal law.[13]

This means that there is a profound difference between a would-be social science and successful natural sciences. The natural scientist can observe relations among phenomena and then set out to develop a theory which, relative to the aims and requirements of scientific work, best accommodate the observed patterns among the phenomena of interest. Indeed, 'for the purpose of science' can be regarded as a criterion which can govern natural scientists' work and one which allows them to classify and measure phenomena with maximum intellectual convenience. Not so with the would-be social science. Explaining the puzzling activities of the Azande or as-yet-to-be-identified chess players is not seeking an explanation which posits causal connections between phenomena but is constrained to try to understand the connections which are, as it were, built into the activity in question. It is trying, to put it another way, to understand relations which are intrinsic to the activity. Someone who wants to understand what chess players are doing wants to capture the sense that their activity has for them, to identify the connections that they see between the various moves they make. As we argued in the previous chapter this does not require 'trying to see into the minds' of the people involved but trying to understand the connections that the participants make because of their participation in the complex of activity, connections which are part of that activity. In the example of chess, we do not come to understand the activity by giving someone a psychological account of the players, but by giving them some explanation of the rules and principles of chess. We do not, to return to a previous example, discover why a car has stopped at a red traffic light by getting into the car and interviewing the driver, but by coming to understand the rules and conventions of traffic lights. Explaining in social science is not by any means a matter of theorising in the sense of building a general theoretical scheme. Rather, it is a matter of describing the complex of activity to which a given action belongs and this is often a matter of specifying the rules which are constituent of it: ones which are already known to the people doing the activities, for they themselves are acting in terms of these rules.

Identifying rules and other cultures

A major question which arises is how one can come to identify the rules which make up a complex of action. It is one thing to appreciate the force of the arguments here by using examples, such as chess or traffic light behaviour, which are familiar to most people because they are examples taken from our own culture. But what about cultures about which we have little familiarity? How can we really understand alien witchcraft practices, irrespective of whether we think them to be true or not, when they belong to a culture which is very different to our own, part of this difference being witchcraft practices?

Some critics of Winch have interpreted his arguments as though he were saying that the only way to understand a complex of activity is to be part of that activity, thus making it impossible to understand a culture very different to our own (see Hollis and Lukes 1982). But this criticism overlooks the fact that Winch's argument with Evans-Pritchard is over the proper or correct understanding of a particular, very different culture, not over the general question of whether understanding another culture is ever possible. Although Winch argues that there are special limiting cases, such as mathematics and music, where to be able to understand the activities involved requires that one be a competent participant in the activity, his main point is that one comes to understand another culture by learning from the members of that culture. One learns the rules of that culture, or a given activity complex, by being taught them, and one can often learn many of these without becoming a member of the group who engage in the activity in just the same way that an anthropologist does.

Once again, a model of social science inquiry based on purportedly scientific conceptions is challenged, namely, the model of the observer recording the occurrences of a phenomenon and seeking to understand them through hypothesising theories. The *actual* practices of social researchers, even when using questionnaires or interviews, is more akin to that of operating as an apprentice to an instructor. They learn, in other words, not by any specifically scientific method but in much the same way that anyone might learn by having things explained to and clarified for them by those who are already familiar with the activity. What is learned does not derive so much from what the social researcher has devised by way of scientific method but from what can be taken from the people being studied and adding this to our own understanding. We may not, in many ways we cannot possibly, ourselves engage in the authentic practices of Azande witchcraft, but we can, nonetheless, through study of them extend our own understanding, stretch the boundaries of our own thought to accommodate a wider understanding of what it is possible for human beings rationally to do. We may not come to understand the Azande better than they do themselves but we understand them better than we did before.

Once again what we have here is a very different conception of the nature of social science and social research from that proposed by positivistic science. Although Winch does not wish entirely to preclude causal analysis of the kind typical of natural science, his argument suggests that this is not likely to solve many of the major problems that puzzle us. Instead, what these need is the descriptive explication of a complex of activities rather than any attempt to identify causes. These arguments, along with related ones discussed in the previous chapter, ally strongly with the view that there is a sharp divide between the natural and the social sciences, a divide which hangs upon the fact that social actors already live in a world which has meaning for them and it is out of this that many of the puzzles for social research arise, puzzles which are not resolvable by theorising or causal analyses.

Now we want to turn to another set of arguments which also raised the spectre of relativism by, according to many of its interpreters, challenging the rationality of science through a study of the development of the natural sciences themselves.

The Kuhnian turn

Despite his own protestations to the contrary, Kuhn was commonly understood as putting forward a relativist and irrational account of science and, eventually, denying that science could make any kind of contact with an 'objective' reality.

The central part of Kuhn's story puts forward an account of the history of science as involving substantial discontinuities rather than, as previous accounts had it and as we discussed in Chapter 4, an evolutionary progression toward better and better theories. Briefly, science is characterised by periods of revolution in which previously dominant research and theories are thrown out in favour of new ones. After such revolutions science then settles down to its 'normal' puzzle-solving phase until, at some point, the conditions are laid for another revolution and the cycle resumes. However, while Kuhn's account was of the historical development of science, in particular the Copernican revolution and the origins of quantum theory, its arguments were directed against various philosophers of science and their accounts of the rationality of science. Not unsurprisingly perhaps in the light of his arguments, Kuhn was widely seen as denying rationality to science whereas, in his own terms, he intended to substitute a different conception of rationality to the prevailing one which he regarded as too limiting to grasp the realities and complexities of the historical changes in science.

One of the elements of the more traditional philosophies of science which Kuhn sought to challenge was the idea of a scientific method, an algorithm of explicit and precise procedure which, if appropriately applied, would enable scientists to determine which of rival theories was the correct one, the one which best represented reality. The search for such an algorithm, Kuhn held, was fruitless, for the choice between rival scientific theories is rarely, if ever, straightforward, clear-cut and unequivocal. As indicated earlier, Kuhn's picture of the development of science is one of alternating periods of 'normal' and 'extraordinary' or revolutionary science. A mature science, such as physics, and unlike sociology which is divided by endless disagreement between different approaches, has (for much of the time and throughout many areas) a basic agreement about fundamentals, about appropriate theories and about effective methods. 'Normal science' takes place in such a settled and consensual period in which a scientist can have a clear idea of what a problem is, how it might be solved, and what it looks like, how it relates to other problems, and so on. It is a 'puzzle-solving' period because scientists have an idea how to solve them, though they may not yet have done so.

However, during such 'settled' periods anomalies to the accepted theories accumulate. Scientists make investigations which do not get the results that, in terms of prevailing theories, are expected. These may not, at first, be regarded as too serious and can be put down to experimental error, or regarded as matters which will eventually be resolved within the received frame of thought. However, some of these anomalies will remain intractable and, at some point, they will come to be seen as posing a profound problem for accepted theories, so throwing the science into crisis. The fact that these anomalies cannot be accommodated within the received theory now begins to suggest that there is possibly something profoundly wrong with it. New theories are necessitated which can deal with the anomalies and the science enters the revolutionary phase. An attempt is made to reorganise the science comprehensively around new theoretical ideas. Moreover, Kuhn argues, the political origin of the term 'revolution' is appropriate since introducing new theories is tantamount to a political struggle whose outcome is not decided on the basis of scientific evidence, but on the basis of power. A scientific revolution does not involve the whole of the scientific community concerned consensually agreeing to abandon the old scheme and bring in the new. Far from it: it results in intense and protracted strife within the science. The common pattern is that radical new ideas get taken up by younger scientists who are at the beginning of their careers and who have yet to develop a serious commitment to old frameworks of thought. Thus, the field becomes, for a time, divided between irreconcilable protagonists of the old and the new, with the outcome eventually being settled by mortality. The new theories finally triumph but not because everyone has been persuaded by it – the older generation may never become reconciled – but because the opposition have retired or died off.

A key element in Kuhn's argument is that the standards or criteria, such as simplicity, comprehensiveness, systematisation, among others, by which scientists are supposed to choose between theories are not so delimiting as to provide, in any particular cases, a conclusive outcome. To advise people that they should prefer the simplest, the most comprehensive and systematic theory may be good advice but it hardly helps when faced with the practical choice between say, three theories, X, Y, and Z where theory X is simpler than Y but not as general nor as systematic as Z, but where Z, while being more systematic and comprehensive than X and Y, is less general than both X and Y. Which criteria is to be given priority: simplicity, generality or systematicity? There are many ways of answering this. Moreover, there are different ways of judging simplicity, comprehensiveness or systematicity and different scientists could well, and reasonably, total up the merits of the competing theories in very different ways, just as those debating the merits of sporting performers can sum up the merits of rival candidates according to very different judgements of respective worth. The dispute over whether one scientific theory is to be preferred over another can be, and has proven to be as a matter of historical fact, an open-ended matter. In any theory-to-theory comparison one is dealing with a long list of assorted pros and cons and, accordingly, even when one theory does eventually triumph this does not mean that there was everything to be said on behalf of the victorious theory and nothing on behalf of the defeated rival. Indeed, Kuhn ironically observes that a supposedly defeated point of view may be somewhat, if not entirely so, rehabilitated in the next revolution.

As we have seen, this picture of normal science contrasts with that put forward by Popper who saw science as an essentially critical activity in which scientists are constantly striving to disprove each other's theories. Accordingly, Kuhn's normal science was, for Popper, an unrepresentative conception of what the essential spirit of science involved. This was a departure from the relentlessly critical attitude proper to the true scientist. Moreover, Kuhn's emphasis on the importance of dogmatic and authoritarian scientific training in which the scientist was required to absorb the orthodox science compliantly and without disagreement as a condition for admission to the scientific community, compounded Kuhn's offence in Popper's eyes.

However, Kuhn is not arguing that those who resist the change in theories do so for narrowly political reasons and only because they have a vested interest in the prevailing organisation of the science, though they may well have such interests. His point is, rather, that a major obstacle to their making a change in their theoretical allegiance is that they find it extremely difficult, if not impossible, to understand the new theory. They cannot see or be persuaded of the merits of the new framework. Change in scientific theories, Kuhn holds, involves changes of meaning. Because theoretical terms take their meaning from the theory they belong to, even when the same words are used in a new theory they will mean something different; they are incommensurate with the same words in the old theory. Thus, a scientist brought up in the old theory can only confront the new theory as if it were a foreign language even when it, on the face of it, uses the same concepts and words. The situation is as much a communication breakdown as it is a revolution.

As far as Kuhn is concerned, his arguments do not claim that the outcome of scientific controversy is just a matter of power and vested interests and is entirely bereft of rationality. He insists that science *is* a rational pursuit and that it makes progress. Thus, Kuhn argues with respect to the Copernican revolution in astronomy that the grounds for the Copernican theory were no better than, and perhaps even poorer than, those favouring the geocentric theory, and that the acceptance of Copernicus's arguments was due to their appeal to some near mystical, not scientific, views then current among some influential astronomers. It was not the obvious empirical and evidential superiority of Copernicus's work which carried the day. However, as things have turned out, the Copernican conception has been vindicated, has proven to be the superior one and there is now overwhelming evidence to support the Copernican position. Thus, astronomy has made progress. But, if science does progress it does not do so in the way that philosophies of science had previously understood. Scientists' judgements about the merits of competing theories are much more complex that the previous picture had allowed. While being quite equivalently rational in their deliberations, scientists can draw very different conclusions in any given case, not least because of the plurality of criteria of theory choice as noted earlier. However, and this is perhaps Kuhn's most acute provocation, progress in science involves much more than rationality in this sense of a theory obtaining a closer grasp on the nature of reality. The key consideration here is language.

Language again

In Kuhn's case the argument against the idea of a new and currently successful theory having a closer grasp on the nature of ultimate reality than its rejected predecessors originates from his rejection of the distinction between 'theory language' and 'observation language' which was a key elements of traditional empiricist philosophy of science, as we have seen. For Kuhn such a distinction cannot be sustained because the language in which observations are reported is itself theory laden. As we saw in the previous chapter in connection with the discussion of the conceptual logic of motives and intentions, these are concepts which enter into the description of actions so that it becomes difficult to sustain a discrete distinction between, to put it this way, a language of behavioural observation and a language of mental states since both belong, to borrow a conception from Wittgenstein, to a 'grammar of action concepts' in which both are intimately intertwined. A similar idea is involved in the notion that the language of observation is theory laden.

The distinction between 'theory' and 'observation' languages was intended to provide an assurance that scientific theories did make connection with the world. In a truly deductively formulated theory, the highly abstract general concepts would systematically connect with observable phenomena – by the intervening, progressively less general levels in the chain of deduced propositions, which leads, eventually to predictions about concrete, specific, observable states of affairs – so ensuring that the theory was responsive to the way the world was and allowing a close comparison, and hoped-for match, between the facts of the world and the claims of the theory. However, and for Kuhn, since actual scientific observation is done in terms of some theory, then the kinds of things that are observed must depend upon the theory. For example, if a physiologist is interested in the effects of a drug on the haemoglobin in the blood stream, then his or her observations are going to be in terms of a theory in which many of the key observational phenomena are already defined. Thus, again for Kuhn, it is not possible to describe the world independently of some theory. More strongly than this, the idea of a world independent of some theory can have no meaning and a scientist can only encounter the world in terms of a theory he or she accepts, a point which Kuhn glosses by describing theoretical protagonists as living in 'different worlds'. Accordingly, the discontinuity between pre- and postrevolutionary phases of scientific change is so great that it makes little sense to talk of one theory giving a better account of the same world than its predecessor. It would be more appropriate to say that the new theory puts us into a different world to that of its predecessor.[14]

The linguistic turn in social research

We said at the beginning of this chapter that the emphasis on meaning as the distinctive characteristic of human social life brought language very much to the fore of social science concerns. In the last two decades or so, a focus on language, especially through the term 'discourse', has been rampant across not only the more traditional disciplines but also newer intellectual infusions such as cultural studies as well as encouraging, paradoxically, a more social turn in those discipline traditionally concerned with the study of language, such as literature studies and linguistics. Language has, in more recent years, become a cross-disciplinary focus.

Although Wittgenstein, Winch, and Kuhn are by no means the only scholars responsible for this emphasis, they were influential figures and can be seen as reminding us that social life and language are interwoven. Language is a social activity. It is something that developed in and as part of social activities and, reciprocally, social activities are carried on through language. Thus, language is a prominent medium of the conduct of social life and, accordingly, the study of social life becomes, in important respects, the study of language use. Wittgenstein's insistence on the diversity of language uses was intended to counter the fixation on those aspects of language which involve 'talking about the world' and, instead, recognise the role language plays in carrying on social relations and activities. This he emphasised by placing sense or meaning as prior to truth in his deliberations on language. Only a statement which has sense, which says something that can be understood, can either be true or false, and the things which determine sense, that is, words having a role in language and activities, are different from those which determine whether what is said is true or false. This was a very different emphasis from that of positivistic or empiricist philosophies which gave priority to truth as the condition of a meaningful statement: a feature particularly prominent in logical positivism and, in social research, an emphasis on testing the truth of theories as the point of research.

In sociology, these views converged with symbolic interactionism and ethnomethodology which had, although from different philosophical inspirations, been long campaigning for adoption of the idea that social life is a linguistically constituted affair and that social life, substantially and centrally, consists in the use of language (see e.g. Lee 1991). A combination of ethnomethodogical and Wittgensteinian influences has resulted in the development of 'conversation analysis' which focuses in great and intense analytic detail on the socially organised character of ordinary talk.[15] In significant respects these developments extend the tradition referred to earlier that grew out of the cultural debates in Germany in the late nineteenth century, debates which tried to forge a principled distinction between the social and the natural sciences.

The issue of relativism and idealism

At the heart of the criticism of Winch and, relatedly, Kuhn, is the issue of whether their arguments invite relativistic conclusions. Much of the effort of positivistic and empiricist philosophies, as it was for rationalistic philosophies, was directed toward securing an absolute basis for scientific knowledge. Winch and Kuhn seem, by some at least, to be denying such ambitions. As we have already pointed out, Winch is often read as arguing that witchcraft is as good as science or, a slightly more cautious position, that there is no independent means of choosing between witchcraft and science.[16] Similarly, Kuhn in his description of the 'different worlds' involved in the revolution between old and new theories, is seen as arguing that it is not reality which determines which theory is right but the decline in vigour of the proponents of the old theory. Hence, since there is no means of determining which theory best compares with reality, relativist conclusions are inevitable.

Certainly, if these were the kind of views that Winch and Kuhn were arguing for then it would be difficult to escape relativist conclusions. However, another charge against both of them, and hence against those of similar views, is their alleged idealism. Kuhn, for example, is often taken as saying that reality is what a particular scientific community hold it to be. The post-revolutionary world of science is different to that of the prerevolutionary. Such idealism elides the difference which is crucial to our rational thought, namely, that there is a difference between the world as we believe it to be and the world as it is. The notion of the world as 'mind independent', regardless of whatever way we believe it to be, is one of the keys to our whole way of thinking and can only be denied at the risk of absurdity. Believing that one has won the lottery is – alas! – obviously not the same as winning the lottery.

Realism

The arguments of Winch and Kuhn are regularly seen as a challenge to materialist and realist positions which premise themselves upon the affirmation of a reality independent of the mind and are, in this respect, part of the legacy of positivism. As in the case of positivism, these philosophical positions sustain certain conceptions of the study of social life as a science like natural science with a key role for theory but within what is hoped to be a more sophisticated view of science itself.

The picture of social science painted by Winch eschewed the idea that social science should be mainly preoccupied with providing causal explanations. Rather, its role was more communicative. In asking for explanations of what others are doing, most of the time what is needed is to find out what it is we do not know but of which they are perfectly aware. If we have chess explained to us what we learn is what chess players already know. Similarly with Azande witchcraft. Accordingly, while social science can find things out, for a large part of the time these will be things that are familiar to those who do the activities but which puzzle us. This is in stark contrast to the notion that the social sciences are, or should be, discovering sciences like other discovering sciences and capable of finding things out that no one knew before their discovery. This was certainly the conception argued for by Durkheim, for example, as we saw in Chapter 2. Marx, though in significantly different ways, also held to the same view. The forces which shape society are deeply rooted and are largely invisible to the members of society until discovered by the application of the method of historical materialism. In just the same way that Darwin discovered the evolutionary origins of life or the way in which Einstein discovered that the speed of light provides the limit of motion, so should the social sciences be.

The concept of social science as a discovering endeavour does not sit easily with allegedly idealist notions that there is no 'mind-independent' reality. If such were the case then there would be no point to science. If reality consists in what we believe then we must be aware of these beliefs and cannot be mistaken about them and if reality is the same as what we believe then, logically, we should know reality itself. There would, as said a moment ago, be no point to science; all we need do is inspect our beliefs. In this respect, Marx and Freud stand as 'proof' that we do not know our minds. Their discoveries showed that our minds are not transparent. We are unconscious of the forces which shape and guide our actions.

Materialism and realism both insist on the indispensability of the gap between the world as we believe it to be and the world as it is; the gap between appearance and reality. For materialism, 'mind' or 'ideas' are immaterial and can play no causal role. Realism, though not committed to the materialist notion that reality consists solely in matter, is no less insistent that although our endeavours may fail to capture the true nature of reality, nonetheless, a distinction must be maintained between beliefs and the way the world is in itself.

Realism and science

An important attempt to recover the lost ground by the attack on positivism, and so retain the idea of a social *science*, was made by Bhaskar (1978) who presented what he termed a 'transcendental realism' which would include the social sciences among the sciences. It would permit, as far as Bhaskar is concerned, the retention of a revised Marxist mode of explanation, along with diagnoses of false consciousness and the political implication of the possibility of emancipation, but is not so easily vulnerable as positivistic conceptions of science to the kind of objections inspired by Winch and others.

Bhaskar holds that science makes discoveries about the nature and the powers of real things, things which exist independently of that science and our knowledge of them and which would continue to exist and behave in the ways they do even if there were no science to explain them. At the same time, Bhaskar also wants to insist that science, that is, what we know and what we can say about the nature and power of real things, is itself contingent, a historically and socially produced phenomenon. Thus, in part, he is prepared to concur with supposedly relativist conclusions but wants to argue that relativism and realism are not in conflict. In Bhaskar's scheme, because the very possibility of science requires the recognition of the existence of a real, mind-independent world which operates according to natural necessity, what we have is an *ontological* realism. However, we also need to recognise that science and its knowledge is a human activity which is culturally and historically shaped. Accordingly, an *epistemological* relativism is also required. There is, to put it another way, a difference between our descriptions of reality and the reality that is described. Although it is only through our scientific descriptions that we know about, insofar as we do know, the things in reality, the kinds of descriptions given in science are themselves historically and social formed products, the result of the work of previous investigators and theorists. It is they who have built whatever terminology we use to talk about reality, and there is no necessity that we should describe the natural, necessary relations among phenomena in the terminology that we happen to have inherited. We might describe these phenomena in other ways, and have known them under different descriptions than those we happen to have. But, this does not mean that the nature of the things known would be different. The nature of the things in reality is not the same as their descriptions. So a description of a thing in one way rather than another does not change the nature of the thing as we alter the language of description.[17]

Within Bhaskar's own 'naturalistic' position, the traditional dualisms of naturalism versus hermeneutics, voluntarism versus reification, and individualism versus collectivism, are not necessary oppositions in which we have to choose one or the other. He treats the opposition between naturalism and hermeneutics as consisting in the two other dualisms and to be overcome through a transformational model of social action. Social structures are not reified as things which possess a life of their own and which determine the actions of individuals as in collectivism. Social structures preexist individual actions and are a precondition for them. They are, at the same time, the products of those actions.[18] Social life is neither something constituted solely by individuals, nor comprised of self-subsistent social wholes but is, instead, a network of social relations, an ensemble of given positions and associated activities and practices, which are occupied by individuals who are agents capable of making decisions and choices and who, consequently, can carry out the requirements of those positions and, thus, may transform the structure that they or others will subsequently occupy.

These arguments ensure, for Bhaskar, that the 'social sciences can be seen as sciences in the same sense as the experimental science of nature, such as organic chemistry, but in ways which are as different from the matter as they are specific to the nature of societies' (Giddens 1986: 93). In other words, the social sciences will have to take into account the kind of phenomena that, for Winch and others, undermined their very status as sciences, such as the understanding of social actors – Bhaskar calls this the 'hermeneutic moment' – and a recognition that social reality consists in part of social actors' concepts and understandings.

Conclusion

We raised, but did not directly answer, the question as to whether Wittgenstein's views about the 'autonomy of grammar' did not result in the disconnection of an 'external reality' of the sort that Bhaskar fears and that he seeks to reconnect with his own statement of an elaborated realism. We did not directly answer the question, but the fact that it does not result in such a disconnection should be fairly apparent. Wittgenstein's argument is, rather, against asking the question about the relationship of language to reality as one to be posed and answered in a general way. Clearly enough, the name 'Fido' is not the same as the dog, Fido, and when we give the name 'Fido' to the dog we do make a connection between something linguistic, a name, and something nonlinguistic, namely, the living dog. Wittgenstein is certainly not contesting such obvious facts. What he is attempting to do, however, is dissuade us from *beginning with* and *focusing exclusively* on facts about giving names to things as if these represented the very essence of language. He wants us, too, to remember that the making of such connections between words and things do not represent the root or the foundation of language, that such connections presuppose the existence of organised human activity of which language is a part. Giving names to dogs is itself a social practice we also extend to other 'pet' animals, but which we do not apply to animals generally. However, the availability of this sociocultural practice is presupposed in the most basic example of relating words to things, such as giving the dog its name. Reflecting on what would be a concise summary of Wittgensteinian, even Kuhnian, views, we might offer: recognition of the importance of the sociocultural context for our linguistic and other practices does not deprive us of the capacity to 'talk about reality' but it endows us with the capacity to do this. We are dependent upon a sociocultural reality for the expression 'talk about reality' to have an intelligible sense and application.

Notes

1. Connolly (1995) suggests that the shift from positivism to post-structuralism is a shift from epistemological to ontological concerns. The positivist project relied upon implicit ontological assumptions that were so deeply entrenched as not to be an issue. Post-structuralism, he contends, questions precisely this assumption.
2. 'Concept' is not the same as 'word'. Someone who goes in for activities akin to prayer and worship would be said to have the concept 'religion' even if their language has, perhaps, no such word.
3. Of course, there is no necessary reason why we should restrict ourselves to a single category. The relevance of descriptions is bound up with the point of view taken with respect to the activity.
4. This point is also applicable within cultures.

5. This view was sufficiently strong as to have convinced Wittgenstein himself in the early part of his divided career. After completing his first book, the *Tractatus Logico-Philosophicus*, and the only one published in his lifetime, he gave up philosophy for a period thinking that he had done with it altogether. When he returned to philosophy he developed a deeply different view which was profoundly critical of his first book. See his *Philosophical Investigations* (1958).

6. An important point to insist upon is if, like the later Wittgenstein, one takes the view that among the several sources of philosophical confusion is the inclination to overgeneralise patterns of language use, then the preoccupation that language is some kind of fully integrated system would be a strong temptation towards premature overgeneralisation.

7. 'Grammar', for Wittgenstein, is not the kind of activity which concerns itself, for example, with classifying parts of speech. It has more to do with what it makes sense to say.

8. It is worth noting, by the way, that Evans-Pritchard himself in other parts of his argument was very close to accepting something like Winch's views. Winch himself says that to a large extent he and Evans-Pritchard are in close agreement but that, in the end, Evans-Pritchard is not in enough agreement. Winch's criticism focuses on a point at which he regards Evans-Pritchard as lapsing into the more disreputable view.

9. Thus Winch is implying that the so-called 'correspondence theory of truth' mentioned earlier, which holds that a statement is true when it corresponds with the facts, is not stating a theory about the relation between two things, statement and facts, but is only restating a meaning equivalence from our ordinary language. 'True' and 'corresponds with the facts' are equivalent and often interchangeable expressions.

10. In some ways, Evans-Pritchard's analysis continues the tradition which sees primitive people's lives as governed by animistic beliefs since they are massively ignorant of the true causes of why things happen in the world around them. As scientific knowledge increases, the phenomena of nature cease to be attributed to spirits. This ignores that such peoples were skilled hunters and metal workers who needed detailed knowledge of nature in order to survive. Also, as Wittgenstein noted, if rain dances, for example, were intended to cause rain we might expect them to be more frequent in times of drought. But they are not. Rather they occur when the rains are coming. They are celebratory not causal. See Wittgenstein (1979) and the excellent chapter 12 in Phillips (1996).

11. Winch is not denying that to give an explanation can be to provide a cause. What he is questioning is that it is the only way.

12. Winch's argument does not require that all regularities in society are rule-governed and that none of them are causal. His point only requires that some, even many important, regularities are 'rule-governed' rather than causal.

13. Since this is not really a task in the sense usually understood by would-be social scientists, Winch's preference was for the expression 'social studies'.

14. Kuhn is aware that such an argument is not to be taken too literally, though some of his followers have not been so cautious. It might be better to formulate it as follows: a post-revolutionary science produces both changes in the way that scientific work is done and the picture of the world that it projects.

15. The founder of conversation analysis was Harvey Sacks. See his collected lectures (Sacks 1995).

16. For Winch, of course, witchcraft and science cannot contradict each other since they are not even speaking 'the same language'.

17. This is a position Kuhn inclined toward, but then retreated from in favour of the idea that the nature of things depended upon our descriptions of them and that, accordingly, changes in ways of describing meant changes in the nature of things. For Bhaskar the different descriptions both try to capture the intrinsic nature of the thing.

18. The notion is not very different from Gidden's concept of 'structuration' in which 'society is both the condition and the outcome of human agency and human agency both the production and reproduction (or transformation) of society' (Giddens 1986: 92).

CHAPTER 8

The evaporation of meaning

The two previous chapters have reviewed the positions which attempt to argue that social phenomena are intrinsically meaningful and that the business of the social sciences should, therefore, primarily be concerned with the study of meaning and meaning making. In the last chapter we raised the question of whether this would lead toward various seemingly undesirable consequences, such as subjectivism, idealism and relativism, and argued that such fears were largely illusory. We suggested that neither the Wittgensteinians' nor the Kuhnians' view carry any such implications. Now, however, we need to consider positions which attempt to go back on the view that social phenomena are *intrinsically* meaningful. Here we present two very different sets of views. First, those of 'postempiricism', a position led by W.V.O. Quine; second, those of European 'poststructuralist' theory through its two most prominent figures, Michel Foucault and Jacques Derrida. For very different reasons, and with very different envisaged consequences, these two approaches involve the idea that the notion of social phenomena as 'intrinsically meaningful' is an essentially metaphysical conception, and that the need for the thorough purging of all metaphysical elements from thought entails the abandonment of the notion of meaning, disposed of by a frontal attack upon previous theories of meaning.

The arguments reviewed in the previous two chapters were concerned to explore the relevance and the implications of the issue of meaning, and hence of language, for the study of social phenomena. In this chapter we want to turn to arguments which seek to deny that social phenomena, especially language, have meaning. Briefly, these tendencies arise from two very distinct, quite unrelated, sources. One originates with European social theory, which tends to include philosophy as much, or even more, than it does sociology, and here the primary influences are 'structuralist' and 'poststructuralist' ideas. The other arises from the mainstream of contemporary Anglo-American philosophy and 'post-empiricist' doctrines with which positivism is often associated.

However, although the arguments are about language and meaning they are also deeply concerned, through these, with the issue of rationality and the nature of science. Winchean arguments had been relativistically interpreted as claiming that there was no absolute standard of rationality and, hence, no secure means of determining an intellectual authority for science. Witchcraft, it was supposed, was no better, and no worse, than science or, to put it more accurately, there was no principled way showing one or another to be better. These tendencies can be seen, in very different ways, as reinforcing, even – in the case of European social theory – taking much further, the supposed consequences of Winch-type views.

Postempiricism

The concern with the meaning of language and the meaning of actions involved, as much as anything else, a response to and critique of behavourist tendencies in the study of social activities. The strategy of behavourism was condemned as a reductionist one in which all activity was accessible to scientific study but only on the condition that all reference to 'mentalistic' elements was eliminated from the description and explanation of the activity.

Behavourism, as we have seen, inherited the Cartesian dualism in at least the sense that it allowed the options to be defined in Cartesian terms of an opposition of 'mind' to 'body'. Cartesians argue that human beings consist of a material, physical and observable body and an immaterial, unobservable, separate and distinct mind. Against that, behaviourists may deny that there is anything other than the body, or insist, more moderately, that the mind is not a possible topic for scientific study. The body is unequivocally within the domain of science. The mind, however, seems to fall outside the sphere of observable physical phenomena and, for the behaviourist, only those phenomena which consist of physical, and publicly observable phenomena can count among the legitimate phenomena of science. The mind must be excluded as a topic of scientific study and as a potentially explanatory factor in the explanation of embodied behaviour, unless, that is, mental phenomena can be shown to be, in effect, products of bodily states.

Quine's behavourism

One of the foremost of contemporary behaviourists is W.V.O. Quine who, at least since the 1960s, has been one of the more influential of Anglo-American philosophers. We have already discussed some of Quine's views in relation to the discussion of science in Chapter 4. However, the way in which Quine has had most impact in the post-1960 period is through his ideas on the nature of language and meaning organised around the issue of 'translation' and involving what must be one of the most frequently debated issues in contemporary philosophy, the 'thesis of the indeterminacy of translation'.

Quine's philosophy is constructed out of a selective adoption of the heritage of empiricism and positivism. In his view, one of the serious consequences of the behaviourist position is that it assumes that the main tasks of philosophy are now predominantly carried out by science. The main aim of philosophy, the objective of its metaphysical concerns, was to tell us what reality ultimately consisted in, a question now suc-cessfully – or as well as is currently possible – answered by the up-to-date findings of science. Another of its main tasks, epistemology, the determination of how it is possible for us to know the nature of the external world, has not yet been handed over to science, but Quine recommends that it should be. Epistemology should be 'naturalised' by being made over into the empirical study of the development of the human cognitive apparatus. Philosophy cannot bid to play a role it has traditionally sought to occupy, that of 'first philosophy' which works out the basis for knowledge and prescribes to science how it should organise itself for success.

However, although Quine reduces philosophy's role considerably, philosophy is not entirely redundant. It can still play the part of clari-fying what it is that science tells us and of checking the way in which we 'ordinarily' speak against the standard that science has set.[1] As far as Quine is concerned, science tells us that there are only physical things and it is this which brings it into conflict with some of the ordinary things that we say. The way that we speak, for example, often postulates things which do not, in fact, exist; which do not, or never have had, physical existence, such as the gods on Mount Olympus, unicorns, or fairies at the bottom of the garden. Indeed, one of the problems of the study of human social life is that this too uses a vocabu-lary of dubious provenance, expressions which purport to explain the activities of human beings but which postulate entities which do not pass the scientific standard of physical existence. The whole 'inten-tional' vocabulary of our ordinary language – of the kind we discussed in Chapter 5 – which appeals to such entities as minds and to thoughts, to motives, to purposes, and so on, and is used to explain conduct, falls into doubt.

Quine's attitude to the vocabulary of science is, in his own words, an 'austere' one requiring the elimination of all 'entities' the postulation of which is unnecessary to the business of science, which mainly means those 'entities' which cannot be cashed out in physical form. The notion of meaning is a term which Quine sees as a candidate expression for the explanation of our linguistic activities through our knowledge of meanings and, therefore, is a concept which bids to be included in any scientific theory of linguistic behaviour (Quine 1953b). However, for Quine, the notion of meaning cannot pass the test of scientific accept-ability and needs to be excluded from a properly scientific vocabulary. In other words, according to science, which is the source of our judge-ments as to what really exists, in Quine's scheme of things, meanings do not exist. There are no such things as meanings any more than there are any other kind of mental entities such as beliefs, thoughts, inten-tions, and so on. These have no identifiable physical existence in the neurophysiological structure of the human animal and, hence, cannot be part of any properly scientific explanation of the behaviour of such animals. As far as explanations of human linguistic and social behavi-our is concerned, we can only begin with any confidence with what is observable and physical, namely, the outward behaviour of the organism – which is why Quine adopts behaviourism – and the inward operation of the physiological system. Thus, the main business of social science must be conducted on behaviourist terms, treating behaviour not as organised through 'inner mental' entities but through the environmental conditioning of the organism's response.

There are some superficial affinities here with Wittgenstein's position, but they are superficial and only in respect of their conclusion that meanings are not some kind of 'mental entity'. The position both Wittgenstein and Quine reject assumes that it is necessary to have access to some mental state or event, such as a 'meaning', in order to fix the meaning of a word or sentence. Quine calls this the 'museum myth' in which 'meaning entities' are arranged as if in a museum exhibition somewhere in the mind and to which words in the language can be connected, so gaining meaning. Wittgenstein concluded that if the meaning of a word was not fixed by reference to any 'mental entities', then it must be settled by some other means, and identified the organisation of language as fixing the meaning of words. Quine goes on to draw an utterly different conclusion: if meaning cannot be fixed by 'mental entities' (which must, given his emphasis on science as the arbiter of reality, really be physical entities, that is, states of the brain or nervous system), then meaning cannot be fixed at all. And since 'mental entities', including meanings, are not physical entities, then meaning cannot be fixed.

The indeterminacy thesis

To understand Quine's argument here we need to examine his thesis of the indeterminacy of translation.[2] The thesis appears to make some drastic claims. In attempting to translate from an alien tongue there is no answer to the question, 'What did the speaker say?', in the sense of 'What did the speaker mean by what he or she said?'. There is no uniquely correct answer to the question. Rather, there are many completely different, even mutually contradictory, answers all of which may be considered as correct answers to the question. The fact that each translation can be considered, in one sense, correct, means that in another sense they cannot. If each rival translation, even the incompatible ones, is just as good, just as correct, as another, then none of them can be said to provide *the* correct translation. None has any more claim than any of the others to capture the meaning intrinsic to the sentence being translated, though they do yield translations which are perfectly adequate for the business of talking to and dealing with speakers of an alien tongue, and who do not conform with what we would normally call evidence for a correct translation.

The indeterminacy of translation results from the fact that it is necessary, and not just convenient, for someone attempting a translation – for Quine this means producing a systematic scheme for translation, what he calls a 'translation manual' – to make major assumptions about the nature of the language being translated in order to develop the translation at all. Different assumptions can be made by different translators which will, at different points and perhaps extensively, result in very different – perhaps entirely incompatible – translations of the same sentence. Using the initial assumptions, the translator will try to check the resulting translations against the speaker's patterns of speech to get the pattern of translation to fit impeccably with the evidence of the speaker's behaviour. However, that a given translator's assumptions yield a scheme for translation which fits with all the evidence about the speech of the indigenous speakers does not mean that another scheme need be any less consistent with the same evidence. Two or more translation schemes could fit equally well, Quine argues, with *all possible* evidence in terms of the language responses of the speakers, and yet, because of the very different assumptions on which the schemes depend, yield incompatible translations of the same sentence.

This marks an important difference for Quine between the 'social sciences' and the natural sciences. There are somewhat comparable situations in the natural sciences where two conflicting theories are equally compatible with the evidence. But, in the physical world both cannot be true for they make competing claims about how the physical facts must be, and there are physical facts which must be one way or the other regardless of our theories about them. Hence, there must be some 'fact of the matter' which will ultimately settle the issue between the rival theories. In the case of the 'social sciences' there are, however, no 'facts of the matter'. Quine has, it must be remembered, denied that there are physical states of the brain and nervous system which correspond to supposed 'mental states' and so there are no physical states which exist independently of, and could eventually be identified and used to adjudicate between, the rival translations. When the rival translators have taken into account all the evidence about the language responses of the indigenous speakers, they will have exhausted all the evidence. There is no further physical evidence to which they might appeal. Accordingly, when two rival linguists have done everything possible to establish that their translations, given their respective assumptions, fit the evidence of the speakers' behaviours, they have done everything that can be done. There is no further court of appeal to which they can turn and no solution to be had as to which is the correct translation. They are left, then, with translations of particular sentences which are yielded by thoroughly coherent translation schemes and which are, in their different ways, each thoroughly compatible with all the evidence of the speakers' behaviour, but which conflict with each other (as a result of the different initial assumptions on which the translation schemes are built) but between which there is no way of choosing. Since there is no 'physical evidence' in the form of states of the brain and nervous system, then the only physical evidence available is that of speakers' behaviour and, *ex hypothesi*, the translation schemes are equally compatible with *all possible* behavioural evidence.

There is something potentially quite misleading about Quine's own use as an example of translation from an alien language for it makes it sound as though the problem is that of translating from a language whose meaning we do not know into one we do, namely, our own. However, Quine's real point is not about translation in this ordinary sense and his argument is only about 'translation' by virtue of a quirk of his in forming his ideas about meaning. For Quine, to give the meaning of one sentence is to offer another sentence purportedly equivalent in meaning. That is, it is to 'translate' a first sentence into a second putatively equivalent one. Thus, in his writing, 'meaning' and 'translation' are entirely interwoven notions. Thus, his point about the indeterminacy of translation is a general one about language and the example is meant to establish the contention that there is no intrinsic meaning to the sentence of *any* language, our own or any other. 'Translation' in Quine encompasses sentences in ostensibly the same language as when, for example, the meaning of one sentence in the English language is restated in another, just as much as it does to the case in which someone is trying to translate from one language into what is ostensibly a quite alien tongue. 'Indeterminacy' applies to all attempts at translation whether performed by the initial speaker or by someone else; that is, the speaker of a language (or a sentence in it) is in no better position than anyone else to know what the sentence means. The speaker is no better placed to answer the question, 'What did you mean by what you said?' that any would-be translator. A translation can be given by the speaker him or herself but it has no privileged or authoritative status, but provides just one possible translation among many. It presents the recipient of any such offered explanation with the same problem, namely, to 'translate' what the other has said into the recipient's own equivalent words. In other words, those of us who speak a language as natives do not know what the words and sentences of our language refer to and mean. We do not know the meaning of our own words, let alone those of anyone else.

However, it is important to be clear about what such a seemingly devastating conclusion amounts to. It does not mean that we are ignorant of the meanings our words have, that we use the words, which have meaning, but we are ignorant or under illusions about this; it is because there is nothing for us to know. The words have no intrinsic meanings, no meanings-in-themselves. Whatever meaning they can have can only be in terms of one or another translation scheme. If to give the meaning of a sentence is supposed to be giving one translation which uniquely matches it, then, in this sense, Quine's indeterminacy case makes the point that there is no such meaning. There is no securely identifiable unique match between two sentences in a language and, therefore, no meaning.[3]

As we indicated earlier, although there are similarities between Quine and Wittgenstein, they depart in crucial ways. For the latter, that 'meaning' is a word in our ordinary language, not some candidate theoretical term, does not entail postulating the existence of any 'meaning entity'.

To talk about the meaning of a word is simply to talk about the part it plays in our language and the kind of things it is used to say. The meaning of a word is fixed by its place in the language and by the 'grammar' that governs its use. To repeat: it is not to talk about any kind of 'mental entity'. It is the assumption that it is necessary to have any kind of 'mental entities' to fix the meaning of a word which is at fault. Accordingly, demonstrating that there are no such meaning entities endowing words with their meaning, as Quine purports to do, does not leave us in the position of denying that words have meaning. Rather, it suggests that the meaning of words is fixed on some other basis than by reference to 'mental entities', namely, the organisation of language itself.

Quine's argument, in what would be Wittgenstein's view, takes him toward an absurdity, that is, that someone could use a word in the same way in every respect as we do, and yet we could not say that they used it with the same meaning. For Wittgenstein, the fact that someone uses a word in the same way as someone else *simply is* our grounds for saying that they mean the same by it. Quine's argument for indeterminacy requires that the postulated rival translations must be compatible with, in its strongest possible formulation, all the possible evidence about the linguistic responses of the speakers and their circumstances. But, and to use Quine's own example, the idea that we could be in possession of all the possible evidence that someone's use of the word 'gavagai' corresponded in every particular with our use of the word 'rabbit', and yet we could still lack conclusive evidence that they meant 'rabbit' by it is, for Wittgenstein, simply inconceivable. Quine seems, in effect, to be the victim of a residual attachment to the conviction that we need access to some mental counterpart of speaking the words of a language in order to accord them meaning: a residual attachment in the sense that he accepts the doctrine's requirement that a mental counterpart would be necessary to fix meaning, then denies the possibility of fulfilling this requirement. This attachment Wittgenstein altogether abandons: the fault is with the very idea that mental counterparts need figure in the issue at all, hence the question of whether or not there are mental counterparts is immaterial to the question of whether words have meaning.

Wittgenstein is not trying to be more behaviourist than Quine when he avers that it is on the basis of what people say, in the circumstances in which they say them, that we decide what they mean. Wittgenstein is not putting forward any kind of theory of meaning but purports to be describing the ways in which we use the word 'meaning' in our ordinary affairs where, routinely and without qualm, we determine whether someone has understood the meaning of a word by seeing how he or she uses that word.[4] If in any doubt we could actively test people to see what they say or do when using the word. If they do not behave in the ways we expect, then we may well conclude that they do not know the meaning of the word. Of course, it is not just a matter of matching someone else's behaviour against our own, but of doing so where our own behaviour can serve to exemplify the norms of the language when we are confident that we use the word correctly. On occasion, of course, we might want to match both our own and someone else's usage against a more decisive authority, such as a dictionary.

Davidson's attack on relativism

Davidson, taking over, in part, some of Quine's positions, attempts to develop them into arguments against relativism of the kind that Winch is seen as holding, that is, that different people comprehend reality differently because they comprehend it in terms of distinct, self-contained 'conceptual schemes' which cannot be compared (Davidson 1980, 1984, Davidson and Hintikka 1975). Such a position does not deny that people are rational. What it does deny is that people are all judged according to one universal standard of rationality. In other words, standards of rationality are diverse in being internal to conceptual schemes. Davidson wants to argue against the idea of there being different conceptual schemes and contends, instead, that people have the same rationality or, and this is an importantly different point, that it must be assumed that others are rational in the same way that we are. This is so because it is involved in our very concept of language.

Davidson follows Quine in assuming that understanding a language is the same as translating it. Similarly he adopts a holistic view of language.[5] Davidson treats the business of understanding others mainly in terms of a trade-off between belief and meaning. In order to understand what someone says, he argues, we have to make assumptions about their beliefs, assuming them to be the same or different from ours. Thus, if someone uses a word which is familiar to us in a way that seems inappropriate, we have a choice: either between supposing that the person has the same beliefs as us and means the same thing by the word but has misapplied it; or supposing that this person has different beliefs from us about what the word means, about what things it applies to, is not misapplying it, but is using the word with a different meaning and, in their understanding, using it correctly. Meaning and belief are inextricably interwoven for we can only try to work out what other people believe on the basis of what they do and, most especially, what they say. But, as mentioned, for Davidson what people believe is involved in determining the meanings of their words, so we cannot establish what people believe or what they mean independently of each other. There are different conclusions we can draw in any given case depending on how we decide to view what they do. Again we are back in the position where there is no unequivocal evidential basis on which to decide what is the correct way to trade off the meanings of their words against their beliefs.

In the face of such circumstances, Davidson recommends the 'principle of charity'. We have to face up to the fact that we have little choice but to use this principle if we want to get anywhere in our dealings with others. We have to assume that their beliefs are much the same as ours in order to understand their words and translate them into our language. If we do not assume this, then we shall be at a loss. We shall be assuming that these people have different beliefs than ours, beliefs which we can only figure out by understanding what they say. But if their beliefs are truly very different, how shall we know how to translate their words? Only by translating their words can we begin to grasp their truly alien beliefs. But if they have truly alien beliefs how are we to start translating their words since, until we have translated some, we cannot find out what their beliefs are, and since the meaning of their words depends upon the beliefs they hold?

The only way to get started in translation is to suppose that other's beliefs are overwhelmingly the same as ours, and to assume that their beliefs are true. We take our own beliefs to be true for that is the nature of belief: we cannot believe something we take to be false – which is not to say that we cannot believe something which is false. Hence, by definition, our own beliefs we take to be true and, since we must assume that others have much the same beliefs as we do, then their beliefs must also be true. Thus, we must, if we are to try to understand others at all, presume that the great majority of their beliefs are true, which is to assume that they are people who hold and act upon true beliefs about the world, that is, that their conduct is rational. To suppose otherwise would be to suggest that the words and beliefs of others, being interdependent, would not be translatable. But since the idea of being translatable is a constituent part of a language, then we would have to conclude that these people do not possess a language. Accordingly, the idea of people possessing a different conceptual scheme, a radically variant set of beliefs, is not thinkable on Davidson's arguments.

Of course, it is important to remember that Davidson's confidence in the inter-translatability of languages goes along with a scepticism that language has any intrinsic meaning[6]. There is no empirical scientific basis for resolving the question as to the trade-off between belief and meaning; there is only practical necessity to make a working assumption about how they do operate, and one which we are more or less compelled to make in terms of the principle of charity. Thus, Davidson's position is essentially pragmatic. It is practically useful to assume that others mean the same as we do and that they have the same beliefs.

Davidson's argument are an attempted rebuttal of arguments of the type put by Winch and Kuhn, or allegedly so, that different kinds of people can have different kinds of 'conceptual schemes', by which Davidson means different collections of beliefs about the nature of the world. If one concedes that people have significantly different systems of belief, then one might be led into the relativist doctrine that they live in different worlds. This gives rise, as Winch and Kuhn are often misunderstood as doing, to the idea that translation is a chronic problem because one cannot find words from within one conceptual scheme to express radically different beliefs held in another, disjunctive scheme. Davidson tries to make translation *the solution* rather than the problem:

the operation of translation simply denies the fact of the existence of different conceptual schemes. Attempting translation simply and necessarily involves assuming sufficient homogeneity in belief between the uses of the two languages to make the notion of 'different conceptual schemes' inapplicable.

Roth's attempt to resolve the struggle about rationality

On the basis of a broadly Quinean approach, Roth (1987) attempts to resolve the *Rationalitätstreit*, that is, the struggle about rationality. Broadly, he argues that the two sides to the controversy stage their confrontation on the basis of a joint assumption, namely, the 'unity of method assumption'. Both took for granted that the sciences should share a single method. Therefore, the social sciences could be a science if it adopted the method of the natural sciences. This was the position adopted by positivism, as we have seen. Alternatively, if the social sciences could not follow the method of the natural sciences, then they would not qualify as sciences. Roth's way of dealing with this dilemma is to recognise that there is no necessary unity of method for the sciences but there can be a plurality of methods.

Roth's argument is worked out in terms of Quinean views about the indeterminacy of translation and, in part, by a critique of Winch. Indeterminacy of translation means that there is no unique right answer to the question, 'What did the speaker say?', where this is understood to ask the same as, 'What did the speaker mean by what he or she said?' The indeterminacy argument should, we suggest, be taken as claiming that there is the possibility of a multiplicity of *right* answers to the question. Quine's point is that there are many different answers which could be right in squaring with all the evidence but, given the way in which the translation process was set up, would give radically different answers to the question. There would be no 'facts of the matter', in Quine's vocabulary, no physical evidence that would enable us to choose between them. There would only be answers relative to one or another 'translation manual'. In this spirit, Roth criticises Winch for 'meaning realism', that is, for arguing about what the right translation of an alien group's practices might consist in. Winch supposes that there is something which speakers *really* mean by their words, something which is determined by the social rules which they follow. But, according to Roth's application of Quine, rules are no more determinate than meanings.

The argument is defused, according to Roth, because the argument is just about translation and there can be no final answer to the question of whether something is the right translation. That is, there is little to distinguish the charge that others are irrational from the claim that what we have is simply a bad translation. Instead of the search for the right answer, the search is for the best, the most empirically adequate translation that we can provide at the time.

Winch's argument over witchcraft, however, is not about the relationship between two empirically equivalent translations, as a Quinean
might put it, but about, in effect, the view that there are reasons to
prefer his interpretation over that of Evans-Pritchard's. Evans-Pritchard's
own evidence, and the way in which he draws comparisons between the
practices of witchcraft and primitive magic and the activities of our
own society, is not entirely compatible with the interpretation that Winch
wants to give. Overall, Winch is arguing that his own interpretation is
more consistent with Evans-Pritchard's own evidence. Winch main-
tains that there is something to choose between his and Evans-Pritchard's
account, on the one very important point of dispute, and that Evans-
Pritchard is, on that point, *mistaken.* Such a case is not of the kind
touched by Quine's indeterminacy thesis which, after all, applies to
translations which are empirically equivalent, which are equally good,
as accounts of all the evidence. But all attempted translations need not
be regarded as empirically equivalent. Roth has both misunderstood
Winch and misapplied Quine.

However, this is not Roth's only attack on Winch. He has criticisms
of Winch's treatment of rule-following, a treatment which he regards as
buttressing the 'meaning realism' he attributes to Winch in which rules
fix determinate meaning. Roth, however, seems to suppose that Winch
is treating rules as a kind of causal mechanism which explain why
people acted in one way or another. But, as we have argued, on Winch's
account rules are not inner mental phenomena but are publicly observable features of social life. The notion of rule following applies to
certain kinds of regularities in social life which contrast with other
kinds of regularities such as causal ones. Their importance is that they
figure in very different kinds of explanations than those which seek, for
example, to provide a causal explanation.

Further Roth persists in begging the question that Winch poses,
namely, whether there is any demonstrable need for the kind of explanations a putative social science would supply? Winch does not offer
rule following as a kind of explanation that social science might give,
but points out its character as the sort of explanation that, as ordinary people in society, *we do give.* The standards which govern such
explanations originate in the practical purposes and social lives of the
people involved in the giving and receiving of these explanations. These
standards are not the same ones which are set by notions of what scientific explanations can provide. Explanations in terms of rules cannot be
found deficient by the standards of science because they are not candidates for the judgements of science. The rules of chess do not constitute
a candidate scientific theory of the game of chess but provide criteria
of what it is to play chess legitimately and properly and, thus, provide
socially sanctioned means by which to talk about the things that people
playing chess are doing, including explaining why they make the moves
they make. For example, there is a difference between explaining to
someone why a player makes a particular move in terms of what
prompts him or her to make that move rather than another, and where

characterological attributes might feature – for instance, the person is a cautious player – and explaining why some move is not allowed within the game – such as moving the castle diagonally. The latter kind of explanation is more likely to be required by a naive onlooker and this is, Winch is saying, much more akin to the kind of thing that would-be social scientists actually go in for when they are engaged in explaining things rather than providing causal explanations for phenomena which *ab initio* lack such causal explanations.[7]

'Semantic nihilism' of the Quine/Davidson/Roth sort derives from a very different source to that of French philosophy and social theory where the notion of meaning has been conceived as, effectively, an ideologically generated illusion. The lesson that is drawn is that we should disrupt language and shatter the illusion of meaning. This marks a turn to the *text* and to the examination of social science as a matter of *writing* and of writing in language which is steeped in ideology. It demands an intensely reflexive and deconstructive approach to the text, towards a disruption of, rather than an attempted capture of, meaning.

Post-structuralism

The ideas summarised in the last part of the paragraph above originate, as the label suggests, in a reaction against French structuralism while retaining many continuities with structuralism. The critique was, in the simplest of terms, that structuralism had failed to clarify the meaning of its own doctrines. In particular, it had not been clear about the extent to which those very doctrines invalidated the idea of 'science' despite insisting that this was its aspiration. Abandoning the idea that one could have a science of language was, in part, motivated by also wishing to abandon the idea that one could progress from ideology to science. Structuralism's problem was its failure fully to understand the extent to which language is ideology: the extent to which notions such as meaning and, especially, reality are themselves ideological notions.

Structuralism was another tactic in the recurrent effort to make the social and cultural studies into sciences by modelling them on another successful science, in this case not a natural science but a human science, namely, linguistics. Linguistics had seemingly achieved a certain measure of hard scientific success through the work of Ferdinand de Saussure (1959) who had argued that the way to understand language was as a self-enclosed system of contrasts. As Wittgenstein later did, Saussure attacked the attempt to understand language in terms of words standing for things. Saussure argued that words do indeed 'stand for things', but this is no basis for a scientific linguistics. The connection between words and the things they stand for is arbitrary as can be seen in the way, in different languages, different words stand for the same thing. The correct way to understand language is as a differentiated system, one within which the units, to be units, must be characterised by their differences, just as, say, the positions in a soccer team are defined by the different roles their occupants are supposed to play. Thus, within the team, positions are identified by contrast with each other and so it is with the words of a language.

The structuralism of Lévi-Strauss

This conception, successfully applied in linguistics, was adopted by an anthropologist, Lévi-Strauss in his studies of culture.[8] Taking the view that, basically, the human mind is everywhere the same, Lévi-Strauss thought that the model of structural linguistics could be applied to anthropology to demonstrate the universality of logical thought. Using the example of myth, he argued that though 'savages' are held to think differently from the way we do, if we examine how mythical stories unfold then we can see that this is not so, or at least only in ways that are superficially different. Their thought is no less logical than our own.

The superficial appearance of difference derives from our possession of science and mathematics, the disciplines which specialise in logical thought and which have developed complex tools to enable us to think in abstractions. Despite their lack of such tools, 'savages', Lévi-Strauss argues, have just the same logical powers as we do, but these are expressed in a different form from our own, for example, in mythical tales. 'Savages', for example, have an immense, thorough and detailed knowledge of the flora and fauna of their world, and it is through their empirical knowledge that they are able to exercise their logical powers. Rather than employing abstract devices, such as mathematics and symbolic logic, the 'savage' operates with concrete materials which finds much of its expression in mythical tales. It is, therefore, less as tales and more as logical constructions that Lévi-Strauss is interested in them. Such myths are comprised of stories which feature phenomena taken from the world around those who recount the myths. Reference to such materials can play the same role that abstractions can play in logic and mathematics except the reasoning is 'concrete' rather than abstract.

The key idea for analysing the logical structure of myth is the same as in Saussure and the school of structural linguistics arising from his work. It is contrast which is important in understanding mythical stories. In other words, the point is to attend to their organisation as a pattern of contrasts, that is, their structure, rather than to their substance. Thus, Lévi-Strauss's method is to ask about the role that, say, a particular kind of animal, person or other phenomenon, plays in a given myth or even in a connected series of them. Through a patient investigation of the intricate pattern comparing all the places and connections that element occupies first in the myth, and then ideally in all the other myths in which it occurs, the 'semantic value' of the item can be worked out.[9] Working out the 'semantic value' is not an end in itself but a means to discover the underlying logic of 'mythical thought' and to exhibit the way in which this thinking comes to grips with some of the profound and perennial problems of human thought.

For a very simple example, Lévi-Strauss notes that myths treat 'above' and 'below' as two contrasts in respect of their relationship on the up–down scale. They are also separate from one another. The 'above' is not accessible to ordinary human beings but is often thought of as the domain of celestial beings. Water, however, is an element which can cross that divide for, in the form of rain, it can pass from above to below. Similarly, 'fog' is halfway between above and below. It has the characteristics of clouds, which are found in the sky, but which itself appears near ground level. Thus, these natural phenomena, by virtue of their natural properties, can be used in the myths to stand for logical relations, such as those of opposition as between 'above' and 'below', or intermediate status 'one-and-the-other' as with water which comes from above to below or neither one nor the other, as fog.

Natural and social phenomena, for the ways and practices of people can also be elements in myths, provide materials with which to present logical relations and, given the availability of these basic, simple resources for logical reasoning, they can be used to build very elaborate patterns. It is following through the working out of these elaborate structures that Lévi-Strauss's main work is devoted.[10]

One of the aspects of myth in which Lévi-Strauss is particularly interested is in the cosmologies it builds which attempt to explain the most general nature of things including, for example, the diversity of things: why are there different kinds of things rather than only one kind of thing? Given that there are diverse kinds of things and that they originated from one thing, then how to deal with the logical puzzle of many originating from one. In *The Story of Lynx,* there is a discussion of the role of unequal twins. In these myths, the twins, though near identical, are not actually so for they have having opposed characteristics: one is bright, the other stupid, one honest, the other a deceiver, and so on. According to Lévi-Strauss, the idea of twins can be used to work out a fundamental structure for the nature of things. He begins:

These myths represent the progressive organisation of the world and of society in the form of a series of dual splits but without the resulting parts of each state ever being truly equal. In one way or another, one is always superior to the other . . .

(Lévi-Strauss 1995: 213)

Earlier he had extracted from other myths a representation of reality in precisely such a series of dual splits (see Figure 8.1), beginning with the original separation of creatures from the creator which exhibits a descending order of contrastive divisions and which form of representation, as unbalanced distinctions, provides for the proper functioning of the system of the world which 'depends on this dynamic disequilibrium, for without it this system would at all times be in danger of falling into a state of inertia'.

He goes on:

What these native myths implicitly state is that the poles between which natural phenomena and social life are organised – such as sky and earth, fire and water,

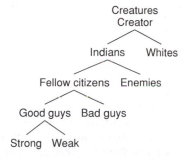

Creatures
Creator

Indians   Whites

Fellow citizens   Enemies

Good guys   Bad guys

Strong   Weak

Figure 8.1 **The structure of myths**
Source: Lévi-Strauss 1995: 213

above and below, Indians and non-Indians, fellow citizens and strangers – could never be twins. The mind attempts to join them without succeeding in establishing a parity between them. This is because it is these cascading distinctive features, such as mythical thought conceives them, that set in motion the machine of the universe.

(Lévi-Strauss 1995: 213)

Thus, the concrete example of unequal twins, who are themselves a case of more than one coming from only one, is used to stand for the 'abstract' idea of unequal opposites, and used to introduce a dynamic element into a nested hierarchy of oppositions.

It is important to emphasise that this is only a very small selection from Lévi-Strauss's account of the structure of mythic thought. Although the example illustrates the way in which the claim for the logical character of mythic thought is evidenced, the rivalry between the twins in the mythic stories is used to work out fundamental cosmological themes, a single element of a much more complex and intricate structure which cannot be presented here.

For the structuralists, one of the key features of Saussure's conceptions had been the way in which they challenged the idea of meaning as produced by the individual; instead meaning was produced by the system of language. Comparable to Bhaskar's realism, the emphasis was on the acting individual as a product of a real, unconsciously operating, system. Lévi-Strauss certainly regards thought as having its own laws which we, the 'savages' who tell myths, operate by even though we are unaware of them. The patterns to be found in myths are not manifest to those who tell the myths but are only revealed through extensive scientific comparative study. Thus, the structuralists were important contributors to the resurgence of intensely anti-individualist themes in social thought. One of the key elements in structuralism was its emphasis on displacing, or 'decentring', to use an often-preferred mode of expression, the subject. That is, the latter is no longer viewed as the·centre and causal source of system of human activity, but as someone whose very existence depends upon and is to be understood in terms of its location within the system. True explanation in the social sciences is not to be sought using concepts such as intentions, purposes, or other so-called subjective states of mind, but in the laws of the differentiated, complex and encompassing structures within which individuals are suspended.

The structuralists saw themselves as giving new content to the ideas of Marx and Freud about the way people are unconscious of the true nature of, and explanations for, their own actions, and Lévi-Strauss's work initiated a boom in structuralist studies. For a brief period it was hailed as providing the possibility of a new and much more rigorous science which provided a method of great generality, and which could be applied to all kinds of cultural products, as well as myths, from all kinds of societies. Thus, in their first flush, structuralist ideas were keenly adopted in literary studies. The unqualified enthusiasm for structuralism, however, was short lived. Even before structuralism's reputation had spread outside France, key figures in the movement were beginning to have second thoughts, and younger academics expressing deep scepticism, largely on the basis that an important requirement of a social theory is that it should be 'reflexive', that is, apply to itself as well as, and in the same way, to those other people that it studies. If a social theory is successfully to lay claim to being comprehensively general, then it should apply to all human activities including that of social theorising. Structuralism had not applied this requirement. While emphasising the ideological character of language and thought, and the unconscious nature of its operation, it did not apply these to itself nor to the venture of science with which it had affiliated itself. It had retained, unexamined, the supposition that its own language, as an instance of that of the language of science, was exempt from such unconscious ideological determination and could, simply and unproblematically, refer to reality itself. Louis Althusser's (1969) work, for example, pivoted on a stark opposition between ideology and science in elucidating those elements of Marx which had broken through into science.

In the hands of the poststructuralists, the requirement of reflexivity collapsed the distinction between science and ideology, so leading to a treatment of the former as the latter. The form this took was to critique science as an instance of the ambitions of reason. Since the Enlightenment, the ideologues of modernity had presented reason as a progressive, emancipatory force but which could be exposed, by poststructuralist critiques, as an instrument of domination within the modern state and not a power for individual freedom. The conception of a coherent history of the Western world, over the last three hundred or so years, as a progressive movement toward liberation through science was termed a 'grand narrative' by Lyotard (1984): an attempt to conceive history in terms of an all-embracing and congruous story. The era of such 'grand narratives', Lyotard maintained, was over. Changing historical circumstances no longer enabled people to believe that history has a meaning, purpose, direction or coherence; it is this 'incredulity' toward 'grand narratives' which is, for Lyotard, the demarcation point between modern and postmodern society.

This critique implies a profound change in the nature of social research. The idea of method is displaced by a conception of confrontation, that is, the breaking up of the unities which the text appears to project, of exposing the ideology which it seeks, surreptitiously, to put across, and destabilising the terms in which it pretends to give a coherent expression of that ideology. In so doing, it rejects the positivist project of seeking a method as but an instance of the Enlightenment project which sought to establish reason as an agent of freedom. The aim is not so much to describe or even to understand the text (with 'text' being here used in a broadened sense to include not just written phenomena but all those, such as social phenomena generally, which need to be interpreted, i.e. 'read') but, rather, to challenge it by using the text against itself, by reading the text in such a way as to bring to the fore all the ways in which the text gives itself away, all the ways in which it manifests incoherence and internal division despite all its efforts to project itself as being coherent and having a unified structure.

To understand the way in which deconstruction treats the requirements of logic and reason, the demands for order and coherence may be easier if an analogy is drawn with the way keeping wild animals in zoos is now criticised. Though originally presented as a way of enabling us to make contact with wild nature, the zoo is now widely seen as a means of domesticating that nature which, in so doing, gives a distorted picture of the nature of the animals it contains by placing them in an unnatural situation. In the same way, logic, reason and their vehicle, method, are not means of bringing out the true nature of phenomena but, rather, a way of domesticating those phenomena by presenting them in contained, controlled but unnatural ways. The implication is not to go along with the demands of reason, to provide new methods to its service as, for example, the positivistic tradition constantly strives to do, but to challenge those very demands (see, e.g. Foucault 1972, 1977). Reason's complicity in oppression needs to be exposed and ways devised to subvert and disrupt the capacity of those methods to project themselves as representations of 'objective realities'. Related to the loss of faith in 'grand narratives' is a 'crisis of representation' in which our culture has collectively lost faith in the capacity of our schemes of thought, especially science, to represent the truth about reality. Post-structuralism is both a further development and a symptom of this loss of faith.

Two figures stand out, Foucault and Derrida. Both aim to provide tools for the subversion of reason's pretensions to rigorous, reality-capturing authoritative methods.

Foucault and the discourses of knowledge and power

Foucault is one of the most prominent poststructuralists and probably the most influential figure in the humanities and the social sciences in recent years. Foucault's case was that the development of knowledge, as exemplified in the fledgling social sciences of the eighteenth century and since, have contributed to the proliferation of power relations in the formation of modern society.

Foucault argued that there has been no diminution in the degree to which power intruded into people's lives in the centuries since the Enlightenment or, as he would call it, the 'Classical Age'. If anything there has been an intensification of such intrusion. Power has permeated into ever more spheres of social life and in ever finer and ever more intricate details. There has, however, been a change in the form in which power appears in our lives. The often brutal power, nakedly exercised, of the absolute monarch has been replaced by the velvet glove of the administrator; manipulation has taken over from coercion. In modern society there has been a proliferation of bureaucracies which operate to extend supervision, through surveillance, throughout society and, in the course of this, generate extensive recording and documentation systems about the lives and activities of innumerable individuals. This regime has developed to serve the purpose of the management of the society and has grown in conjunction with the introduction of techniques of organisation, in the military, at work, in schooling, for example, all of which make individuals more tractable to more management through inculcating discipline: regimes of detailed control whose objective was the transmutation of control into self-control, so making the individual a willing accomplice in the requirements of power. The would-be social sciences have played a crucial role in these developments in shaping the management of the population by reference to ideas of 'normality'. The control, even manipulation, of people is justified in terms of the development and maintenance of their 'normality', with even more rigorous control over those deemed 'abnormal'.

Foucault was also putting a strongly historicist position. The 'historicist' on some central meanings of this term is one who regards the meaning of ideas as something which is thoroughly historically contexted and, thus, restricted in scope. The ideas can only have a specific meaning in certain sociohistorical circumstances, and hence can only be truly understood *and believed* by those who inhabit just those specific sociohistorical circumstances. If those necessarily relevant circumstances change, then the ideas can no longer make the same sense and, hence, cannot any longer be authentically believed. Thus, the notion that the 'same' ideas can be shared across drastically different historical periods, that there can be perennially true and universally accepted ideas is denied. It is not possible for them to be the same ideas, even if they superficially look the same.

The poststructuralists are not alone among those with some inclination to contemporary historicism. For example, we have already met an element of this in Kuhn's arguments about the 'incommensurability' of scientific theories and the 'breakdowns of communication' which arise between different generations of scientists. The philosopher Richard Rorty (1991a, 1991b) has argued that the idea that philosophy deals with 'eternal' questions, and is always addressing basically the same questions throughout its history – a very common way of portraying the history of philosophy – is just false and that there are radical discontinuities in the nature of philosophical problems, with new problems appearing and displacing old ones. Such transitions are the result of sociohistorical change, for it is only possible to *think*, i.e. conceive of something as a problem, and to think about that problem under certain conditions. Similarly, though differently inspired, the historian of political thought, Quentin Skinner, has argued for a thorough re-examination of crucial phases in the history of political theory.[11] Skinner argues that there has been a serious misunderstanding of major and much studied figures, such as Thomas Hobbes and Niccolò Machiavelli, because it was thought that their meanings could be established by reading their texts alone to ascertain the extent to which they 'speak to us' across centuries and formulate purportedly general arguments about the universal problems of political life. Skinner complains, however, that this treatment distorts the actual meaning of the classic texts because it is given in ignorance of the very specific conditions under which the texts were created, and the ways in which they relate to, and are about, particular and local problems of their time and place.

For Foucault, then, the growth of the social sciences, like all other events in the history of thought, was purely and entirely a product of a particular phase in history, one in a series of successive 'epistemes', as he called them. Each 'episteme' was self-contained, enclosed against and entirely discontinuous with its successors and predecessors. They were complex structures which determined the possibility of thought but which, being the structures within which thought takes place, were not available to conscious thought. The 'episteme' which supported the social sciences, the idea that there was an underlying and unifying phenomenon of study, that of the study of 'man' or humanity, had lasted for three hundred years but its days were now drawing to a close. The thought of Marx, of Freud and, more recently the structuralists, had all prefigured the displacement of the notion of 'man' by that of 'structure'.

Foucault, like so many of the prominent thinkers of the latter part of the twentieth century, puts language (or, better, language and other forms of representation) at the centre, in Foucault's case, as 'discourse'. A discourse is a complex structure governed by a system of rules which identifies the things that can be talked about, the things that can be said about them, which things can be said by which kinds of persons, and so on. For brief and simplified example, in the discourse of psychiatry the things which can be talked about are, prominently, 'mental illnesses' and 'mental patients', the latter's symptoms and treatment, and so forth. What can be said about them varies with different therapies. The people involved in this discourse stand in different positions within it. Those designated 'patients' have their speech understood as expressing symptoms, while those designated 'psychiatrists' diagnose and prescribe treatment.

Such discourses, Foucault seeks to demonstrate, are contingent. They come into being only under highly specific sociohistorical conditions and form in the context of the thoroughly contingent development of organisational structures and ways of organising activities. The discourse of psychiatry, for example, arose in conjunction with the formation of the hospital and the inclusion of the 'mad' within the category of those considered in need of 'treatment'. But, initially this outcome was very delicately balanced in that the 'mad' might possibly have been brought under the designation 'criminal' and taken under the jurisdiction of the newly developing prison system.

It is the specific and contingent circumstances which provide the conditions under which the vehicle of thought, the discourse, can come into, albeit transient, existence. Thus, Foucault takes a view of language as creating or producing the things whereof it speaks and, as such, he is another of the opponents of the view that the relation between language and the world consists in the giving of names to objects which preexist the language. Instead, his emphasis is upon the way in which the development of a discourse, a protracted and diffuse process, creates the possibility of there being certain kinds of objects such as, again for example, the 'mental patient'. It is not as if the 'mental patient' could preexist the development of psychiatric discourse, for the idea that 'madness' was a type of illness was itself historically late. Moreover, the idea that illness was itself something to be dealt with by placing people into the category of 'patient' also awaited the development of an organisational form of medical treatment. The practices of hospitalisation are post-seventeenth century developments. But it was these developments which created the possibility of there being such a thing as the 'mental patient', the possibility of our ever speaking of such an 'object'. Since the formation of objects is integral to the development of discourse, this means that it is intimately connected with power. Accordingly, the categories of language, the way in which language classifies, are not demarcating what is there naturally but is, instead, an imposition on the world with the result that, in social life, the language of normality and pathology is not the expression of reason's grasp, through science, of the nature of things in themselves but is really only the language of social control.

Foucault's purpose is, in part, a political one. The point of the exercise is not just to analyse and describe objects but, in important respects, to discredit them by making things which had seemed 'natural' or 'logical' into things which are seen to be 'contingent' and 'arbitrary'. Foucault does not suppose that by exposing them in this way, he thereby makes them easier to overthrow, let alone engenders their immediate collapse. The movements of thought and patterns of change which he depicts are ones which, after all, take place outside of human control and direction. He supposes that only the revelation of the 'contingent' or 'arbitrary' form of these seemingly 'natural' and 'logical' forms of knowledge erodes both their social and their intellectual authority. Revealing that patterns of organisation of our life which we have treated as natural and logical are not only contingent and arbitrary, but also authoritarian, repressive and even cruel, should divest them of their hold over us, make unthinking compliance with them more difficult, and make transgression of them easier. Foucault does not think that such 'resistance' as his work encourages can, however, overthrow the system or even come close. It can only provoke localised and specific oppositions to the most concentrated foci of repression and cruelty.[12] The erosion of the authority of our instituted frameworks for thought through a demonstration of the way in which their fundamental form is rooted in sociohistorical structures of which we are unconscious is meant to attack, among other things, what is imagined to be one of the keystones of our society's way of thinking, that is, the notion that we can grasp, through thought, the ultimate nature of reality itself.

If the postempiricists have treated science as fulfilling the role metaphysics aimed to play, namely, that of capturing the nature of reality itself, then the poststructuralists, to the contrary, deny that the ambition of metaphysics can ever be fulfilled. The nature of reality can never be captured in thought. The determinants of the nature of thought itself are not, as Foucault's ideas attempt to make plain, those of reality itself but, rather, they are the sociohistorical conditions under which thinking is done: sociohistorical conditions which change in drastic and unforeseen ways because of shifts which cannot be understood by human beings. Thus, Foucault's key idea is reflection of the view of language, and the categories and schemes of thought seen as having, or at least eventually attaining, the status of 'representations', that is, media in which the nature of reality itself may be re-presented or portrayed. In many ways this is regarded as the prime illusion of the Enlightenment legacy: that rational thought can produce authentic representations of reality itself. Such an idea is, in Foucault's scheme, manifestly a nonsense and is one reason why the main exercise in much recent social thought has been the critique of 'representation' and why there is much talk of the present period as being one in which we confront the 'crisis of representation'.

Another key figure in provoking the sense of a 'crisis of representation' is Foucault's Parisian contemporary and sometimes antagonist, Jacques Derrida. The coinage 'deconstruction', now a household word though one usually meaning just the 'destruction' or 'demolition' of someone's position rather than the more technical sense it has for Derrida, certainly conveys the implication of disruption and subversion which it is intended to carry.

Derrida and deconstruction

The notion of 'deconstruction', the coinage of the literary critic, Paul de Man, and the philosopher, Jacques Derrida, takes a drastic line toward the possibility of meaning.[13] Derrida's endeavour is nothing less than a critique of the whole of the Western philosophical tradition as the leading representative of the idea of reason and as a quest for the impossible. In some respects he begins from the same point as Hegel by noting that philosophy is preoccupied with oppositions, with the true against the false, the beautiful against the ugly, the mental against the physical, the finite against the infinite, and so on. Hegel tried to show how these oppositions could be overcome, even reconciled. But Derrida's very different purpose is to show that they can be undermined. The oppositions do not just involve counterposing opposites, Derrida argues, for they are characteristically ordered hierarchically with one element of the pair deemed superior to the other, and this reflects the depth to which domination is rooted in Western thought.

The key oppositions which Derrida focuses upon are two related pairs: presence and absence, and speaking and writing. As just noted, these are not just opposed but are also hierarchically connected. Presence is preferred over absence, speaking over writing, not least because the latter pair are seen as instantiating the former pair. In Western philosophy's treatment of knowledge and certainty, it is that which is 'present' which promises true and certain knowledge. In positivist and empiricist philosophies, for example, the search was for those 'brute facts' with which we have immediate contact and about which we can have no doubts, a search for things that were unquestionably 'present' and which were often found in our 'sense experience'. However, Saussurian linguistics, reconstructed by Derrida, subverts this idea. The whole point about the meaning of a word being given through a series of contrasts implies that the meaning of a particular word, if that is present for us, depends upon things which are *absent*. The meaning of a spoken word is determined by a contrast with other words which are not now being spoken, ones which could have been used but which were not. This undermines the idea of opposition and hierarchy between the categories of 'presence' and 'absence' for the very nature of what is present to us is determined by what is not present; it is presence and absence *together* which determine the meaning of a word, and this means that presence cannot be preferred over absence.

The distinction between speech and writing, as we remarked, also embodies the traditional hierarchical opposition of presence and absence, with speech being present, the voice immediate to us as it is produced in the presence of the hearer. Writing has been viewed as something secondary to and derivative from speech and which represents speech to make it present when it is absent. By its very nature writing involves absence since the writer is not available to the reader in the way that the speaker is available to the hearer. This means, also, that it is not possible to determine the meaning of that which is written in the way that it is of something said. One can check with a speaker whether one has understood his or her meaning by asking questions, for example, but one cannot ask the author of a written piece who may, after all, have been dead for some centuries.

Derrida questions the opposition of speech and writing by trying to reverse and abolish it. He wants to say that it is speech which is derivative of writing and to do this is to take away the difference between them, making speech a form of writing. He does not give up on the idea that it is problematic to establish the definitive meaning of a text since this is the platform of all his work. Instead, he proposes that there is no difference between speaking and writing on this point, that it is impossible to determine meaning conclusively. And the reason lies in the nature of language.

The crucial point of difference between the structuralists and the deconstructionists is not that the latter deny that it is contrasts that matter in language. What is denied is the structuralist's treatment of these contrasts as if they were in a closed system. Language is not, in Derrida's view, a closed system but a proliferating one within which the possibilities of contrast are open-ended. This means that it is not possible to exhaust the contrasts relative to a determination of meaning; it is impossible to identify a determinate set of stably related contrasts and thus attain a closure of meaning. It must be left as uncertain and unresolved – open-ended, so to speak – what exactly the meaning is.

Accordingly, the quest of traditional philosophy for a determinate, final meaning is a search for that which, in the very nature of language, does not exist. The next step in the programme is to demonstrate that a coherent, settled meaning cannot be attained, and to highlight the extent to which the attempt to provide definitive interpretations involves a gratuitous imposition – it is often condemned as a form of violence – that exaggerates the determinativeness, and suppresses the extent to which such attempts manifest openness, indeterminacy and contrast. Insofar as many philosophical texts are organised around and dependent upon hierarchical oppositions, such a procedure will show these to be spurious and demonstrate how they collapse in on themselves. Thus, the method of deconstruction is essentially that of allowing the text itself, so to speak, to bring out its own indefinite, uncertain and internally divided character: to display, that is, its own disunities. This is not directed at identifying faults, infelicities of expression, for example, which can be put right, for that would be to remain in the frame of mind which considers that meaning can be determinate. Rather, the aim is to effect a change in frame of mind, to bring out that it is futile to suppose that these internal disunities are only incidental features of the text which can be eliminated. Any attempt at putting things right will simply generate further disunities of its own.

Like Foucault, Derrida regards the attempt to apply a notion of rational order in the traditional sense of a logically coherent and systematic scheme as essentially an autocratic operation, one which is false to the heterogeneity of things. It involves the suppression, the denial, of that which cannot conveniently be incorporated within the scheme. This denial of the 'other' subordinates and excludes those who do not fit within the scheme, the reduction of the different and the dissident to silence and echoes Durkheim's ideas about the way that cohesion is achieved through contrast, and how social solidarity involves the expulsion of persons and their transformation into what is nowadays termed 'The Other'.

In practice, then, the mode of deconstruction goes directly against the whole traditional mode of research which is toward unity and accumulation and where the point of interpreting a text is presumed to be that of searching out a single, coherent interpretation to arrive at some resolution, draw the research to a close and endow it with a positive outcome. Deconstruction involves precisely the opposite. It seeks to bring out disunities and contradictions within the text to break down its very unity as a single text. It seeks to uncover the extent to which a given text is a composite of elements from and relations to other texts, its 'intextuality'. Deconstruction does not move toward closure or conclusion but away from it. It encourages proliferation, with deconstructions themselves further grist to the deconstruction mill. Deconstruction is a matter of bringing out the unresolved and unresolvable tensions and contradictions which, though pressed into the margins of the text, are nonetheless disruptive of its purposive integrity. The lesson is, of course, that we cannot master the prolific energies of language, and our very attempt to do so (and note the gender connotations of the very term 'master') merely exhibits and reproduces our culturally deep-rooted ideological drive toward domination and oppression, toward making the world conform to our ideas of order even if that means that we must reshape it so that it will do so. The desire to have things neatly contained and tidily concluded is part of that same 'logocentric' drive and is such a persistent drive that deconstruction runs the risk of being brought back within the fold. Resistance to this logocentric demand must be tireless and endless since it is a constant, continuing demonstration of the tentacular ways in which logocentrism seeks to extend itself over the whole of language and, at the same time, the ultimate futility of this effort. Logocentrism is based on suppositions about how language works which are contrary to the ways in which it actually does. Thus, a book about Derrida ends, in Derridean spirit, by declaring the ultimate elusiveness of his thought and the extent to which the book itself is an attempt at something which cannot be done:

> Trying to repeat faithfully the essential features of Derrida's thought, we have betrayed him . . . we have aborted Derrida, his singularity and his signature, the event we were so keen to tell you about into a textuality in which he may well have disappeared . . . Double bind in which our absolute fidelity has been infidelity itself. This is why this book will be of no use to you others, or to you, other . . .
>
> (Bennington and Derrida 1992: 316)

Derrida's arguments have had an immense impact upon literary criticism, especially in the United States where his works are often regarded as a major contribution to the 'culture wars' recently raging within the academy, but somewhat less so in the social sciences. Nonetheless, he has helped to encourage a notion, which is prominent in cultural studies, that the phenomenon under investigation is the 'text'. Under Derrida's guidance, 'text' has been extended beyond its more traditional meaning to include all kinds of phenomena and activities, and the purpose of inquiry is to give a reading of the text. It is not, as said earlier, to give a definitive or final reading of the text but to give variant and dissenting ones, ones which will disturb, disrupt and dismantle the more conventional readings. Very often the aim is to give rereadings rather than first readings, and to give them in terms which would characteristically be denied or excluded from the usual interpretations of those texts. Thus, the socially marginalised – gays, women, blacks, and so on – are to be revealed as the unmentioned 'others', at the margins of the text.

Similarly, in social and cultural anthropology there has been an enthusiastic discovery in some parts of the discipline, that anthropology is a matter of writing and that the aspirations of the anthropological text for a coherent, objective account, has been an expression of the imperialist mentality seeking to subordinate all reality to the single voice of the author on behalf of Western imperialism: a voice which subordinates and denies the 'natives' even as it writes about them. This is to be corrected only by pluralising voice, by removing the anthropologists/authors from a privileged position of speaking for anyone other than themselves, situating them within a dialogical relationship to 'the natives'.[14] Diversity and disparity need to be brought to the forefront, giving all parties the opportunity to speak for themselves and be acknowledged as independent equals.

Conclusion

In some respects Derrida and Wittgenstein are in agreement about the nature of language. Wittgenstein would agree, for example, that language is not a closed system but proliferates. Wittgenstein's own analogy, as we described earlier, is that language is like a large city which has evolved over many years. Although it is a whole it is not any thoroughly integrated whole. There are districts and zones, some of which are neat and tidy, others which are degenerating and messy, some of which are spacious while others are overcrowded, and so on. From the point of view of a high flying aircraft one gets little sense of the variety and the character of the various areas of the city. From within the city itself, that is, from within language, one absorbs the flavour and the detail but lacks an overall picture. Wittgenstein would also agree with Derrida that meaning is not intrinsic to the word in isolation: meaning belongs to language itself. Where the profound disagreements arise would be over the issue that there is any one principle, such as that of opposition, which is a candidate for fixing the meaning of a word within language. For Wittgenstein, meaning derives from the use of language in ordinary ways, and out of the organisation and needs of the activities within which words (together with meanings) originate. Language is not a self-subsistent system, but is something which is thoroughly interwoven with peoples' activities, and its parts derive their character from the way they are involved in those activities. For example, the very identity of words such as 'love', 'deuce', 'advantage', and so on, is as terms for calling the scores in tennis. Troubles arise when language 'goes on holiday', when, for example, philosophers take concepts out of their ordinary usage, forget the close connection that these words have in the context of activities, and thus lose track of the sense of those words. In other words, Wittgenstein's attack is directed toward the idea that we need a theory of meaning. Instead, what we require to dissolve our philosophical puzzles about meaning is a 'perspicuous view' of the use of words within the activities where they have their home. Derrida's effort to see in language an overarching principle of organisation around oppositions, presence and absence, is to offer a theory of meaning which is unnecessary to the practices of language. The problem of the lack of a 'definitive meaning' arises only if we think that such a thing is necessary for language to have meaning. We do not, however, have to start with this assumption nor, if rejected, take the diametrically opposed view that if language can have no 'definitive meaning' then it is meaningless.

Notes

1. This is akin to the 'underlabourer' conception of philosophy proposed by John Locke. See Chapter 1.
2. The thesis has proven difficult for other philosophers to give a formulation of the thesis to which Quine assents, and equally difficult for other philosophers to find what they can recognise as clarity and consistency in Quine's own formulations. We have done our best.
3. The idiosyncrasy about Quine's notion of meaning and translation when used in this way is an issue we cannot go into here save to note that it is a product of his broader philosophical views.
4. Quine himself agrees that this is the way in which we do carry on and, indeed, have to carry on. He explicitly says that his arguments make no difference to anything we practically do when 'translating', and that his indeterminacy thesis makes 'only a philosophical point': that is, it tells us that we have not established anything 'objective' by translating, have not identified any 'fact of the matter' in his sense, which supports the statement of meaning (or, as he would have it, 'translation') we have made. A Wittgensteinian approach simply questions whether the contention that there is no 'fact of the matter' is anything more than a gratuitous intrusion into discussions of the objectivity of translations. The fact that there is no 'fact of the matter' does not detract from anyone's actual translation activities nor, as Quine himself agrees, is there any reason why it should. Thus, all that Quine's talk of indeterminacy does is seemingly cast a shadow across the business of translation (or giving meanings) such that it will seem immensely more problematical than it ordinarily does but which, on closer inspection, proves to do nothing of the sort. Translation could not, in practice, be otherwise than it is. If the absence of a 'fact of the matter' disqualifies translation from the status of a scientific pursuit, then who has ever supposed that it required such a status, apart from Quine that is? The fact that the long history of translation practice has managed without access to any 'facts of the matter', or the realisation that any might be

needed, does not imply that we must now review all the translations that have been made. As Quine himself acknowledges, the lack of access to 'facts of the matter' makes no difference to past, present of future practice. Translation may not be a scientific pursuit, but that does not make it an unscientific one.

5. Davidson departs from Quine in important respects in the way that he applies his holism, though these are not relevant here.

6. He is, like Quine, a 'semantic nihilist'.

7. However, defending Winch against criticisms which seem to misunderstand his problem and position, and which do not really counter the underlying Wittgensteinian ideas which motivate that argument but simply beg them, is very different from presenting a rebuttal of the 'indeterminacy of translation' thesis which has proved extraordinarily difficult to do. The fact that Quine's position has withstood numerous attempts at dismissal does not, however, necessarily testify to the strength of the argument but may just manifest its elusiveness. Though we have given a sketch of the argument in a general way, it is another thing to detail it in such specific ways that one can say what kind of objections would count decisively against it, especially as, as for example Kirk (1986) has observed, Quine himself is prone to keep restating the argument in terms sufficiently different to amount to different theses. The attempt to say what is wrong with the 'indeterminacy thesis' is entangled with the effort to say what the thesis definitely states.

8. The work of Lévi-Strauss is voluminous. But see, for example, Lévi-Strauss (1966, 1968, 1969, 1970).

9. The 'semantic value' need not remain constant over different myths.

10. This now totals nearly 4,000 published pages.

11. Skinner (1985). There are chapters on Lévi-Strauss, Derrida, Kuhn and Foucault and an introduction which outlines how grand theorising has again taken centre stage after the demise of positivism.

12. He himself was an activist for prisoners' rights.

13. Here we draw upon Derrida's version. See Derrida (1976).

14. This deconstructionist emphasis has led to the rediscovery of the Russian thinker, Bhatkin, who argued for the idea that any given text is actually a polyphony composed of an assortment of different, interacting voices.

CHAPTER 9

Conclusion

In this book we have tried to trace some of the many and multifarious connections between philosophy and social research and, now, we should say something on our own behalf about this topic. We have not tried to disguise our own sympathies in our discussion, though neither have we sought to give them much prominence.

The pivot of the organisation of the book is the key event for the social sciences in the latter half of the twentieth century, though the seeds were laid earlier, namely, the reaction against and rejection of positivist doctrines. This reaction represents in the social sciences a pattern of movement which had already been taking place in philosophy, a turning against what we have termed 'foundationalist' doctrines which were most prominently represented in the social sciences by positivism. To an important extent, the fate of foundationalist doctrines is interwoven with philosophical views about the nature of science. The achievements of post-seventeenth century natural science are widely seen as quite special, with foundationalists tending to see these as being the closest candidates to the certain truths that they seek. The achievements of science are seen at least as the best possible candidates we can have for knowledge and, if they are to stand as the exemplars of proper knowledge, then they need to be supplied with the necessary foundations. Unavoidably, then, the rejection of foundationalism goes along with a demotion of science in terms of its philosophical status.

It is important to emphasise the difference between 'science' and philosophical ideas about the nature and worth of science, since various criticisms are often taken as if they were criticisms *of science* when, in fact, they are criticisms of philosophical views *about science*. We ourselves doubt whether it is helpful to talk about 'science' since this can well suggest a much more unified and coherent venture integrated around a single, focused task, than is manifested by the variegated assortment of largely unrelated disciplines which now operate as sciences (Dupré 1993). When philosophy talks about 'science' it is often really only talking about physics. This might seem to be a perfectly reasonable thing to do on the grounds that it is the exceptional achievement of physics which mainly endows the sciences with their air of distinctiveness from other forms of thought. However, it needs to be borne in mind that the achievements of physics are *exceptional within science* and, accordingly, focusing solely on this discipline can be misleading, and in an unproductive way. It can be argued that physics has achieved its great successes by avoiding the difficult and complex questions by leaving them to others. These have been 'farmed out', as it were, to disciplines such as geology which, while a respectable enough science in its own right, comes nowhere near the supposed ideals which philosophers have extracted from physics.[1]

If there is any validity to the above argument, then it follows that social science's aspiration to model itself on the advanced sciences would have required the sacrifice of many of the things which social scientists regard as their subject matter, especially those to do with historical questions. Geology, not theoretical physics, might be a better picture of the kind of natural science that the social sciences could come to resemble. Had the social sciences measured themselves against one or other of the natural sciences apart from physics, such as astronomy, botany or geology, for example, rather than against the abstract picture of 'science' painted by philosophers of science, then the status of the social sciences *as sciences* might have seemed a good deal less problematic.

Among the views we have covered in the book are the ideas of Wittgenstein and his follower, Winch, and these are ideas with which we ourselves have the greatest sympathy. The problem which Winch poses for the social sciences – using sociology as his leading example – is not one which we have so far discussed, nor one which is usually considered in relation to his work, where 'rule following' and 'understanding a primitive society' are the topics which tend to get all the attention. We see the important argument in Winch as being his claim that the social sciences are not really sciences, but are philosophy's foster children and that sociology is, in many main respects, nothing other than 'misbegotten epistemology'.

It is easy to react against arguments like Winch's by describing them as 'antiscientific' and many of his critics have not hesitated to stoop so low. The very tendency to put arguments in terms of the dualism of 'proscientific' or 'antiscientific' is typically to transgress the distinction we have been trying to make between science and philosophical views about science. The fact that some philosophical positions identify themselves with science – not unlike, perhaps, the way in which some politicians unscrupulously wrap themselves in the national flag – serves only to cloud the issues. Some philosophers are enthusiastic for science, so much so that they become virtual spokespersons for 'the scientific point of view', advocating its dissemination throughout all areas of life. These philosophers are not, of course, scientists.[2] However, the attempted association, even identification, of their philosophy with science can make it seem that an attack on their views is an attack on science itself. This need not, of course, be the case for criticism can precisely be on the claim that these views provide anything like an accurate characterisation of 'science'.

This was, as we have seen, precisely the problem with positivism in the social sciences. It was apt to present itself as *the* philosophy of science: the philosophy upon which science was built, the philosophy according to which science was practised, and the philosophy that would transform the social sciences in the direction of science itself. The effect was to induce confusion by, in effect, conflating the following kind of arguments.

First, that the social sciences could not be sciences because they could not comply with positivism, and should not want to be sciences because this implied, or seemed to, a misguided or unpleasant view of human beings. Second, the picture of what it takes to be a science as presented by positivism was itself a misleading and impractical one. The trouble with positivism is that it proved to be anything but a prescription for turning the social sciences into sciences. The positivist project was, as we have suggested, a conspicuous failure *as a project*.

Thus, it is necessary to recognise that criticism of philosophers such as Winch for being 'antiscientific' may well just be restatements of philosophical views of the kind that Winch is questioning. The notion that favouring the idea of a social science puts one 'on the side of science' involves, rather, just a tacit subscription to the philosophical presupposition that science is the only true form of understanding, and that if we do not possess a scientific theory of a phenomenon then we just do not understand it.[3] The complaint of being 'antiscientific' may also carry the message that someone like Winch is attempting to obstruct the legitimate progress of science, and is doing so in an obscurantist fashion, seeking to protect certain areas of existence from the scrutiny of science. Again, however, it is important to be aware of the following assumptions.

First, that somehow there is a 'natural' progress to science whereby it extends its domain across all spheres and, therefore, must include human existence and social life. Second, since it is only through science that understanding can be attained, the attempt to exclude things from the purview of science is the attempt to assert that they can defy our attempts at understanding, perhaps as a kind of mystical denial of science.

In our view, Winch's arguments involve nothing of the sort. He only treats the issue of the extent to which the writ of science runs as one which is open to argument, and not one which is preempted by prior – and nonscientific – presuppositions about the nature and possibility of our understanding. Winch's central case is about the diversity of the forms which understanding takes, and of the risks of overstating the claims of science to be the sole or preeminent source of understanding. Part of Winch's point about the inapplicability of the supposed 'scientific' – that is, positivistic – type of understanding to many puzzles about social life is that it is *superfluous*. It is not that social life *defies* the understanding of science, but that many of the things which are important in social life are already understood in that acquiring an understanding of these is part of living a social life: mastering concepts and rules, the practice of giving explanations by reasons, using language, and so on. Such understanding comes through participation in social life, not by the adoption of the attitudes and procedures of science.

It should be noted that 'explanation by rule' and 'explanation by reason', to mention but two, are not proposed as the kinds of explanations that social scientists should adopt instead of causal explanations, but as kinds of explanations that, as members of society, we give each other. The explanations in terms of rules and reasons are ones which are given for, and often resolve, the kinds of puzzles, problems and bafflements that arise for us *as part of our everyday existence*. They are ways of answering questions which are *not themselves scientific* in nature and, hence, do not and cannot take answers which *are* scientific in nature. Thus, the idea that the social scientist's kinds of explanations, whatever those might be, might be in competition with those we ordinarily give each other – a conception which many social scientists cherish – now seems quite odd. The power of 'explanation by rule' is not due to its justification by epistemological argument, but due to the way in which organising affairs in terms of rules is a prominent practice in society itself, a widespread way of setting up and coordinating other practices. Creating a game, for example, may be nothing other than setting out a set of rules for it, and developing a game around those rules ensures that appeals to those rules will, thereafter, have all kinds of potentially explanatory roles in relation to the playing of and talking about the game.

The attempts to construct 'social science' have been conspicuous failures. We say this advisedly, and as we did with respect to criticism of the positivist project, that is, with respect to the very great ambitions which would-be social science has entertained. This is far from saying that the social sciences are not worth the paper that they are written on, that the game is not worth the candle, that they amount to nothing at all.[4] What needs to be emphasised is how very large are the ambitions which social scientists often envisage for their discipline. Auguste Comte wanted it to be not only one of the sciences, but to be the greatest of the sciences and their crowning achievement. This is not altogether absent from sociology where the idea that it is a discipline which can assess and criticise all the other disciplines persists in some parts. If everything is social – a treasured premise of some sociologists – then everything is suitable material for sociological comment. In addition to these large cognitive ambitions, sociologists have often seen their acquisition of knowledge as done for the purpose of moral improvement – and not on a small scale either – as providing the resources out of which the whole fate of humanity as a whole will be decided. This, again, is no trivial or modest aspiration but an aim of the grandest kind.

It is not unfair, we think, to suggest that these grandiose ambitions often serve as alibis for failure on the grounds that frustrations and problems are inevitable when one reaches for the stars. Even the weakest and smallest achievements can be vested with a greater value for they are, after all, contributions to a great and high-minded cause. They are the first and early steps to satisfying the highest standards of intellectual life, namely, the rigorous standards of science, and to fulfil the noblest of ambitions, the emancipation of all humankind.

While it is true that a journey of a thousand miles must begin with a single step, it is also equally true that someone who jumps a few feet in the air is not taking the first step toward a muscle-powered leap to the moon. There is, that is, another view of social science's great ambitions not as utopian even but merely as premature and even utterly unrealistic. These ambitions might invest routine and limited research with a sense of greater purpose, but they can equally well, and almost at the same time, induce and perpetuate the sense of failure and crisis. The fact is that having set such great objectives the social sciences fail to make significant movement out of the starting gate and are hard pressed to demonstrate real progress.

In its more ambitious and sustained efforts to go after the big targets such as, for example, the development of a quantitative social science by positivists, or the theoretical schemes contrived by Karl Marx or Sigmund Freud, it is possible to argue that these efforts often turn out to be not even promising. In the case of the positivist, measurement-minded project, its results have turned out to be more like a formalistic and superficial compliance with examples taken from the natural sciences, rather than genuine rigorous and fertile achievements in measurement, as protagonists of positivistic and quantitative views are themselves often quick to realise. In the case of the grand theories, such as those of Marx and Freud, these remain debatable as to their scientific character and value. Both have probably been more productive of debate about whether they are proper sciences, or only exercises in metaphysics, and about what their theories, be they scientific or metaphysical, actually say and mean.[5]

We do not want to suggest that this is an especially regrettable state of affairs nor that it has been a waste of time arguing over the merits and meanings of such as Marx and Freud. Our point is that these activities, described in this way, sound empty and valueless only if it is supposed that what one should be doing is getting on with the only truly serious business, namely, that of building a proper science. It is only if one sets a ludicrously large scale for the assessment of the activities of fairly fledgling ventures that their activities will seem to be relatively insignificant.

There are, we want to suggest, at least two ways of thinking about the plight of the would-be social sciences.[6] One is to see the social sciences as currently representing the nadir of failure. After long effort they have made no real progress. Indeed, much of the main movement of recent years has been, we have documented with deconstructionism, that of retreat, of undermining themselves and fearing, even proclaiming, their own futility. Their current activities, unless they are modelled after something like the positivist conception, are a time-wasting distraction and not worth pursuing. This conviction can be held both by those who maintain that the aim must be to attain scientific

status and that it is only because we have not yet found the right for-
mula, or have not made the right and sufficient efforts in applying it,
that we have not made better progress; and by those who see the current
plight as meaning that they can never be real sciences and might as
well be abandoned altogether.

Another view is to see the debates over the old texts, and so on, not
as distractions from the real purposes, not as misplaced activities
obstructing the right route to scientific status, but as just the kinds of
things which are characteristic and appropriate to the 'social sciences'.
If they do not look much like 'scientific activities' as these are depicted
in the positivist literature, then this is perhaps because they are not
much like scientific activities and the misconception is to think that
they should or could be.

We have argued elsewhere that the social sciences are often much
more like philosophy than they are like physics (Anderson *et al*. 1985).
This is, we think, very much Winch's· own point. Winch's mentor,
Wittgenstein, was apt to sloganise his approach to philosophy as that of
'showing the fly out of the fly bottle', by which he meant that his
argument was designed to show people that one of the reasons why
they were not making progress in solving a particular philosophical
problem was because they were following the wrong method. The fly
tries to escape by battering against the glass, when it could escape
just by retracing the way it got into the bottle in the first place. One
prominent and inappropriate method is that of attempting to solve philosophical problems (which, on Wittgenstein's view, are not empirical in
nature) by empirical, especially scientific, means. Winch's argument is
just of this form.

It does not mean that *all* the problems of the social sciences are
philosophical rather than empirical or scientific in nature, for there
clearly are all kinds of empirical investigations that can be and are
made. Winch's contention is that many of the main problems of the
social sciences are not empirical or scientific in nature. Examples of
what this could mean should already be familiar. The argument over
reasons and causes is not an empirical argument about the cause of or
the reason for anything in particular. The argument is not about whether
the government's monetary policy is the cause of inflation as opposed,
say, to the pressures arising from international trade, or about whether
Henry VIII's reason for divorcing Queen Katherine was dynastic rather
than, say, religious. These are empirical questions and can be investigated by looking at the evidence. The argument about 'reasons' and
'causes', however, takes it for granted that we can attribute reasons in
some cases and causes in others. What it argues about is whether or not
when we attribute a reason we are giving a similar kind of explanation
as when we give a causal one. Is a reason a cause or not? This kind of
question cannot be answered by empirical investigations of any particular cause or reason.

The same point can be made about the question of whether sociology
– or for that matter any other of the social sciences – is a science. When

we argue that sociology is as much concerned with asking questions about its own identity as is it about any empirical understanding of the world, we are not accusing it of a frivolous disregard of duty. Rather, we would regard this as additional support for a Winchean position for philosophy, too, is just as preoccupied about its own identity. Philosophical argument on *any* topic is likely to function most importantly for philosophical purposes as a demonstration of the value and fertility of the philosophical view that it expresses: as evidence, that is, that *this* view is the best exemplification of the nature of philosophy. We have made the point that social science researches are often undertaken as applications, illustrations or demonstrations of method, as manifestations of the philosophical conceptions of science and knowledge which inform them and which prescribe the shape of the method being followed. All of this could indicate that the resemblance with philosophy's preoccupation with its own nature on the part of the social sciences is more than superficial or accidental.

The very constant preoccupation with social science's own would-be scientific status gives rise to philosophical questions: What is the nature of science? What kinds of methods are distinctive to it? Could these methods be applied effectively to social life? What is the nature of social phenomena? What kind of relationships obtain in social life? Are they, must they be, causal or are they of some other kind, such as 'rule following'? Is 'rule following' some kind of causal occurrence or is it very different from a causal occurrence? And so on.

There is another battery of heavily epistemological questions which also predominate: Is science a special kind of knowledge distinct from other kinds? Does science have a distinctively objective nature? What assures its objectivity? Is objective knowledge only possible through the application of scientific methods? Are people other than scientists doomed only to 'subjective' opinions rather than objective knowledge? Is truth a relationship between something external to thought and thought itself, or is there no reality external to thought? And so on.

The difference between Winch and many of his critics is not that he thinks, and they doubt, that the above are philosophical questions; the dispute is with those who have already decided that the social sciences are, must be, sciences. They indeed engage with philosophical issues, but they do so on the basis of assuming that this is a kind of preliminary work that must be done prior to the formation of the hoped-for science. It is through taking on, and purportedly resolving, these philosophical topics that the way is prepared for empirical work.

This view is not only strange but also a strangely impractical one. After all, it is a strange assumption that sciences are put together 'from the top down', so to speak, as if they were constructed according to a master plan which was laid down before they began. It is also counter to recent work in the philosophy of science which casts doubt on the existence of any general scientific method but which presents the growth of science as an *ad hoc* affair. Further, insofar as philosophical problems of this kind have ensnared and engaged philosophers for centuries, it is also an optimistic supposition that current interventions are easily going to resolve the issues and license the move to full blown empirical inquiry. It is just as likely that the philosophical problems will produce a 'tar baby' effect and that having become involved with them, one will become more and more caught up in them.

For Winch, such philosophical issues are not preliminaries to addressing the real scientific problems. These are the problems and insofar as they are recurrent and pervasive preoccupations of social science, which permeate into conceptions of method and purportedly give point to empirical research, then sociology is 'misbegotten epistemology', that is, philosophy presented in the guise of science.[7]

The idea of method in the social sciences, then, is only superficially about the design and development of actual research procedures. It is in a profound sense much more motivated by foundationalist suppositions. The attempt to specify 'method' for the social sciences is the attempt to locate an epistemologically secure starting point for these candidate sciences. The very idea of 'the scientific method' did not arise as an attempt to provide a generalised characterisation of how scientists went about their inquiries, but on the basis that the successes of the natural sciences embodied a proven method which, if identified and generally adopted, would provide an assured means of gaining knowledge. This is why the growing conviction, within the philosophy of science as a cumulative effect of the works of Popper, Kuhn and Feyerabend, that there is no scientific method is such a damaging conclusion for foundationalism.

One piece of advice Wittgenstein gave to philosophers amounted to: 'don't oppose philosophical positions'. This did not mean accept philosophical positions without question. What it meant was do not suppose that the way in which to disagree with a given philosophical position is to develop an alternative solution to its problems. The rationale for this advice was that in opposing a philosophical position by offering a rival solution to its problems is to concede too much to that initial position, by retaining and carrying over some of its key misconceptions into one's own thinking. The point, for Wittgenstein, was to dispel, not replace, philosophical positions by liquidating them altogether rather than perpetuating elements of them in some supposedly improved scheme. The shift from 'foundationalism' to 'antifoundationalism' which occurs in the book between the discussion of positivism and the discussion of its alternatives exhibit well what Wittgenstein saw to be one of the dangers of opposing philosophical positions, namely, that it results in a movement between extremes. (Wittgenstein 1958, 1969).

We ourselves are, as Wittgenstein himself was, 'antifoundationalist', but only in the sense that we do not – as he did not – accept foundationalism. The trouble with foundationalism is not, however, that it failed to fulfil its ambitions. This would be to concede too much to foundationalism in accepting its idea of the nature of knowledge that it should depend upon the identification of categorical certainties. If we accept that idea, then opposition to foundationalism will almost inevitably –

as it had done in large parts of fashionable philosophy and social science – induce the sense of crisis. If foundationalism has failed to fulfil its ambitions, if it is realised that these ambitions cannot be fulfilled, then we are left bereft of foundations. Knowledge, and science as the leading exemplar of knowledge, must be in crisis. We cannot invest in them the kind of certainty that we used to endow them with for they lack secure foundations and the essential epistemological authority. Thus, the antifoundationalists become the mirror image of the foundationalists in sharing the same fundamental preconception: if knowledge, or science, cannot be provided with sound epistemological foundations, then it is unjustified because it cannot be shown to originate in indubitable certainties.

Both foundationalists and antifoundationalists share the above assumption, but differ on what its implications might be. Foundationalists suppose, or hope, that the requisite certainties can be identified; the antifoundationalists doubt, or deny, that they can be found. Both agree, however, that if such certainties do not exist, then knowledge, especially science, is unjustified. For the antifoundationalists this means coming to terms with the failure of foundationalism. We must learn to live in a world which is bereft of certainties and we must adopt a much more sceptical approach to all questions of knowledge. We must instead emphasise the uncertainty and undecidability of everything that might be taken for knowledge. In this way, antifoundationalist conclusions are straightforward deductions from key foundationalist premises.

Wittgenstein was of the view that 'philosophy leaves everything as it is', a remark which, in the highly politicised climate of philosophy and the social sciences in the past few decades, has led to him being condemned as a conservative, as though his argument were about the possibility of sociopolitical change. However, the kind of thing that Wittgenstein meant by this remark can perhaps be seen in the example of foundationalism. The debate between foundationalists and antifoundationalists sounds as if it should make a difference, and a huge difference at that. Certainly, antifoundationalists are often keen to give advice on lifestyle, to tell us how we should change our ways of living in the light of a world bereft of certainties. What could be a greater difference than a world in which things are absolutely certain, and a world in which nothing is certain? However, if we take Wittgenstein's remark to the effect that philosophy leaves everything as it is, then accepting or giving up on foundationalism should not, does not, materially change the certainty of, say, the findings of science.

It is important to note here that the certainty which foundationalists wanted to vest in the results of science was not one derived from actually existing or, more accurately, actually identified, foundations of knowledge. The philosophical problem was, after all, to identify the requisite foundations. The aim in doing so was validated by the notion that, in the case of the sciences, this was a worthwhile effort since these were the exemplars of true knowledge. Thus, it was the certainty vested in the findings of science which was the occasion for foundationalist thinking, not the other way around. The certainty of scientific knowledge was adjudicated independently of, and prior to, the formulation of these supposed certainties.

Foundationalism saw itself as defending the certainties of knowledge against persistent scepticism. However, Wittgenstein's point about conceding too much to the initial position applies. Insofar as foundationalism originates in an attempt to respond to the sceptic, then it concedes already too much to the sceptic. It allows that the sceptic has posed a valid challenge to whatever certainties are the sceptic's target. In so doing, of course, one must accept – if one is to respond to them meaningfully – some of the sceptic's terms for setting the problem, for ascertaining whether, for example, we can ever be certain of anything. Wittgenstein denied that the sceptic's position is an authentic one, denies, that is, that the sceptic has any genuine doubts to raise. The sceptic's 'doubts' are not doubts at all but pretences of doubt. The sceptic's arguments can really be granted for the purposes of argument only, which means that they are not granted at all. Indeed, it is difficult to find actual philosophical sceptics even though philosophers deem it necessary to try to find answers to scepticism. Descartes, whose method of systematic doubt became the leading technique of sceptical argument, did not apply the method out of his own sceptical convictions, but out of a concern to counter the possibility of scepticism. His method of systematic doubt was his attempt to give his opponent's arguements their best shot. Note once again, foundationalism and scepticism are interwoven. Foundationalism is partly developed as a response to the imagined threat of scepticism which makes it unsurprising that antifoundationalism itself involves a large measure of scepticism.

The rarity of the genuine sceptic is further demonstration of Wittgenstein's point that the certainty of knowledge in general, or of scientific knowledge in particular, is not a real contest between the foundationalist and the sceptic, with both sides accepting the difficulty of seriously asserting sceptical arguments, for that would require genuine, substantial and not just "for the sake of argument", doubts. Thus, neither the foundationalism nor scepticism envisages doubts that make a tangible difference.

There have been doubts, for example, about the foundations of mathematics. Suppose, the worry goes, that there was an undetected contradiction in mathematics, a contradiction in something as basic as arithmetic. Is it possible to prove logically that mathematics, even simple arithmetic, is not inconsistent? Note that this doubt does not suggest that there *is* such an inconsistency. It has no basis for suggesting, and certainly not for identifying, any particular inconsistency in arithmetic. All that is being complained of is the lack of any general method of ruling out all possibility of inconsistency. But saying that arithmetic has not been proven to be consistent is a long way from saying, from being able to say, that arithmetic is inconsistent. That we cannot prove arithmetic to be consistent does not provide a reason for thinking that it is inconsistent. But imagine. What if there were an inconsistency in arithmetic? Consider how much about our lives is built upon arithmetic, and what would happen if it turned out there was such an inconsistency? Perhaps bridges built according to its calculations would start to fall down, computers suddenly crash, financial transaction no longer make sense? If this were true, if there were any real reason for supposing that there might be an inconsistency in arithmetic, then surely those who thought so should be out campaigning to get its use stopped and start redesigning bridges, computers and financial systems. However, sceptical arguments which promise genuinely catastrophic results from the neglect of them do not seem to be taken seriously enough to occasion attempts to avert the potential catastrophes. Of course, no one is really expecting such catastrophes. Nor need they. We build all kinds of buildings and bridges, write all kinds of computer programs, carry on all kinds of financial transactions using arithmetic calculations. Some bridges fall down, many computer programs go wrong and many financial transactions go awry. But, equally, many do not. If there were a contradiction in arithmetic, then it would have been there all along; it would have been built into the bridges and buildings, programs and financial systems. If the consequences of such a contradiction were catastrophic, then such catastrophes would have been happening all along. Hence, the fact of a contradiction in arithmetic might make little practical difference to an awful lot of what we do since what we have done with arithmetic hitherto has worked fine for most of the time, just as Newton's physics can go on being used for all sorts of purposes in physics despite being surpassed, in certain connections, by the work of Einstein.

The tangible difference between the foundationalist and the sceptic now seems a very diminished one and, moreover, one which is not manifested in any tangible differences in the actual world. Even if one did acknowledge the possibility of the sceptical position, even if one did agree, say, that there might be a fatal connection at the heart of mathematics, little of significance follows from this acknowledgement. Unless one knows where the contradiction lies, what kind of contradiction this is, there is nothing that one can do in response to it, no way in which to scope the consequences, take action against it, or put the contradiction right. In Wittgenstein's view, attempts to acknowledge the possibility of the kinds of doubts the sceptic tries to pose can only comprise empty rituals which otherwise make no difference to, have no leverage with, how one carries on doing things.

Thus, the certainty which we vest in scientific findings, commonsense understandings, and the rest, is certainty which is vested in them *independently* of the proven existence of foundations and of sceptical arguments. The idea that certainty requires, and can have, *rational justification* has itself been called into question but it is a mistake to suppose that this means that certainty is *without* rational justification, that it is, in a word, *irrational*. This conclusion would be to concede too much to foundationalism and scepticism by supposing that the notion of 'rational justification' is a cogent one in this context to begin with. To repeat a figure of an argument: that I do not have a justification does not mean the same as, I am without, lacking or in need of a justification.[8]

Wittgenstein's attempted erosion of foundationalist ideas is complex and itself contains unresolved arguments. But a main point of his platform is that those things of which we are most certain are things *which we cannot say we know*. To emphasise: he does not mean, if we cannot say we know them, then we must say that we do not know them. Rather, it means that the connection between 'know' and 'certain' which is, of course, the absolute linchpin of foundationalism, has been cut. Foundationalists and sceptics say that we can only truly say that we know about those things of which we are absolutely certain. Wittgenstein says that we can only say that we know in cases where we can acknowledge the possibility of doubt. His celebrated argument about 'pain' provides a good example. One is in no doubt that one has a pain, a certainty which is expressed by the person saying, 'I have a pain' or 'My arm hurts'. This does not entitle the person to say, 'I know I have a pain'. We cannot intelligibly say, 'I know I have a pain' because this does not equate with, 'I do not know I have a pain', for there is no doubt that the person is in pain. The inapplicability of 'know' here connects only to the fact that we have no ways of doubting whether one is having the pain that one is feeling, of checking whether the pain one is ostensibly feeling is one's own pain. Thus, there is no room for doubt, that is, no way of sensibly introducing doubts which people can check out and which, if confirmed, would show they were mistaken. Someone can doubt whether the pain he or she is feeling in the left eye is due to sinusitis or a bad tooth, and can say, 'I know my pain is due to sinusitis, not toothache' and can be wrong, of course, because the cause of the pain unlike the fact of its possession can be investigated and confirmed.

If there is anything to these Wittgensteinian lines of argument, then to reject foundationalism does not equate with the diminishment of our certainties. Foundationalism should be abandoned not because it is wrong in its arguments about what foundations are, and whether they can be found, but because it is *superfluous*. The trouble is with the whole idea that foundations are required at all, that our certainties do, or should, derive from deeper, more objectively secured certainties. Giving up on foundationalism does not leave us bereft of certainties for that would be to credit foundationalism with much more success in its venture than it is entitled to. It would suppose that the certainties we do have did depend on foundations, that foundationalism itself was a kind of foundation for our historical and contemporary certainties and that, therefore, we only vested our certainties in, say, the findings of science because of a tacit acceptance of the foundationalist doctrines about science. Only then could the idea of pulling away foundationalism be seen in any way as involving pulling away some, if not the whole, of the support for those certainties. If, however, foundationalism is only an ornamental feature of our thought and not a structural support, then the removal of foundationalism will have no further effects. As argued here, the certainties of our lives have *never* needed nor depended upon foundationalism.

Earlier we noted the distinction between philosophical conceptions of the nature of science and the sciences themselves, and suggested that ostensible attacks on the latter are often really attacks on the former as, we think, has been the case in the reaction against positivism. Positivism sought to advance itself as 'the scientific point of view' when it was only a philosophical account of science and had no more connection with science than any other philosophy. Even if some scientists declared themselves positivists or, later, and with enthusiasm, Popperians, this did not mean that science was therefore based upon and conducted in terms of positivism or Popperianism. The same science is conducted by scientists of different philosophy of science convictions and scientists with no such convictions, just as it is conducted by convinced atheists as well as by those who are devoutly religious. The sciences are not conducted on the basis of any philosophy, do not depend upon the support of any philosophy of science, positivistic or otherwise. The attack on positivism is not an attack on science but an attack on a philosophy of science. The attack is misguided if it is thought that it is an attack on the natural sciences as a model for the social sciences, for it is, or ought to be, an attack upon the account that positivism gives of the natural sciences and, thus, of 'science in general'.

The more general problem is not with science but with *scientism*. That is, with those philosophies, such as positivism, which seek to present themselves as having a close affiliation with the sciences and to speak in their name, and which then go on to fetishise the so-called scientific standpoint, arguing for its unlimited and universal applicability. The simple truth is that the undoubted successes of the leading natural sciences do not add any weight to such arguments. The fact that the natural sciences have had some remarkable, even unprecedented and unmatched successes, does not mean that these must be followed elsewhere. Arguing that the natural science approach, assuming that there is such a method, will eventually have the same success in explaining human behaviour as it has had in explaining that of inanimate phenomena is not one strengthened by the success it has had in explaining inanimate phenomena. There is no scientific evidence to support such claims for, of course, they are not scientific claims at all but philosophical speculations. Further, one might argue that the fact that the remarkable successes of the leading natural sciences have not been followed up in all other spheres, despite tremendous efforts to do so, is just as much evidence against this self-styled optimistic idea. The important lesson is to refuse to accede any of the authority that one might concede to a science to those philosophers who seek to carry its weight by purportedly acting in its name. Equally, one might also refuse to accede a similar authority to those who wish to deny science in the name of a rejection of the excessive claims of a philosophy of science. Indeed, one might refuse to accede an authority to any attempt to revise the sciences on epistemological grounds.

Notes

1. See Miller (1987) and, in a more popular vein, Ridley (1984).
2. Even if they have or have had distinguished careers as scientists. A scientist writing on philosophical topics is not contributing to science, is not carrying out scientific work, but is acting as a philosopher and, hence, propounding not 'the viewpoint of science' but a 'philosophical viewpoint about the nature and significance of science'.
3. This is, of course, the prejudice – more kindly, presupposition – which has so favoured the cause of 'theory' in not only the social sciences but also in the humanities in recent decades. The absence of theory in literary studies, for example, has been one of the most influential arguments on behalf of the need for theory.
4. After all, if the social sciences were pervasively moronic and devoid of all worthwhile ideas, we ourselves would have found little interest in them!
5. Indeed, the recent literature on Freud has tended to accuse him of being a self-conscious and calculating fraud. See Masson (1984).
6. We are mindful of the fact that, as the old saw has it, those exercises which have 'science' in their name are usually not sciences at all – library science, domestic science, Christian Science, and so on – even though they may well be respectable enough activities in their own terms. Winch suggests that 'social studies' is a better title than 'social science'. In either case, then, continuing to call them 'social sciences' is compatible with their being disciplines which do not have an authentically scientific character in the manner of, say, physics, while designating them as 'social studies' avoids all risk of gratuitously supposing that the title 'social science' does indicate some inherent connection with scientific aspirations.
7. Thus, one of the major contemporary bones of contention in sociological theory is the 'structure' versus 'agency' question. However, the argument is only in relatively small part about the empirical adequacy of distinct explanatory theories. Rather, it is a rerun, with respect to the relationship of the individual and society, of the long-standing, and entirely philosophical, 'free will' versus 'determinism' debate.
8. See the excellent Chapter 13 in Phillips (1996) where he argues, in a discussion on foundationalism, that the fall of metaphysical absolutes does not entail the fall of nonmetaphysical absolutes. 'Within moral, political, aesthetic and religious perspectives, people may adhere to absolute values. If philosophers deny this possibility because they think that *metaphysical* absolutes are absent, this shows that they are still in the grip of the metaphysics they think they have rejected. In order for an absolute to mean anything for them it *would* have to be a metaphysical absolute. But ordinary absolutes are untouched by the demise of the latter' (pp. 188–9).

REFERENCES

Achinstein, P. and Barker, F. (eds) (1969) *The Legacy of Logical Positivism*, Baltimore: The Johns Hopkins Press.

Ackroyd, S. and Hughes, J.A. (1991) *Data Collection in Context*, 2nd rev. edn, London: Longman.

Althusser, L. (1969) *For Marx*, Harmondsworth: Penguin.

Anderson, R.J., Hughes, J.A. and Sharrock, W.W. (1985) *The Sociology Game: an Introduction to Sociological Reasoning*, London: Longman.

Anderson, R.J., Hughes, J.A. and Sharrock, W.W. (1986) *Philosophy and the Human Sciences*, London: Routledge.

Anderson, R.J., Hughes, J.A. and Sharrock, W.W. (1988) 'Some thoughts on the nature of economic theorising', *Journal of Interdisciplinary Economics*, 2: 307–20.

Anderson, R.J. and Sharrock, W.W. (1986) *The Ethnomethodologists*, London: Tavistock.

Anscombe, G.E. (1957–8) 'On brute facts', *Analysis*, **11**: 69–72.

Aron, R. (1970) *Main Currents of Sociological Thought*, Vol. II, Harmondsworth: Penguin.

Atkinson, J.F.M. (1971) 'Societal reactions to suicide: the role of coroner's definitions', in S. Cohen (ed.) *Images of Deviance*, Harmondsworth: Penguin.

Atkinson, J.F.M. (1978) *Discovering Suicide*, London: Macmillan.

Austin, J.L. (1961) *Philosophical Papers* (ed. J. Urmson and G. Warnock), Oxford: Oxford University Press.

Ayer, A.J. (1946) *Language, Truth and Logic*, 2nd edn, London: Gollanz.

Ayer, A.J. (ed.) (1959) *Logical Positivism*, New York: Free Press.

Ayer, A.J. (1990) 'The elimination of metaphysics', in R. Ammerman (ed.) *Classics of Analytical Philosophy*, Indianapolis: Hackett Publishing.

Baccus, H.D. (1986) 'Sociological indication and the visibility criterion of real world social theorising', in H. Garfinkel (ed.) *Ethnomethodological Studies of Work*, London: Routledge and Kegan Paul.

Bauman, Z. (1978) *Hermeneutics and Social Science*, London: Hutchinson.

Becker, C.L. (1932) *The Heavenly City of the Eighteenth Century Philosophers*, New Haven, Connecticut: Yale University Press.

Bennington, G. and Derrida, J. (1992) *Jacques Derrida*, Chicago: University of Chicago Press.

Benson, D. and Hughes, J.A. (1991) 'Evidence and inference', in G. Button (ed.) *Ethnomethodology and the Human Sciences*, Cambridge: Cambridge University Press.

Berelson, B. and Steiner, G.A. (1967) *Human Behaviour*, shorter edn, New York: Harcourt, Brace and World.

Bhaskar, R. (1978) *A Realist Theory of Science*, 2nd edn, Sussex: Harvester Press.

Blalock, H. (1982) *Conceptualization and Measurement in Social Science*, London: Sage.

Blalock, H. (1984) *Basic Dilemmas in the Social Sciences*, London: Sage.

Bloor, D. (1976) *Knowledge and Social Imagery*, London: Routledge and Kegan Paul.

Bloor, D. (1981) 'The strengths of the strong programme', *Philosophy of the Social Sciences*, **11**: 199–213.

Blumer, H. (1956) 'Sociological analysis and the variable', *American Sociological Review*, **21**: 68–90.

Bridgeman, P. (1927) *The Logic of Modern Physics*, New York: Macmillan.

Brown, R. (1973) *Rules and Laws in Sociology*, London: Routledge and Kegan Paul.

Bulmer, M. (1984) *The Chicago School of Sociology: Institutionalization, Diversity and the Rise of Sociological Research*, Chicago: University of Chicago Press.

Burger, T. (1976) *Max Weber's Theory of Concept Formation: History, Laws and Ideal Types*, Durham, North Carolina: Duke University Press.

Button, G. (ed.) (1991) *Ethnomethodology and the Human Sciences*, Cambridge: Cambridge University Press.

Campbell, N.F. (1957) *Foundations of Science*, New York: Dover.

Carnap, R. (1967) *The Logical Structure of the World*, London: Routledge and Kegan Paul.

Cartwright, N. (1983) *How the Laws of Physics Lie*, Oxford: Oxford University Press.

Cicourel, A.V. (1964) *Method and Measurement in Sociology*, New York: The Free Press.

Cicourel, A.V. (1968) *The Social Organisation of Juvenile Justice*, New York: Wiley.

Cicourel, A.V. (1973) *Theory and Method in a Study of Argentine Fertility*, New York: Wiley.

Connolly, W. (1995) 'Nothing is fundamental . . .' in W. Connolly *The Ethos of Pluralization*, Minneapolis: University of Minnesota Press.

Coulter, J. (1973) *Approaches to Insanity*, London: Martin Robertson.

Coulter, J. (1982) 'Remarks on the conceptualization of social structure', *Philosophy of the Social Sciences*, **12**: 33–46.

Coulter, J. (1989) *Mind in Action*, Cambridge: Polity Press.

Coulter, J. (1979) *The Social Construction of Mind*, London: Macmillan.

Curtis, J.E. and Petras, J. (eds) (1970) *The Sociology of Knowledge: A Reader*, London: Duckworth.

Dallmyr, F.R. and McCarthy, T.A. (eds) (1977) *Understanding and Social Inquiry*, New York: Notre Dame Press.

Davidson, D. (1980) *Essays on Actions and Events*, Oxford: Clarendon.

Davidson, D. (1984) *Inquiries into Truth and Interpretation*, Oxford: Oxford University Press.

Davidson, D. and Hintikka, J. (eds) (1975) *Words and Objections: Essays on the Work of W.V.O. Quine*, Dordrecht: Reidel.

Davis, J.A. (1971) *Elementary Survey Analysis*, Englewood Cliffs, New Jersey: Prentice Hall.

Derrida, J. (1976) *Of Grammatology* (trans. G.C. Spivak), Baltimore: Johns Hopkins University Press.

Deutscher, I. (1973) *What We Say, What We Do*, Glenview, Illinois: Scott, Foresman.

Duncan, O.D. (1984) *Notes on Social Measurement: Historical and Critical*, New York: Sage.

Dupré, J. (1993) *The Disorder of Things: Metaphysical Foundations of the Disunity of Science*, Cambridge, Massachusetts: Harvard University Press.

Durkheim, E. (1952) *Suicide* (trans. J. Spaulding and G. Simpson), London: Routledge and Kegan Paul.

Durkheim, E. (1953) *Sociology and Philosophy* (trans. P.F. Pocock), London: Cohen and West.

Durkheim, E. (1966) *The Rules of Sociological Method* (ed. G. Catlin), New York: Free Press.

Eglin, P. (1987) 'The meaning and use of official statistics in the explanation of suicide' in R.J. Anderson, J.A. Hughes and W.W. Sharrock (eds) *Classic Disputes in Sociology*, London: George Allen and Unwin.

Evans-Pritchard, E.E. (1965) *Witchcraft, Oracles and Magic Among the Azande*, Oxford: Clarendon Press.

Feyerabend, P. (1975) *Against Method: Outline of an Anarchist Theory of Knowledge*, London: New Left Books.

Foucault, M. (1972) *The Archeology of Knowledge* (trans. A. Sheridan), London: Tavistock.

Foucault, M. (1977) *Discipline and Punish: The Birth of the Prison* (trans. A. Sheridan), London: Allen Lane.

Gadamer, H-D. (1975) *Truth and Method*, London: Sheed and Ward.

Garfinkel, H. (1967) *Studies in Ethnomethodology*, Englewood Cliffs, New Jersey: Prentice Hall.

Giddens, A. (1977) 'Positivism and its critics', in A. Giddens *Studies in Social and Political Theory*, London: Hutchinson.

Giddens, A. (1986) *Constitution of Society*, Cambridge: Polity Press.

Habermas, J. (1971) *Knowledge and Human Interests*, London: Hutchinson.

Hacking, I. (1981) *Scientific Revolutions*: Cambridge, Cambridge University Press.

Hacking, I. (1983) *Representing and Intervening*, Oxford: Oxford University Press.

Halfpenny, P. (1982) *Positivism and Sociology*, London: Allen and Unwin.

Harré, R. (1972) *The Philosophies of Science*, Oxford: Oxford University Press.

Hart, H.L.A. (1961) *The Concept of Law*, Oxford: Oxford University Press.

Hayek, F.A. (1964) *The Counter-Revolution of Science*, New York: Free Press.

Held, D. (1978) *Introduction to Critical Theory*, London: Hutchinson.

Heritage, J. (1978) 'Aspects of the flexibility of language use', *Sociology*, **12**: 79–103.

Hollis, M. and Lukes, S. (eds) (1982) *Rationality and Relativism*, Oxford: Blackwell.

Homans, G.C. (1967) *The Nature of Social Science*, New York: Harcourt, Brace and World.

Horton, R. and Finnegan, R. (eds) (1973) *Modes of Thought: Essays on Thinking in Western and Non-Western Societies*, London: Faber and Faber.

Hughes, H.S. (1967) *Consciousness and Society: The Reorientation of European Social Thought, 1890–1930*, London: MacGibbon and Kee.

Hughes, J.A., Martin, P. and Sharrock, W.W. (1995) *Understanding Classical Theory: Marx, Weber and Durkheim*, London: Sage.

Hume, D. (1975) *Enquiry Concerning Human Understanding* (ed. L.A. Selby-Bigge, rev. text P.H. Niddick), Oxford: Clarendon.

Hume, D. (1987) *A Treatise of Human Nature*, 2nd edn, Oxford: Oxford University Press.

Keat, R. and Urry, J. (1975) *Social Theory as Science*, London: Routledge and Kegan Paul.

Kirk, R. (1986) *Translation Determined*, Oxford: Oxford University Press.

Kuhn, T. (1974) 'Second thoughts on paradigms', in F. Suppe (ed.) *The Structure of Scientific Theories*, Urbana: University of Illinois Press.

Kuhn, T. (1977) *The Essential Tension*, Chicago: University of Chicago Press.

Kuhn, T. (1996) *The Structure of Scientific Revolutions*, 3rd edn, Chicago: University of Chicago Press.

Lakatos, I. (1978, 1984) *Collected Papers*, Vols 1 and 2, Cambridge: Cambridge University Press.

Lakatos, I. and Musgrave, A. (eds) (1970) *Criticism and the Growth of Knowledge*, Cambridge: Cambridge University Press.

Lassman, P. and Velody, I. (eds) (1989) *Max Weber's 'Science as a Vocation'*, London: Unwin Hyman.

Laudan, L. (1977) *Progress and its Problems: Toward a Theory of Scientific Growth*, Berkeley: University of California Press.

Law, J. and Lodge, P. (1984) *Science for Social Scientists*, London: Macmillan.

Lazarsfeld, P.F. and Menzel, H. (1969) 'On the relation between individual and collective properties', in A. Etzioni (ed.) *Complex Organizations: A Sociological Reader*, New York: Holt, Rinehart and Winston.

Lazarsfeld, P. and Rosenberg, M. (eds) (1955) *The Language of Social Research*, New York: Free Press.

Lee, J. (1991) 'Language and culture: the linguistic analysis of culture' in G. Button (ed.) *Ethnomethodology and the Human Sciences*, Cambridge: Cambridge University Press.

Lessnoff, M. (1974) *The Structure of Social Science*, London: Allen and Unwin.

Lévi-Strauss, C. (1966) *The Savage Mind*, London: Weidenfeld and Nicolson.

Lévi-Strauss, C. (1968) *Structural Anthropology*, London: Allen Lane.

Lévi-Strauss, C. (1969) *Totemism*, Harmondsworth: Penguin.

Lévi-Strauss, C. (1970) *The Raw and the Cooked: Introduction to a Science of Myth*, London: Jonathan Cape.

Lévi-Strauss, C. (1995) *The Story of Lynx*, Chicago: University of Chicago Press.

Lieberson, S. (1985) *Making it Count: The Improvement of Social Research and Theory*, Berkeley: University of California Press.

Luckmann, T. (ed.) (1978) *Phenomenology and Sociology*, Harmondsworth: Penguin.

Lukes, S. (1970) 'Methodological individualism reconsidered', in D. Emmet and A. MacIntyre (eds) *Sociological Theory and Philosophical Analysis*, London: Macmillan.

Lukes, S. (1973) *Emile Durkheim: His Life and Work*, London: Allen Lane.

Lyotard, J-F. (1984) *The Postmodern Condition: A Report on Knowledge* (trans. G. Bennington and B. Massumi), Manchester: Manchester University Press.

MacIntyre, A. (1977) 'The idea of a social science', in B. Wilson (ed.) *Rationality*, Oxford: Blackwell.

Mandelbaum, M. (1955) 'Social facts', *British Journal of Sociology*, **6**: 312.

Manicas, P.T. (1987) *A History and Philosophy of the Social Sciences*, Oxford: Blackwell.

Marsh, C. (1982) *The Survey Method: The Contribution of Surveys to Sociological Explanation*, London: Allen and Unwin.

Masson, J. (1984) *Freud: The Assault on Truth*, London: Faber.

Mead, G.H. (1934) *Mind, Self and Society*, Chicago: University of Chicago Press.

Mill, J.S. (1961) *A System of Logic*, London: Longman.

Miller, R.W. (1987) *Fact and Method: Explanation, Confirmation and Reality in the Natural and Social Sciences*, New Haven, Connecticut: Princeton University Press.

Mommsen, W.J. and Osterhammel, J. (1987) *Max Weber and his Contemporaries*, London: Unwin Hyman.

Mueller-Vollmer, K. (ed.) (1985) *The Hermeneutic Reader: Texts of the German Tradition from the Enlightenment to the Present*, Oxford: Blackwell.

Nagel, E. (1961) *The Structure of Science*, London: Routledge and Kegan Paul.

Natanson, M. (ed.) (1970) *Phenomenology and Social Reality*, The Hague: Nijhoff.

Neurath, M. (1973) 'Empirical sociology', in M. Neurath and R.S. Cohen (eds) *Empiricism and Sociology*, Dordrecht: Reidel.

Nisbet, R. (1974) *The Social Philosophers*, London: Heinemann.

O'Neill, J. (ed.) (1973) *Modes of Individualism and Collectivism*, London: Heinemann.

Outhwaite, W. (1987) 'Laws and explanations' in R.J. Anderson, J.A. Hughes and W.W. Sharrock (eds) *Classic Disputes in Sociology*, London: George Allen and Unwin.

Papineau, D. (1978) *For Science in the Social Sciences*, London: Macmillan.

Pawson, R. (1989) *A Measure for Measures: A Manifesto for Empirical Sociology*, London: Routledge and Kegan Paul.

Pearson, K. (1911) *The Grammar of Science*, 2nd edn, London: Adam and Charles.

Peters, R.S. (1960) *The Concept of Motivation*, London: Routledge and Kegan Paul.

Phillips, D. (1971) *Knowledge from What?*, Chicago: Rand McNally.

Phillips, D.C. (1987) 'The demise of positivism', in D.C. Phillips *Philosophy, Science and Social Inquiry*, Oxford: Pergamon.

Phillips, D.Z. (1996) *Introducing Philosophy*, Oxford: Blackwell.

Pitkin, H. (1972) *Wittgenstein and Justice*, Berkeley: University of California Press.

Plummer, K. (ed.) *Symbolic Interactionism*, Vol. 1, Cheltenham: Edward Elgar.

Popper, K. (1945) *The Open Society and its Enemies*, 2 vols, London: Routledge and Kegan Paul.

Popper, K. (1959) *The Logic of Scientific Discovery*, London: Hutchinson.

Popper, K. (1965) *Conjectures and Refutations*, 2nd edn, New York: Harper and Row.

Popper, K. (1972) *Objective Knowledge: An Evolutionary Approach*, London: Oxford University Press.

Putnam, H. (1975) *Mathematics, Matter and Method*, Cambridge: Cambridge University Press.

Putnam, H. (1978) *Realism and Reason*, Cambridge: Cambridge University Press.

Quine, W.V.O. (1953a) *From a Logical Point of View*, Cambridge, Massachusetts: Harvard University Press.

Quine, W.V.O. (1953b) 'Two dogmas of empiricism', in W.V.O. Quine *From a Logical Point of View*, Cambridge, Massachusetts: Harvard University Press.

Quine, W.V.O. (1960) *Word and Object*, Cambridge, Massachusetts: MIT Press.

Quine, W.V.O. (1969) *Ontological Relativity and Other Essays*, New York: Columbia University Press.

Quinton, A. (1973) *The Nature of Things*, London: Routledge and Kegan Paul.

Rawls, J. (1955) 'The two concepts of rules', *Philosophical Review*, **64**: 9–11.

Ridley, B.K. (1984) *Space, Time and Things*, 2nd edn, Cambridge: Cambridge University Press.

Robinson, W.S. (1950) 'Ecological correlations and the behaviour of individuals', *American Sociological Review*, **15**: 351–7.

Rosenberg, M. (1955) 'Faith in people and success orientation', in P. Lazarfeld and M. Rosenberg (eds), *The Language of Social Research*, New York: Free Press.

Rorty, R. (1991a) *Philosophy and the Mirror of Nature*, Oxford: Blackwell.

Rorty, R. (1991b) 'Solidarity or objectivity', in R. Rorty *Objectivity, Relativism and Truth: Philosophical Papers*, Vol. 1, Cambridge: Cambridge University Press.

Roth, P. (1987) *Method and Meaning in the Social Sciences*, Ithaca, New York: Cornell University Press.

Ryan, A. (1970) *The Philosophy of the Social Sciences*, London: Macmillan.

Ryle, G. (1966) 'The world of science and the everyday world', in G. Ryle *Dilemmas*, Cambridge: Cambridge University Press.

Sacks, H. (1995) *Lectures on Conversation*, Vols 1 and 2 (ed. G. Jefferson, intro. E.A. Schegloff), Oxford: Blackwell.

Saussure, F. (1959) *Course in General Linguistics* (trans. W. Baskin), New York: The Philosophical Library.

Schnädelbach, H. (1984) *Philosophy in Germany, 1831–1933* (trans. E. Matthews), Cambridge: Cambridge University Press.

Schutz, A. (1962) 'Commonsense and scientific interpretation of human action', *Collected Papers: The Problem of Social Reality*, The Hague: Martinus Nijhoff.

Schutz, A. (1963) 'Concept and theory formation in the social sciences', in M. Natanson (ed.) *Philosophy of the Social Sciences*, New York: Random House.

Searle, J. (1969) *Speech Acts*, Cambridge: Cambridge University Press.

Shapin, S. (1982) 'History of science and its sociological reconstructions', *History of Science*, XX: 157–211.

Sharrock, W.W. (1987) 'Individual and society' in R.J. Anderson, J.A. Hughes and W.W. Sharrock (eds) *Classic Disputes in Sociology*, London: George Allen and Unwin.

Shaw, M. and Miles, I. (1979) 'The social role of statistical knowledge', in J. Irvine, I. Miles and J. Evans (eds) *Demystifying Social Statistics*, London: Pluto Press.

Skinner, Q. (ed.) (1985) *The Return to Grand Theory in the Social Sciences*, Cambridge: Cambridge University Press.

Smelser, N.J. (1968) *Essays in Sociological Explanation*, Englewood Cliffs, New Jersey: Prentice Hall.

Smith, A. (1970) *The Wealth of Nations* (ed. A. Skinner), Harmondsworth: Penguin.

Smith, R. (1997) *The Fontana History of the Human Sciences*, London: Fontana Press.

Storer, N. (ed.) (1973) *The Sociology of Science*, Chicago: University of Chicago Press.

Stouffer, S.A. (1962) *Social Research to Test Ideas: Selected Writings*, New York: Free Press.

Taylor, C. (1978) 'Interpretation and the sciences of man', in R. Beehler and A.R. Drengson (eds) *Philosophy of Society*, London: Methuen.

Toulmin, S. (1972) *Human Understanding*, Vol. 1, Oxford: Oxford University Press.

Toulmin, S. and Goodfield, J. (1965) *The Discovery of Time*, London: Hutchinson.

Torgerson, W.S. (1958) *Theory and Method of Scaling*, New York: Wiley.

Turner, S.P. (1987) 'Underdetermination and the promise of statistical sociology', *Sociological Theory*, **5**: 172–84.

Turner, S.P. and Turner, J.H. (1990) *The Impossible Science: An Institutional Analysis of American Sociology*, Newbury Park, California: Sage.

Urry, J. (1973) 'Thomas Kuhn as a sociologist of knowledge', *British Journal of Sociology*, **24**: 462–73.

Waismann, F. (1951) 'Verifiability', in A. Flew (ed.) *Logic and Language*, Oxford: Blackwell.

Weber, M. (1949) *The Methodology of the Social Sciences* (trans. E. Shills and M.A. Finch), New York: Free Press.

Weber, M. (1960) *The Protestant Ethic and the Spirit of Capitalism* (trans. T. Parsons), London: Allen and Unwin.

Weber, M. (1969) *The Theory of Social and Economic Organisation* (ed. T. Parsons), New York: Free Press.

Weber, M. (1975) 'Knies and the problem of irrationality' in M. Weber *Roscher and Knies: The Logical Problem of Historical Economics* (trans. G. Oakes), New York: Free Press.

Weber, M. (1978) *Economy and Society* (eds G. Roth and C. Wittich, trans. I. Fischoff), Berkeley: University of California Press.

Weider, L. (1974) *Language and Social Reality*, The Hague: Mouton.

Whorf, B.L. (1956) *Language, Thought and Reality* (ed. J.B. Carroll), Cambridge, Massachusetts: MIT Press.

Willer, D. and Willer, J. (1973) *Systematic Empiricism*, Englewood Cliffs, New Jersey: Prentice Hall.

Wilson, T.P. (1974) 'Normative and interpretative paradigms in sociology', in J.D. Douglas (ed.) *Understanding Everyday Life*, London: Routledge and Kegan Paul.

Winch, P. (1990) *The Idea of a Social Science*, London: Routledge and Kegan Paul.

Winch, P. (1977) 'Understanding a primitive society', in B. Wilson (ed.) *Rationality*, Oxford: Blackwell.

Wittgenstein, L. (1958) *Philosophical Investigations* (trans. and ed. G.E.M. Anscombe and G. von Wright), Oxford: Blackwell.

Wittgenstein, L. (1969) *On Certainty* (trans. and ed. G.E.M. Anscombe and G. von Wright), Oxford: Blackwell.

Wittgenstein, L. (1979) 'Remarks on Frazer's *Golden Bough*' in C.G. Luckhardt (ed.) *Wittgenstein: Sources and Perspectives*, Hassocks: Harvester Press.

Wolin, S. (1973) 'Political theory as a vocation', in M. Fleischer (ed.) *Machiavelli and the Nature of Political Thought*, London: Croom Helm.

Woolgar, S. (1981) 'Interests and explanations in the social study of science', *Social Studies of Science*, **11**: 365–94.

INDEX